Goodbye
Ole
Miss

Goodbye
Ole
Miss

by
Carroll Seabrook Leatherman

Cover Portrait by
Charles Inzer

Cover design by
Jacob Fasano
&
Graeme Parsons

ISBN NUMBER 0-9748243-0-5

Second Printing
Printed in the United States of America

Toof Printing Company
670 South Cooper Street
Memphis, TN 38104

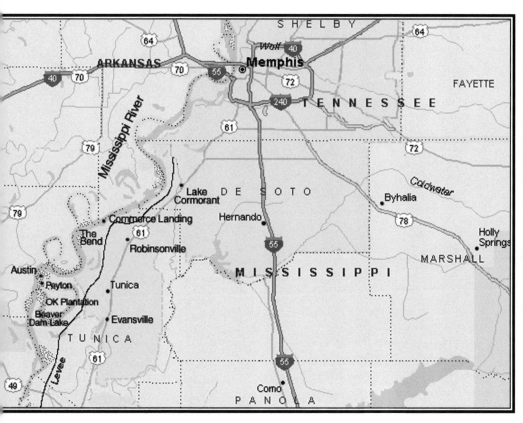

Area Map of Memphis, Tennessee and parts of North Mississippi that helped trace my family history.

Dedication

This book is dedicated to my deceased son, Samuel Richard Leatherman IV. Late each afternoon, Dick would call me from his furniture manufacturing company in Bruce, Mississippi. Now that he does not call, I sit by the phone late afternoons and his spirit sends me courage to write this book. One of Dick's favorite sayings came from *Baja Oklahoma*, a book by Dan Jenkins: "If the phone don't ring, you'll know it's me."

My Special Thanks

My special thanks to my husband, Samuel Richard Leatherman, III. Without his support and knowledge I could not have written this book.

Table of Contents

Introduction

Introduction

In my mother's garden was a lovely fish pond. I liked to sit there in a tall-backed lawn chair that Mother and I had painted so often with a dripping brush that it resembled icing on a cake. We sat there together one mid-summer evening. The garden sprinkler threw water on the flowers, cooling the air a bit. It was not yet dark, and I could hear the crickets chirping as the goldfish swam into their porcelain castle in the fish pond at the end of the day. Curled up there next to Mother as the sun began to wane, I felt a peace and joy I had never before experienced. It was one of those bench-mark moments–perhaps you would even call it an epiphany– when you feel a complete and utter harmony with the universe, with God. Next, I remember wondering, for the first time, about death–someone else's, of course, not my own. After all, I was only five, with an awareness of few things beyond my backyard fence.

In September 2000, my doctor told me I was terminally ill. I awoke late one night and went into my powder room for a glass of water. The window was open to the mild Memphis night, and I could hear clearly the crickets outside. The sound of those crickets chirping, singing their song to the night sky made me realize that I was not immortal and that I would be leaving my earthly home–the Delta South that I love so dearly.

In this book, I hope I have captured some of the things I saw and experienced, things that have come and gone. Some were for the better, and some were not, to my great sorrow. And I hope I have found my true voice as a narrator, because I have many wonderful things to tell you about the history of Memphis, Tennessee, and the north part of the Mississippi Delta. I want to share tales that have been handed down for generations. I will try to be accurate where history is concerned. Dates are important, and I will include some, but my hope is to convey to you a slice of Delta life—what I've heard people say and do—their customs, ceremonies, and behavior. Perhaps you will be moved by what I saw take place on the richest soil in the world, that of the Mississippi Delta, as its people evolved from a Native American culture to the pioneers who came to the land, cut trees, settled, and eked out a very modest and sometimes intolerable existence. I will drop back in history–I might even dream and go forward.

I will tell you about how my Southern world has changed from when I was a child growing up in Memphis and on two Mississippi family farms. Later as a young married woman on yet another Mississippi plantation, I watched agriculture progress from mule farming and laborers to sophisticated mechanized farming.

I'll talk about how the Delta has changed in attitude, from sharecropping to migration and integration, to the gambling industry that has now found its way to the shores of the Mississippi River. Where once the Indians stood, there are now casinos with more hotel rooms than there are in the Caribbean.

My family has owned land in Mississippi for almost 200 years. If I were in a doctor's office and they drew blood, they would find muddy water, for I am a daughter of the land—and if you could listen to my heart, you would hear songs of jubilation and of sorrow, Indian war whoops, rebel yells, and perhaps the most important, black spirituals and the world-famous Delta blues. So if you dare, come with me on a visit to the Old South, as we move forward through the humor and heartbreak of my life to the South of today.

Chapter 1

Southern Childhood in the City During the Depression

The deed from 1875 representing the purchase by my great grandmother, Emily Carruthers Withers, of her brother's share of the Carter Plantation in Buckingham County, Virginia.

Southern Childhood in the City During the Depression

There is so much of the old South in my life that as late as 1977, my houseman and right hand, Israel "Wink" Clark, still called me "Ole Miss." It was an old Southern custom to call the "top lady" on a plantation "Ole Miss." It is a compliment, a token of respect and a term of endearment. This custom is so ingrained in Mississippi history that the University of Mississippi is affectionately called "Ole Miss" by all who love it.

Though his job title was "chauffeur" and he wore a uniform—the kind delivery men wear, the gray Eisenhower jacket, pants to match, black tie, and a black ensign's hat—Wink, despite being crippled due to a bad break in his leg that had never been set, wore his uniform with dignity. Both Wink and I had grown up barefoot, with mud between our toes, on family plantations in the northern Mississippi county of Tunica, just 40 miles south of Memphis, Tennessee. Wink became my right-hand man after mechanized farming took over, when his extraordinary skill with mules could not keep his tractor out of the shop.

One morning I was working in the garden behind my English-style house in Memphis, when I heard Wink call out, "Better come in, Ole Miss! It's some gent'man on the phone, long distance. He's still on the line and keeps saying he'll wait."

Had it been a close friend, even one as far away as New York, they would have known Wink and that he could be trusted to take a message.

Wink was not good at reading or writing, but if the person spoke slowly, like molasses poured from a jar on a cold day, he could write a name and number down. So I knew it was a stranger, and I was curious enough to come in out of the garden and answer the call.

"Mrs. Leatherman, my name is William Stadiem," the caller began. "I am calling because *Town and Country* magazine is doing an issue on the Southern way of life. There will be a long and very important article about the prestigious first families of the South. After many calls and eleven years of research, I believe that you are a 'must have.' Everyone I have spoken with tells me that you are one of the best raconteurs and could be a big help with my article."

In his article "The First Families of the South," Stadiem couldn't come closer to the truth when he says, "One of the South's favorite topics of conversation is family. For all Southern institutions, family is the most revered. And the oldest, most distinguished, most eccentric, then so much the better."[1]

He said he called me because he had learned that I am a descendant of the Carrolls, Seabrooks, Breathitts, Eatons, Bradfords, Montgomerys, Whites, Woods and Withers families, and I married a Leatherman—all old Southern family names. He found that I was a direct descendant of Daniel Carroll, a signer of the Constitution. When we visited on the phone, he asked me if I was a member of the D.A.R. or the Colonial Dames. Much to his surprise, I replied that although both my grandmothers had been members, I did not belong to either, nor had I ever submitted even one of the many applications sent to me for listing in the Social Register, commonly referred to as the "Blue Book," or *Who's Who*.

"I am, however, a member of AA," I said.

Stadiem burst into laughter and said, "I doubt that would read well in an article written for *Town and Country*."

"The fact is," I said, "my grandfather used to say that aristocratic families are like turnips. The best part is always under the ground."

I thank Mr. Stadiem for giving me a good place to begin my story, but then, he owes me one. He used my quotation as the lead to his magazine article.

We *were* proud of our Southern heritage, but at this stage, most of the glory—and a great deal of the money—were like the turnips: under the ground. "Old" wealth, position and genealogy were revered, but family talk during my childhood certainly was not about ancestors. Most discussions revolved around strained family finances and the subject of the day, the Great Depression. I heard more about the scarcity of money than the privilege of it—stories like when Daddy had to sell his father's gold watch to have a tooth pulled. Of course, our experience wasn't the extreme poverty many families suffered; we were quite lucky to avoid WPA and soup lines. Fortunate or not, the Depression brought great changes in the South, and my parents, like most Southerners, learned to live a much simpler lifestyle because of it.

As a child, I would never have known that we were leading simpler lives, had I not heard it in conversations. I overheard pawnshop stories, for every family seemed to have one. Many a gun and Oriental rug were hocked, only to be retrieved in the nick of time. Whole sets of porcelain and china were sold to send sons and daughters to fine boarding schools and colleges. A close friend told me that his family's silver flatware was pawned so many times that they never knew if they'd be eating dinner with a silver fork or with their fingers. While other family treasures revolved through the pawnshop door, the portraits of our ancestors stayed on the walls – not because people were too proud to sell them, but because no one would buy them.

I was born September 27, 1928, in Memphis, Tennessee, and named for both my parents, Carroll Breathitt Seabrook and Mary White Withers. They brought me home from the hospital to a charming, two-story stucco home they had built at 2231 Court Avenue, west of East Parkway North. My parents' first house, a bungalow on Cleveland Street, was a wedding gift from my father's parents, who lived next door. Not to be outdone by the other side of the family, my maternal grandfather, Captain John Paxton Withers, built them an English-style house on South Parkway. Then my parents, with the help of a good architect, built their third house on Court. The Withers' family farms supplied most of the cypress lumber for this house, the first on the 2200 block of Court.

A deep front porch with a waist-high railing stretched the length of the house. An exquisite wrought iron screen door protected the tall, arched French front door, flanked by matching French windows.

Screened-in porches were vital to Southerners in the days before air conditioning. My upstairs bedroom had a sleeping porch, which was later enclosed to become another large bedroom and bath. On the east side of the house was a delightful screened porch shaded by huge overhanging oaks. I learned that a porch is always situated on the east in order to catch the morning sun instead of the blistering afternoon sun. The front door opened to the living room and behind that was what we called the "second parlor," which led to the back yard and a well-kept and much-loved garden. A hammock, strung between two of the backyard oaks, was a perfect place for two or three children to swing.

My favorite spot in the house was one of the built-in window seats in the living room on either side of the front door, where I curled up on dark red velvet cushions, drew shut the heavy matching velvet draperies, and read. Often a crackling fire in the living room fireplace made my hideaway even cozier.

Even during the worst days of the Great Depression, we were never so poor or never so hard up that we could not have big fires burning in the living room. There was land in Mother's family, and though they were mortgaged for a time, the farms provided us with plenty of firewood, fresh vegetables and canned goods that we shared with our neighbors, friends, and help.

I was considered a "late child" in those days because my mother was 35 and my father was 40 when I was born. Mother lost her first two daughters in childbirth. I had two brothers: Jack, 12 years older, and Sterling, five years older. Being the only daughter and the youngest, I was more than pampered. One of my earliest memories was bouncing on my father's crossed legs as if they were a horse to songs like "This is the way the ladies ride…farmers ride…men ride…and the cowboys ride." My favorite ditty was "Froggy went a courtin', he did ride, with a sword and a pistol by his side."

Not all games went as smoothly with my two big brothers, who often teased me. Once I hit my brother Sterling in the head with a toy shovel, and he played dead. I shrieked and cried until he moved, then hit him in the head again for playing such a mean trick. Another time I swallowed a nickel and Sterling told me that I was certain to die. After a few minutes of thinking how much the neighborhood gang would miss me, I walked to Mother, who was chatting on the hallway telephone, and solemnly told her of my impending doom. She interrupted her conversation only long enough to tell Sterling to feed me some white bread. More than once, having been scolded, I ran away until Sterling would come and find me. Teaser that he was, Sterling did protect me in neighborhood games like hide and seek, so I stayed close to him.

My other brother, John William Seabrook, "Jack," was named for his two grandfathers, John Withers and William Seabrook. Both of my parents had family names—maybe that's why doting relatives financed three of their houses. Brother Sterling was named for my wealthy bachelor uncle, Sterling Adolphus Withers, which proved to be an advantage to him, too. Southerners seem to have a propensity for naming children after the wealthiest kin, or at least making them godparents.

At an early age, my two brothers started calling me by a nickname. It was pronounced "Shugsie" but spelled "Sugsie." I had become the family mascot, and it seemed as though the entire neighborhood depended on "Sugsie" for entertainment. As for the nickname, I can't tell you where it all started. Some say it was because I was as sweet as sugar, while others might say it was because as a little girl, I loved sweets: banana taffy squares, gumballs out of a penny machine, and long red and black licorice twists. I was always eating candy, though with plenty of spirit and vigor, I had no weight problem. Though I do not know why I was called Sugsie, I can tell you this: I hated the name. It took forty years of my earnest requests to shed this despised pet name.

Jack left home at age 12 to live with my maternal grandmother on OK Plantation in Tunica County, Mississippi. One weekend he went to visit grandmother and decided to stay. Who could blame him? It was heaven for a young boy who loved to hunt and fish and ride horses, and my grandmother, my Aunt Camilla and Uncle Sterling treated him like a prince. My mother and father, to the amazement of many, seemed to find the arrangement agreeable, and from then on, Jack only came to Memphis to visit. Being 12 years my senior, Jack seemed more like an uncle than a brother. In very different ways, I was close to both of my brothers. Sterling and I grew up as true siblings in the house on Court Avenue, until he left for Columbia Military Academy in the ninth grade.

****

In the 1930s and 1940s, my neighborhood was part of my family. It was safe, and this gave us the freedom to roam wherever adventure took us. We children met every morning at the corner, where we planned our activities: building a tree house, going swimming in the bayou, or playing kick-the-can. On rainy days, we played inside games. At dusk, we would know when to return home by our fathers' whistles from front porches.

We also celebrated holidays together. Halloween was our chance to "trick" the neighbors we thought were the strictest—the ones who objected to us playing football in their yards, drawing little chalk squares on their sidewalks for hopscotch, or tracing circles in their dirt for marbles. At Christmas, we caroled; on the Fourth of July, we shot fireworks, which proved to be dangerous for Sterling when a Roman candle exploded in his hand.

In our neighborhood, wealth and position went unnoticed except for my next-door neighbor, who had his own goat cart. Winston's toys and clothes singled him out as a rich, only child. Not only did he have a goat cart, but he also wore a tuxedo and a tall silk hat and showed horses for his wealthy uncle. His family could afford two fulltime servants. Their houseman Pal made home brew in his quarters that adjoined the garage, and we sampled it with no shame. By today's standards it seems strange, but our parents had no qualms about our playing unsupervised in the neighborhood. They turned us over to the care of these trusted black servants without a second thought.

I also had a very rich cousin on my father's side in Memphis. When first dropped off to spend a day with Peter, I was timid, but soon realized that Peter had even more toys than Winston, plus he played a guitar and had a bright red go-kart fire engine, the first of its kind. I crashed the fire truck into a tree after Peter made me visit his creepy snake farm, which he kept in his grandmother's garage. Peter's unique talents and interests—like snakes and crayfish in his pool—made him much different from my usual neighborhood gang. For one, he had asthma, and because of this disease, he was often whisked off in a chauffeur-driven Rolls Royce, not to a hospital, but to the largest and most famous hotel in the South, the Peabody in downtown Memphis. Why the hotel instead of the hospital? It was air-conditioned. Poor Peter had to stay in the hotel until his asthma subsided. It was then I decided that only the rich had strange diseases, for none of my poorer friends had such ailments.

Back in our neighborhood, I learned I might not be rich enough to have asthma but was wealthy enough to hurt myself. First, I broke my right arm in a fall from a swing. Then, while roller-skating, I hit a crack in the sidewalk, fell, and chipped my front tooth. Lamenting the possible marriage consequences of this new disfigurement, my older brother Sterling announced loudly to my mother, "Oh, now we'll never get rid of her!"

No one in the neighborhood had a private swimming pool, but we often cooled off by wading in our backyard fish pond or playing under a garden water hose. At age four, a young boy from down the street and I were caught cavorting naked under the water hose, until my nurse came in the yard and spanked me. Years later, at a swank party in Palm Beach, Florida, I saw the young man, now famous for his risque' films in the entertainment world, and I reminded him of his first nude scene.

My best friend then, Betty, was the daughter of my mother's best friend. When in Memphis during the summer, I spent almost every night with Betty. I was lucky to have Betty for a best friend, because she always had two of everything–two dogs, two swings, two ponies. Every morning, we rode "Chick" and "Buddy," fat brown-and-white ponies, down the bridle paths on the parkways with Betty's doting father before he went to practice law.

Overton Square, the closest thing we had to a shopping mall in the 1930s, was only a few blocks from home and an easy walk, skate or bicycle ride. On the corner facing the Number Two streetcar track was the Purdy Jester drug store. It was here that neighbors gathered to exchange gossip and to buy everything from nickel ice cream cones to 50-cent bottles of paregoric, an opium derivative which could be purchased without a prescription. We flocked to the soda fountain like movie stars to the Plaza Hotel in New York. We bought ice cream sodas for 15 cents, and on very special occasions, a banana split for a quarter. Besides the soda fountain stools, there were a few round tables and ice cream chairs. Many an early romance began at Purdy Jester while the young lovers sipped nickel fountain Cokes through a straw. The magazine rack was a wonder, with dime comic books the rage; *Betty Boop* was the girls' favorite, while the boys preferred *Superman*.

Nearby was Burkle's Bakery, where you could buy salt rising bread and gingerbread men. On Fridays, you could get "Surprise Cake," made from all the week's leftover cake mixes. Our birthday cakes were made of sponge cake, so our mothers could slip boiled coins, a nickel or dime, in them before Mr. Burkles slathered thick icing on top. This was the beginning of our family tradition of money cakes.

Until the age of 12, I wore my hair in a short bob that I kept trimmed at Ledbetter Barber Shop. Later when my fine, thick hair grew long, Mother let me get a shampoo at La Vogue Beauty Shop for 50 cents. She hated to hear me cry when she tried to comb out my tangles. The vinegar rinse she used did not a lick of good, and I detested the smell.

By far the most important thing at Overton Square to us children was *The Memphian*, our neighborhood movie theater, or as they say in the Deep South, the "picture show." On Saturday, a child could see a double feature, cartoons, previews and newsreel for a dime. The newsreels were very important to us during World War II, for we had no television. On rare Saturdays, you could see two movies for a just a nickel, and this was named the "Nickel Roar," because there was a theater full of children, roaring with laughter. With any luck we had money left over for treats like nickel candy bars and Cracker Jacks.

Not far away was our neighborhood East End Swimming Pool. We wore wool bathing suits and wrung them out by putting them through rollers that squeezed out the water. East End Skating Rink, although it had no ice, had a slick wooden floor. The luckiest girls had their own white lace-up skating boots. Music was piped in, and at the end of the afternoon, we all skated to the Grand March. I had my 12th birthday there, celebrating with my older cousin John.

John was one of my cousins whose family was hit hard by the Depression. His mother Lucy was born a Dabney and like my mother, she was used to nice things. She married a Catholic man and had five children. He died at the beginning of the Depression, leaving her with a house full of kids and scant resources. Lucy was angry with God for taking her husband from her and angry with the Catholic Church, and she promptly went back to being a Protestant. Lucy supported her whole family by making fine baby and children's clothes. Many a night she sewed until dawn. Mother and I would always bring things from the farm to share with them, and Lucy would make christening dresses while I sewed to fill my doll's blue steamer trunk, complete with hangers.

Lucy was one of a number of strong women in my life. At an early age and because of the Depression, I knew the strength and fight of the Southern woman, so wrongly portrayed in books and novels. For this and many reasons, I favor equal opportunity for women, because they certainly have equal misfortune.

* * * *

It is hard to believe that we could afford household help when we were in financial straits, but the cost was relative. For example, our housekeeper earned a dollar a day and carfare, typical for the time. Many a Southern woman took a job in a department store or 10-cent store, making $12 a week as extra income for her family, and then spent three or four dollars for part-time help.

Economic times improved at the inception of World War II, when I was 12. With more money coming into our household, my parents hired a houseman, Bird Tuttle, who was a great help in stoking the coal-burning furnace in the basement. A coal truck would back up to a basement window and shovel coal to the basement floor. My brother was pleased that Bird was there to relieve him of this chore. Bird Tuttle later became one of the most influential black insurance men in Memphis.

In our neighborhood, vegetable vendors would stroll down our street with produce on their heads, hollering, "Fresh tomatoes, okra, corn, field peas," and you simply went out of your house and bargained with the vendor. A truck that came down the street carrying blocks of ice for iceboxes made for an excellent amusement ride. Children, on the hottest summer days, would jump on the ice truck, climb up where it was cool, and relax for two or three blocks.

The zoo was only two blocks from my house, and from my upstairs bedroom window, I could hear the lions roar. We were proud that Leo, the famous lion we saw and heard on the screen before every MGM movie, lived at our Memphis zoo where he later sired a cub, Dynamite. When we were old enough to ride bicycles, we would pedal over to the Overton Park Zoo almost daily. It was there we learned the name of every animal and bird. The decadent monkey house kept our adolescent attention as the chimpanzees made passes at each other. Because of Peter, I never cared for the snake house, but I did love the birds, butterflies, and most of all, the greenhouses.

I have always been interested in flowers because my mother and father, who were incompatible in almost every other way, had one common interest: horticulture. They won many ribbons for roses and peonies in flower shows. My father always worked in the garden at least one hour before he showered, dressed immaculately, and went to work. The bloom came off the roses when I remember him leaving long must-do lists each morning for my mother. Together, Mother and I would trek into the bad area of town to pick up our gardener, who would work through the list, breaking only for a lunch of cabbage or turnip greens and cornbread.

Because of the Depression, my father's occupation—and through that, my parents' social life—had changed. Once a Front Street cotton broker, Daddy lost his business in the financial crash. Cotton was indeed king in the South, and Memphis was the largest inland cotton market in the country. It ranked along with New Orleans, Louisiana, and Houston, Texas, in cotton sales.

Times were hard at Mother's family farms in Mississippi, too. Most banks would not loan money on land in those days, but with the help of one of Uncle Sterling's friends who worked for the Whitney Bank in New Orleans, they were able to get a mortgage and save the family farms. For the first time, my mother's family could not indulge its beautiful Southern-belle daughter with houses, furniture, cars, clothes, servants and vacations.

So when our neighbor (and my godfather), Mayor Watkins Overton, came over one afternoon about cocktail time and offered Daddy the position of either hospital administrator or beer and wine commissioner, it was welcome news. This was an easy choice for Daddy; he would not even slow down when passing a hospital, much less go in one. Blessed with good health, Daddy believed illness was all in the mind. He told his ailing elder sister at age 93, "Ida, do not go to a hospital. At your age, those fools will be compelled to tell you something is wrong."

Once, I fell and cut my head in the shower. Bleeding, I went to my father for comfort, but he grew red in the face and said, "How could you do such a stupid thing? Don't bleed here in the parlor on the rug. Go out back to the tile bathroom, and I'll call your mother in from the garden." I learned at an early age that I was rewarded for being careful but bled alone if I slipped on the soap.

When he died at age 95, Daddy still had his tonsils, appendix and most of his teeth. He had never been treated at a hospital, except when he broke his collarbone in a high school football game. At his death, he was the oldest alumnus of Memphis University School, one of the most prestigious private boys' schools in Memphis.

Though Daddy detested hospitals, he *would* go in them to check on Mother and to view his newborns. If the baby was pretty, he declared the new offspring to be the spitting image of his side of the family. This decision made, he dashed to the hospital drugstore, purchased quantities of Havanas, and was soon parading up and down cotton row on Front Street passing out cigars. The merchants would have much preferred Mother, famous for her beautiful legs, to promenade down the streets, giving them an excuse to stop grading cotton—or playing gin rummy.

In 1933, Daddy accepted the position of city beer and wine commissioner and began his long adventure in what was known as the Crump Machine. Edward Hull Crump was a Mississippi politician, businessman and former mayor who rose in power to become a benevolent dictator of sorts in Memphis. Though he did not hold public office after 1916, Crump's power went undisputed. He was the boss of a well-oiled political machine until his death in 1954.

I will not dare and could not explain what the Crump Machine did or how it worked—all I know is that I was raised in times when Memphis knew nothing else. Even as a child, it was obvious that what Mr. Crump said, the city of Memphis did. Even so, most of the time the citizens were pleased with his dictates.

I believed then as now that the Crump administration had many honest and able men. During the Depression, many such men were out of work, my father being one of them, as were two of my uncles by marriage. Hugh Mageveny served as judge, and Guy Joyner was sheriff during the Crump years.

Crump owned a large insurance agency, which enjoyed a tremendous advantage from his rise to political power. Anyone in his right mind would buy his policy from Boss Crump. Your lights may not have been turned off if you didn't, but they would flicker, and you certainly would feel the difference if you needed a political favor.

The history of Beale Street is entwined with the history of Boss Crump.

Back in his early days in public office and campaigning as a reformer, Crump hired a young, black musician named W.C. Handy to help promote his candidacy. Handy sang, tongue-in-cheek:

Mr. Crump don't allow no easy riders here,
Mr. Crump don't allow no easy riders here,
I don't care what Crump don't allow,
I'm gonna barrelhouse anyhow.
Mr. Crump don't allow no easy riders here.

Barrelhousin'–drinking, dancing, and gambling–was rampant in Memphis until shortly before World War II, when Crump, who stalled on his campaign promises of reform during the '20s and '30s, had an inexplicable change of heart and actually cleaned up Memphis. Nevertheless, there was a price to pay: the city lost many of the historic buildings on Beale Street. Though he was simply carrying out Crump's orders, the last thing my father or anyone else should have done was to raze Beale Street practically down to the pavement. Many of the more notorious landmarks were purged, and this did make for a safer city. It's interesting to note that at the time the Crump Machine cleaned up Beale Street, there were more murders on a single Saturday night on Beale than in a whole year on the British Isles.

As hard as Boss Crump and my father might have tried, they really never stopped all the drinking, gambling and bootlegging. Some of the most prominent families in Memphis today started as bootleggers. By the end of the '30s, the brothels were gone, the saloons were closed, and there were only a few pawnshops and clothing stores left on Beale Street. However, there was no stopping the birth of the blues, and W.C. Handy and many others like Robert Johnson and Memphis Minnie kept the music alive.

Delta musicians all met at Beale Street to play music and gamble, gamble, gamble. Crap games were the most popular. Dice were dropped into a large leather "dice horn," a cone-shaped leather cup with strips of leather across the opening to make the dice bounce out of the cup. The horn was used to prevent crooked gamblers from winning with weighted dice. When Daddy became the Chief of Police, his office was quickly filled with illegal dice confiscated from Beale. Serious crapshooters, like today, wanted to hear the dice rattling loudly in the thrower's hand, followed by a snap of his fingers. This became a Southern slogan: "rattle and snap."

Reform couldn't quash the Memphis sense of humor, either. One speakeasy had a sign that read, "Come on in, take off your shoes, and have a stinking good time." Even though Beale Street is now just a shell of what it once was, it has become one of the most popular tourist attractions in the United States.

* * * *

I grew up in the days before television, but in the heyday of radio. As I sat cross-legged in front of the large brown radio situated in one corner of our dining room, shows like "Orphan Annie" and "The Lone Ranger" kept my young ears entertained. When the children's stories were over, the most exciting program of the week came on: "Gangbusters," the real-life drama about which criminals had been found, who had been arrested, and in what part of the country. One particular episode of "Gangbusters" featured the capture of George Kelly Barnes, alias Machine Gun Kelly. I was so excited when the show described how Kelly, a bank robber and kidnapping desperado, was captured in Memphis by the F.B.I and local Police Chief Carroll Seabrook on September 26, 1933.

Kelly was reared in Memphis and went to Central High School, the most prestigious public school in the city. This man, known as the most wanted criminal in America, was captured without a shootout, surprising to all because of his bloody record of mowing down victims with his sawed-off shotgun.

Daddy and the F.B.I. thought that Kelly might return to Memphis, his childhood home, so they were on the lookout. My father was soon tipped off about where Kelly was staying. Caught unaware, Kelly was surrounded by local police and the FBI. When he saw that the situation was hopeless, he cried out, "Don't shoot, G-men! Don't shoot, G-men!" The phrase uttered by Machine Gun Kelly that early morning in Memphis gave federal agents their colorful nickname: "G-Man."

I was thrilled to hear my Daddy's name on the radio, but though it was news of national importance, it had barely been mentioned at home. Having been schooled by Boss Crump, my father didn't say a word about the case. Some claimed Boss Crump was so secretive that when he had a conference with someone, it often took place in the garden behind his home on Peabody Avenue, in the dead of night, with only his flashlight burning. Crump's proverb was, "What's writ is there; what's said is air."

* * * *

During my early childhood, we took our vacations on the Gulf Coast in Biloxi, Mississippi. When I was five, my mother had a small boat made for me there. It was on that trip that I first saw Shirley Temple in a movie, and I wrote her a letter. I never liked Shirley Temple after that summer. First, she never answered my letter; and second, when I thought I was so lucky to find a Shirley doll that some child had left in the lobby of the hotel next to our cottage, I was punished for stealing it. My parents made me return the collectible to the lost and found. A hotel guest who overheard the fiasco asked my mother if he could treat me to the Shirley Temple movie playing at the local theater. This lovely gentleman was a Godsend. He gave me face and let me know he thought I was a good child. Today, a mother would not dare to let a child go to a movie with any stranger.

It was at Biloxi that I contracted the dread disease of the time, malaria. Bear in mind, almost every child I knew had malaria in the South. It was as common to take quinine as it was to take cough syrup. Luckily, my teeth were spared the unsightly stripes that quinine sometimes leaves. My malaria was quickly complicated by strep throat, and I remember being lifted out of the back of a car and into a New Orleans hospital as I convulsed. There, I had my first experience with a good, kind Jewish doctor. His name was Dr. Bloom, but I called him "Dr. Balloon." To this day, because of Dr. Bloom, I have great confidence in Jewish doctors, and I still have the treasured china doll I named in his honor, "Bloom."

After a long recuperation, I began the first grade in Memphis almost a year behind. Sterling and I and most of the neighborhood children, went to a public school called Lennox that was four or five blocks from home. On my first day of school I trembled with excitement. I trembled with anger, too. Mother was too busy—too busy with gardening, too busy with church work, too busy talking on the telephone—to take me to school. It fell to Sterling to walk me there and take me into the first grade. I was furious that Mother didn't go with me and embarrassed that I didn't know how to fill out the forms. Luckily, a kind neighbor lady who had a child entering the same grade helped me enroll. Mind you, I knew my name, and I knew my age, but at that time, I had no idea what my father's occupation was. I only knew that I loved him.

The first day of school, I was given a coloring book to bring home and told to color only one page a day for a week. Because Mother had not taken me to school, I colored every page in the book with rage. When Daddy came home, I showed him the book, and, not knowing I had disregarded the assignment, he complimented me on my coloring skills.

Though he was not a tall man, my father had even, chiseled features, straight coal black hair, brown eyes, and he walked erect. The one thing wrong with my father's build, which Mother was so quick to point out, was Daddy's bowlegs, and she was proud that I had not inherited them.

Unlike my father, Mother was a natural artist, creative and spontaneous. She did flower arrangements, wrote poetry, cooked, decorated, entertained, and dressed beautifully, though a little on the flamboyant side. Hats, some veiled, were a must for women then, even for an errand to the grocery store in this period, but my mother's love for hats exceeded that of her contemporaries. She must have had 20 or 30 which she kept in labeled hat boxes stuffed under her bed. Furs and gloves were also very much in style. I can see my exquisite blond, green-eyed mother, with her beautiful neck and shoulders, wrapped in great, white fox furs and ermine stoles. There were fur coats with hats to match. Smoking was not frowned upon, but it puzzled me how these ladies could smoke, eat, and drink while wearing those veils. Mother smoked only at parties, to show off her beautiful hands and manicured nails painted with "moons and tips."

Though going out socially came to a screeching halt when my father entered public life, Mother was still able to enjoy the cocktail hour, a daily ritual in our house and in our neighborhood, with neighbors coming and going between each other's homes. At our house, traditionally on Sunday after church, there was a long cocktail hour followed by a huge sit-down dinner, the size and extent of a Thanksgiving or Christmas meal.

Mother dressed stylishly, and since Daddy was so often unavailable as a companion, she traveled extensively in the States and abroad with her bachelor brother, Sterling Withers. They never missed the Kentucky Derby. Once as she entered Uncle Sterling's box at the Derby, she was mistaken for Mae West.

Mother was lively and funny and had a lust for life. She was also volatile and not always easy to get along with, but there has never been anyone who enjoyed life like this beautiful woman. She had a keen sense of humor and could imitate anyone. The most charming thing about Mother was that she enjoyed herself. After she would tell a story, sometimes even before she finished, she would throw back her head, showing her pearly white teeth, and laugh and laugh, simply because she had amused herself telling the story. My daughter Mary and I inherited her face and this trait, and from family photos of my grandmother, it appears that we are the fourth generation to look alike.

Mother knew what really counted. One of my happiest memories is that she would come in where I was studying–though I usually had a good book hidden behind my textbook–and say, "Stop studying. We've got things to do. That school work can wait." If we had something fun to do, it certainly took precedence over anything *silly* like cleaning house or studying.

She made Christmases very special. In an attic room upstairs, she would have card tables arrayed with hundreds of choices of paper and ribbon. We started preparing for Christmas the very day after Thanksgiving.

My first memories of Christmas are that I would go to bed on Christmas Eve with the house looking just as it had the day before: the fire burning, no tree, only a wreath on the front door. On Christmas morning when I woke up, the tree was up and decorated and all the gifts were under it. Santa Claus had magically done it all while I was sleeping. My favorite Christmas of all was the year I slept downstairs on Christmas Eve. I awoke and crept upstairs to discover a freshly decorated bedroom. Hidden in the attic were new draperies, rugs, and furniture, which Santa Claus had magically used to redecorate.

The dining table was set with beautiful china, and after opening gifts, we would have a large breakfast of wild quail from the farm. There were dishes of sausage, bacon, homemade biscuits, waffles, and hot bread, all served with champagne and eggnog so rich you had to eat it with a spoon.

This eggnog, full of whiskey, rum, and bourbon, taught me my first lesson about being, as we say in the South, "over-served." The Christmas that Santa brought me my Dionne Quintuplet dolls, all five in a big box with clothes, and my favorite Didee doll (the first dolls that would wet themselves so you could change their diapers), I discovered that the eggnog was better than any ice cream and I had several helpings. No one noticed until I stepped in the middle of my box of Dionnes. Everyone thought this most amusing, and I was soon dressed in a black velvet dress with a lace collar and we went off to church.

We did not have fancy handmade stockings decorated with sequined Christmas trees. Instead, we used the biggest silk hose we could find. On Christmas morning, we would find them stuffed with simple things like a ruler, eraser, new pencils and crayons, oranges, nuts, candy, and a shiny silver dollar in the toe.

The Christmas season did *not* include taking gifts from people who wanted to gain favor with Daddy. Daddy told our housekeeper and me never to accept any gift left at our home, no matter how tempting. At Christmas, we would turn away everything from ivory mahjong sets to fancy cakes and cases of whiskey and champagne. Once a pawnbroker came to our door to give me a bracelet with a tiny gold charm shaped like a church. When you looked in the tiny glass door, you could see the Lord's Prayer engraved inside. How I coveted that little bracelet! But then I remembered what Shirley Temple would do, so I simply smiled and said, "I cannot accept your gift, but I wish you a merry Christmas."

****

It didn't take long for Mother to realize I wasn't doing well at the public school, so she enrolled me in the small private school Betty attended. Instead of a big public school with a basement bathroom that reeked like steak and kidney pie, I found myself in a delightful little white cottage on Peabody Avenue with green shutters and a tiny front porch. This was "Miss Eva Lee's School of Childhood." Miss Lee could not afford a room for each class. Only the first grade had its individual room. The rest of the pupils sat at small desks with two or three grades in a room. It was Miss Lee who told me I had a fine mind and that I would soon catch up and even surpass the other students.

In appearance, Miss Lee was an unkempt, disheveled dumpling of a woman with gray hair that she pulled up and fastened with one hairpin. The wayward strands went spiraling out in all directions. Her rumpled clothes appeared to have come from a rummage sale, and her slip always showed five or six inches below the hem of her skirt. She rolled her stockings to the knee, knotted to the side, and when she raised her arms to write on the chalkboard, you could see her wrinkled knees. She had a trained, theatrical voice and was a born storyteller and reader.

One of my favorite things was that Miss Lee would suddenly appear, throw open the swinging door that separated two adjoining classrooms, and with great authority look everyone over and say, "Put your head on your desk. It is time for me to read to you."

When Miss Lee read, you were transported to another world. She had started us off with *Little Women* and *Little Men*, and proceeded to Greek mythology and beyond. We learned to perform simple plays in French. She loved to show off her pupils, and we were carted to every woman's club in Memphis, where we performed our plays and gave our poetic readings. We began every day with a hearty rendition of the French anthem, the Pledge of Allegiance, and "God Bless America."

Holidays were big events for Miss Lee, and I do not necessarily mean traditional ones. For example, we celebrated the birthdays of the famous, with Robert E. Lee's birthday being the biggest event. Miss Lee, who claimed to be kin, kept a portrait of the general on a little easel topped by a curtain rod that supported a gauze drape. On that special day, the drape was drawn to cover the portrait, but at the appointed moment—after we all had turned to face south and sung "Dixie"—some privileged favorite of Miss Lee's got to pull the cord, and there was General Lee staring out at us.

We had a kiddie band, complete with recorders, bells, and drums. Our gold uniforms included circus-monkey hats, and the coveted baton was passed around so each child could be the conductor. Piano lessons were given on "imitation" keyboards, long pieces of cardboard with the keys marked on them, because Miss Lee could only afford one real piano. A few days before the annual Christmas pageant, I convinced my Aunt Camilla to give me private piano lessons as a gift. Visions of playing "Silent Night" came true, the only problem being that in such a short time, I had only learned the first two bars, leaving the students repeating over and over again "Silent Night, Holy Night" as parents and faculty waited anxiously for the rest of the carol.

Another year, we performed *A Christmas Carol*, and I played the part of Tiny Tim's mother. Mother was assigned the task of picking up a fowl from Miss Lee's local grocer and bringing it to the school to be used as a prop for the play. The naked, unbaked bird sat on the table as we children blew our noses and coughed. After an outstanding performance, Mother and I dutifully returned the poor, infected bird back to Miss Lee's butcher.

Health code violations or not, it was a life worth living to be with Miss Lee.

Miss Lee dealt with us in ways that she would probably be sued for today. She once asked us to raise our hands if our parents belonged to a private club. You see, Miss Lee had just told us about Roman baths, that they were like clubs. Only one child raised his hand, so our feelings were not hurt. In these homogeneous days, she would have been labeled cruel for asking a question that might single someone out. Once, a child did not have his homework. She did not scold him, but instead announced to the class that his parents were "social" and perhaps went out at night too often to make sure their son completed his assignments. Another time a little boy spit on a classmate, and she made the offender spit in a bucket most of the afternoon, as the rest of the class stood around drinking water in front of the poor kid. Ironically enough, the worst behaved troublemaker, who was exiled daily to a small porch that adjoined the classroom, ended up becoming the mayor of Memphis.

Perhaps the story I remember best about Miss Lee was when she said in front of the class that a certain child's father had been a poor butcher but was now one of the richest men in the world, because he came out from behind the grocery store counter and let people chose their own food and then check out. She was referring to Clarence Saunders, who revolution-ized the grocery business with his "supermarket" concept, "Piggly Wiggly."

At Miss Lee's we brought our own lunches, and if you did not, with one nickel you could buy a hot dog. However, lunch boxes became very bor-ing, and the smell of Ovaltine repulses me to this day. Peanut butter was the rage. And like Elvis Presley, we thought peanut butter and banana was the top dish, as a sandwich or salad. If we had friends for lunch on Saturday, we always had a split banana with peanut butter, store-bought mayonnaise, and crushed peanuts on top. It was the best fare we could offer each other.

Local businessmen conceived the Memphis Cotton Carnival in 1931 to improve and promote Memphis business. The celebration was in its hey-day during my years at Miss Lee's. My last year, 1941, the Cotton Carnival was so big, and such a part of Memphis, that they had a children's parade and a children's ball. I won the honor of riding the float in the children's parade representing Miss Lee's School. I don't suppose it hurt my vote that Mother made the float. It was a simple affair, covered with daisies. My costume had an attractive bonnet with a big black satin bow tied under my chin, and I wore black lace mitts. I carried a basket of flowers and a parasol and waved the "Miss America" wave, holding my arm stiff and moving my hand only slightly from left to right. I felt like a princess and I loved being in the spotlight.

The little boys of Miss Lee's School, wearing pressed white shirts, long white trousers, and wide yellow sashes, pulled the float like horses. High school bands came from all over the Mid-South to march in the parade. It was a beautiful Saturday morning with a bright sun shining. As we neared the street corner of the police station where my father's office was, I asked the boys to slow down the float. As I passed under his window, I waved to my father. A star was born.

Mother also did all the work for Miss Lee's annual seated Thanksgiving feast. She always brought flowers from her garden for May Day, Mothers' Day and graduation. She spent hours decorating our simple little school for the programs. She knew every child's name and sent each one a card and a 10-cent gift at Christmas. Mother allowed me to form clubs and give parties, where I could serve any food I wanted to my friends.

During the summer after the fifth grade, Miss Lee offered a three-week-long camp for girls at a place only a Southern girl would feel comfortable: the Civil War's famous graveyard, Shiloh National Cemetery. In addition to usual camp activities such as canoeing, hiking, and arts and crafts, we spent hours riding on horseback between the headstones and historical markers. I felt a closeness to this place, having played with the miniball that had killed one of my Seabrook kin. Come dusk at Shiloh, some chubby camper with more spirit than skill managed to play "Taps" as we stood in reverence to the lowering of the American flag. Miss Lee always reminded us of Robert E. Lee's General Order No. 9 and his post-surrender appeal for his Confederate troops to become good United States citizens now that the war was lost. Not all of our camp life was so serious, though, for it was here I heard my first dirty joke. After we had all undressed and were wearing only nightgowns, we would ask a girl to peek down her gown and spell the word "attic" aloud: A–TT–I–C! The most important piece of mail I received at camp came from Betty, who revealed her earth-moving first purchase of a junior brassiere.

All too soon, the time had arrived to decide what poem each student would read at our sixth-grade graduation. The ceremony was held at Miss Lee's church. The girls dressed in all-white party dresses, and the boys were in long white pants, starched shirts without ties, and white jackets. After we marched in to "Pomp and Circumstance," each child stood before the audience and recited a poem of his or her choice. My piece was the Rudyard Kipling poem, "If," a copy of which my father had framed for my bedroom wall.

After Mother left me in the line to march down the church aisle, my good friend Kay, a redhead who had moved to Memphis from Mississippi four years prior, and I had a plan. Just before the procession started, Kay and I both put on "Raven Red" lipstick borrowed from her older sister's dressing table. On went the bright, red lipstick, and we even added some to our cheeks. Marching down the aisle, I dared not look at Mother. When I recited, having practiced for hours in front of the mirror, Sara Bernhardt herself could not have been more theatrical—or more made-up. Mother's only comment was, "Mary Carroll, take that makeup off before we go to your class luncheon."

Joyfully, I received my diploma with tears running down my face and walked out of the church into another world. The following fall, I entered Miss Hutchison's School for Girls, a new planet as far as my previous experience was concerned.

[1] "The First Families of the South." *Town & Country*, November 1977, William Stadiem.

Chapter 2

Aristocratic Families Are Like Turnips

—

The Best Part Is Always Under The Ground

Aristocratic Families Are Like Turnips — The Best Part Is Always Under The Ground

While other young girls dressed carefully casual and waited on Sunday afternoons for boys to come calling, I was–with the bad luck of good weather–carted to as many as four cemeteries by my dear mother. Two of these cities of the dead were in Memphis and two in North Mississippi. All had one thing in common: the headstones of my ancestors. In studying family history, I have learned that for every honor, there are an equal number of embarrassments and tragedies. I have ancestors who signed the *Constitution*, the *Articles of Confederation*, and who served honorably in the American Revolution and the Civil War, but I wholeheartedly subscribe to the old saw: just about everyone who studies genealogy discovers they have "an aunt who was a whore in Leadville [Colorado]".

To be truthful, I think my mother visited the graves to say thank you to our people, who in different ways left us traits, gifts, addictions and best of all, some good Delta land. The stories I pass along are about people whose portraits I still have, jewelry I still wear, and reputations I try— though not hard—to live down or live up to.

The "new" cemetery in the family is Forest Hill in Memphis, added because of my mother's sister, Ada. After an 11-year engagement, Ada married her cousin, Sid Dabney, of Florence, Alabama, only to die a year after the wedding in the flu epidemic of 1918. The marriage was put off for so many years because her parents, like most Southern families, disapproved of unions between cousins, despite the fact that the relation was distant and the groom was a successful and distinguished citizen. My dear friend Tennie (my grandmother's housekeeper) told me that Aunt Camilla so objected to the marriage that she left instructions with the kitchen help that when Mr. Sid visited, he was to be served skim milk and not rich cream with his cereals and coffee.

As the story goes, the newlyweds were driving through Forest Hill Cemetery, when Ada shared with her groom that the blooming dogwoods made this the most beautiful place she had ever seen. Sid buried his bride there, miles away from the Mississippi cemeteries where the rest of her family lies, and I can't help but wonder whether this might have been in retaliation for his long engagement and the skim milk.

Ada's father, Captain Withers, bought an adjoining plot so his daughter would not be buried in Tennessee alone. The groom, so distraught that he tried to jump in his dead wife's grave the day of the funeral, remarried within a year and handed over his plot with an enormous monument to Captain Withers, giving the family 16 spaces. That's how our Mississippi family came to be buried in Memphis instead of Hernando Baptist Cemetery or Spring Hills Cemetery in Holly Springs.

In the attic of our Court Street house in Memphis sat several trunks containing Aunt Ada's lovely wedding trousseau, still packed away many years after her death. The only thing I was allowed to play with was Aunt Ada's tiny black riding boots, which fit me when I was about eight.

Having cut flowers from the garden and put them in big buckets, and with me assigned to steady them in the back seat with the help of sandbags, we headed first to historic Elmwood Cemetery Memphis, where my father's families, the Carrolls and Seabrooks, are buried.

Elmwood Cemetery, established 1852, is interesting for many reasons. For starters, it was never segregated, and since its pre-Civil War inception, it has represented a broad spectrum of Memphis history. In addition to a section for Confederate soldiers—for there are more than 20 generals buried throughout the cemetery—there are special sections for gypsies, Chinese, Japanese, Oddfellows, Masons, and others. Slipped in among the tombs of great civic and military leaders, and the nuns and whores (both groups equally the heroines of Memphis' yellow fever epidemics), lie the remains of many faithful pets. One, a French poodle named Roux that belonged to an uncle, was "potted" in a ball of dirt beneath a holly bush used to beautify the family lot.

Although my great-great-grandfather, Governor William Carroll, is buried in City Cemetery on the river in Nashville, three of his sons are at Elmwood: Charles Montgomery Carroll, Thomas Carroll (a former mayor of Memphis), and my great-grandfather, William Henry Carroll, the Confederate brigadier general at whose feet are buried my two infant sisters.

William Henry Carroll was a direct descendant of Daniel Carroll, a signer of the *Constitution*. According to Mr. Stadiem, who researched my family before including us in his *Town and Country* article about the first families of the South, my Carroll line extends even farther than the *Constitution*.

To me, it was always somewhat eerie to walk Elmwood's narrow paths, originally designed for horse-drawn carriages. But there was a time when families actually "visited" the dead, sitting on benches and making a pleasant family outing of it. The magnificent landscape at Elmwood boasts over 60 species of native trees that survived only because they were growing in a graveyard and were protected from cutting. The arboretum is named after my first cousin Carlisle Page, and believe me, I knew more about these trees than any teenager wanted to.

It was Elmwood where Mother took me to learn to drive a car. Things were going well until I put the car in reverse by accident and instead of going forward as I expected, we backed into a marble angel protecting a child's grave. The little angel toppled over into the child's cradle grave and reposed there, lying in state like it was the poor dead child. Mother was undone and told me to move out of the driver's seat. We headed out of the gates of Elmwood before the gates closed at four, and have told no one until now.

Little did I know as a teenager that my son Dick would be buried in the Leatherman ancestral plot, which was purchased by Davidson M. Leatherman, president of Elmwood's first board of trustees. On this lot stands Elmwood's first mausoleum, sealed in 1937. Since that time family members have been buried in graves surrounding the mausoleum.

Because my husband's mother, Irene McNeal Morrow, was a direct descendant of Ezekiel Polk (grandfather of President James K. Polk), we are eligible to be buried in the famous Polk Cemetery, in Bolivar, Tennessee. There is a saying in the South that it is easier to get into heaven than into the Polk Cemetery. But as for me, I do not want to be buried there. Our heritage is more akin to Memphis and the Mississippi Delta than Bolivar. So I say, why should I lie dead with the very people I have not know well while I was alive? I will be buried next to my son Dick in Elmwood.

Mother was no slouch at genealogy, and at a very early age, I learned I was the great-great-granddaughter of William Carroll, a colorful man in Tennessee history. A friend and contemporary of Andrew Jackson, he was a general during the War of 1812, served six terms as governor of Tennessee, and was land agent for the sale of Indian lands in northern Mississippi by the Treaty of Pontotoc, 1832.

William Carroll certainly benefited from his position as land agent. He purchased several sections of land in the Mississippi counties of Yalobusha and Panola. What interested me as a little girl was that he bought the land from an Indian woman named Istimipacha. She had been given title to the land after the Treaty of Pontotoc between the Chickasaw Indians and the United States. This entitled her to sell it, if she wanted to, and that she did to my paternal great-great-grandfather "and his heirs." That is how the deed dated January 14, 1837, reads. Because she could neither read nor write, after my grandfather had given her cash in the amount of $1,600, "in hand paid to her," she signed the deed with an "x" and her seal. Beneath her mark the chiefs of her tribe certified that she was "sane of mind" and capable of selling her land. I was saddened that 130 years after Istimipacha made her "x," we still had household help who could neither read nor write.

By coincidence, John Paxton Carruthers, my great-great-grandfather on my *mother's* side, purchased land—which we still own and farm today—from the Indians through this same treaty arranged by Carroll, my great-great-grandfather on my *father's* side. The grantor was She-mul-ta-yea.

Governor William Carroll, my great-great grandfather, became one of the heroes of the Battle of New Orleans. Because of creeks flooded by heavy rain, Carroll disobeyed Andrew Jackson's orders to follow the land route from Nashville to Natchez, and he went the long way around on the Cumberland River in boats, reaching the battleground at just the decisive time to be instrumental in the victory. One of the largest streets in New Orleans is named Carrollton in his honor, and throughout the country there are streets and counties named for the Carroll family. Being the only daughter, I've inherited keepsakes from both sides of the family.

Traditionally, females are keepers of family treasures. The Carroll family favorite keepsakes are silver goblets that are said to have been used when Major John H. Eaton of Franklin, the Secretary of War under Jackson, entertained the great Lafayette. Pauline Eaton Carroll, wife of Governor William Carroll, inherited these through the Eaton family. Like the proverbial fur coat that has been passed down through so many heirs that it is now merely a muff, the number of goblets became fewer as they were passed from generation to generation. It's hard to set a table with one or two goblets, so someone had the bright idea of having copies made, which gave more of the family bragging rights to the ancestral silver.

Governor William Carroll was given a gold-handled sword by the state of Tennessee in recognition of his gallantry at the Battle of New Orleans. I wish our family would adopt the tradition of one Memphis family in which the brides use Confederate swords to cut the wedding cakes. We could certainly one-up them with a sword from the War of 1812.

Meanwhile, back at the graveyard, my paternal grandparents, William Henry Seabrook, and his wife, Katherine Carroll Seabrook (daughter of William Henry Carroll and Elizabeth Jane Breathitt), were the subject of Mother's many tales. Our Seabrook family in America dates back to Thomas Seabrook, who emigrated from England in 1664 and purchased land on what is now Long Island, New York. Successive generations migrated to New Jersey, South Carolina (Seabrook Island off the coast of Charleston is named for the family) and Virginia. Some were prosperous ship builders and prominent landowners, but by the time my Seabrook ancestors made it to Memphis, something had gone wrong in the turnip patch, and my grandfather was left in the care of a guardian, who treated the boy like a son and paid for his education at a Nashville boarding school. William Henry went on to become the proprietor of W.H. Seabrook & Company, a successful wholesale and retail drugstore he operated for 35 years at Main Street and Union Avenue in Memphis.

To the Seabrooks and Carrolls, pedigree was important. So what if your great-grandfather was a rounder? William Henry Carroll was a Confederate general, and in the South, it is far better to have a question-able Confederate general in your family than no general at all.

To paraphrase William Stadiem, aristocratic families have more skele-tons than there are closets to put them in. I stand by my statement to Stadiem that like all aristocrats, the best of my ancestry is under the ground. Upon reflection, a few bad turnips are resting in Elmwood.

For example, Brigadier General Carroll was forced to live in Canada after the Civil War until his death. He served for a time in East Tennessee, there incurring the hatred of the Northern Army for hanging Union sol-diers he caught burning Southern bridges. He was later accused of drunk-enness by General Braxton Bragg and fled to Canada to avoid President Andrew Johnson's most-wanted list. There, he joined his wife and chil-dren, who had been sent to Montreal for safety early in the conflict. Many Southerners sent their families to live in Canada during the Civil War. In Montreal, Katherine Carroll attended Sacred Heart Academy, where her roommate was Jefferson Davis' daughter. I have some of Grandmother's letters in which she wrote that Jefferson Davis was not a kind man.

At William Henry Carroll's death in 1866, his body was returned to Memphis and interred at Elmwood. After the Civil War, his wife and sur-viving family returned to their Memphis home on Court Street, which had been used as a headquarters by the Yankees. Every Southern family has a story about silver hidden beneath the floorboards and portraits shot by Yankee bullets, and ours is no exception. It was in the William Henry Carroll house that this may have taken place. The portrait of my grand-mother today hangs on my guest room wall. I can't swear the Yankees did it, but it *is* damaged. Like most Southern families, I wouldn't dream of having it repaired. Dents and scratches are part of a family's history.

Only this summer, a newspaper column "Bygone Days," detailing 100 years ago, recalled that my great-uncle Col. William Henry Carroll and his wife and daughter were going to spend a year abroad. There must have been gold hidden under some board!

My mother used to tell the story of a Southern man who married a Northern girl. Returning home from his business one day, his young wife surprised him by handing over a present. She had taken his family's silver baby cup and had the dents repaired and the finish buffed until it shone like new.

"How *dare* you do such a thing?" said her enraged groom. "Five generations of my family have teethed and banged that cup, and now it looks like it came from a catalogue!"

Exploring tombstones and paper deeds and family portraits might help you understand the family tree, but there is no link to the past more powerful than the land. To stand on land owned by your predecessors for almost 200 years would cause anyone to tremble with awe. You can pick up a handful of soil and *feel* your ancestors; their hopes and dreams trickle between your fingers.

The wind, rain, the sun and moon all belong to God, and we just borrow the land for a short time. Six generations of my family have borrowed this little bit of God's green earth. Land is indeed our metaphor for Southern culture and history.

After the flowers were distributed and the stories told, we left Elmwood, driving past the bell that tolls the dead. We crossed the historical bridge, where caissons, two-wheeled horse drawn carts used to carry coffins, had traversed decades ago, and re-entered the world of the living.

Chapter 3

*Leaving The Cotton City for The
Cotton Land of The Delta*

Leaving The Cotton City for The Cotton Land of The Delta

One weekend, before Mother and I headed to Mississippi, we stopped by the Peabody for a luncheon. No description of life in Memphis, Tennessee, is complete without stories involving the Peabody Hotel. On certain afternoons after school at Miss Lee's, Mother would take me to a spinster who taught elocution in a small room off the mezzanine of the famous hotel. Mother would not park the car but simply slow down on Third Street, and I would hop out under the watchful eye of a liveried doorman. He wore a red, double-breasted coat with tails and brass buttons and a tall black top hat, and greeted me with, "Good afternoon, princess," as he pushed open the polished brass door to the foyer and elegant lobby.

On one side of the south lobby was a well-known photographer's shop, and I would always slow down to see whose portrait was on display. Several would be in the corner window, some facing the lobby and others looking out on Third Street. There were society matrons, politicians, mothers with babies, debutantes, brides and grooms, and prosperous businessmen and professionals. There was a lot of Memphis under the roof of the Peabody.

Elocution came easy for me, but I learned more by watching all the very dressed-up people at the Peabody and eavesdropping on their conversations. Like Federal Express today, the Peabody was the hub of the tri-states.

People of worth and events of interest seemed to start at the Peabody and then branch out to the rest of the world, and those of the rest of the world seemed to end up at the fountain where the ducks swam. Memphis is known as the city where the Peabody ducks splash about in the lobby fountain after making a grand entrance from their home on the roof, paraded by the eminent duckmaster Edward Pembroke down the elevator and across a red carpet to the fountain.

The first ducks were introduced to the Peabody fountain in the early 1930s by Frank Schutt, then the hotel's manager, and by "Chip" Barwick, a Memphis auto dealer, after they returned from a hunting trip. It was still legal to use live ducks as decoys in those days, and so the two came back to the hotel with three live ducks. As a prank, they placed the ducks in the fountain pool. The decoys quickly became at home in the pool. At first, they were called "Peabody," "Chisca," and "Gayoso," after the three hotels owned by the Memphis Hotel Company. Later they were named "Bed," "Bath," and "Bedlam," and then "Ruby," "Pearl," and "George."[1] Even the water fowl had personality at the Peabody.

On the ground floor was the Little Tea Shop, famous for its turnip greens and corn pone. There was a wonderful bakery, a beauty salon, and best of all, one of the top ladies hat shops of the South, where, with the help of "Miss Mattie," fashionable women designed their own hats to match their ensembles. There was a jewelry shop where men and women spent far more than they would have in their Arkansas or Mississippi hometowns, for it was more fun to go to Memphis and play the big spender—it was also a safer place to buy for a secret lover. Some planters might have had to mortgage the farm that year, but a night at the Peabody being pampered like royalty would have them fantasizing about better times. A bumper, or large, cotton crop was every Delta farmer's dream, as my father-in-law used to say when he wanted to put a problem in perspective, "It's nothing that two bales of cotton to the acre wouldn't cure." Being at the Peabody could make you feel like you had made a bumper crop and had sold it for top dollar on Front Street.

One of the standout Peabody events for me was my brother Jack's marriage at age 19 in a large suite with a Mississippi Methodist preacher officiating. I was so impressed when he and his bride left for a honeymoon trip to New Orleans in a new Ford that cost $1,000.

As a little girl, I started going to fancy luncheons with Mother at the Peabody Skyway, a very elegant restaurant, where live music, dancing, and food filled the top floor of the hotel. It was a must for bridal luncheons to be given at the Peabody. The particular affair one day was in honor of the daughter of an Englishman, who like many other foreigners of the time had come to Memphis because of its importance as a cotton financial center. Plans for the bride's upcoming evening garden wedding would be well hashed over by the attendees at these prenuptial parties.

While Champagne cocktails were served in an upstairs suite (Tennessee was a "dry" state, so liquor by the drink was illegal), I drank a "Shirley Temple" made of ginger ale and fruit syrup. Next the guests adjourned to the top terrace of the Skyway for a long and—to me, a child—boring luncheon.

Lonzo, the head waiter and maitre'd, passed the inevitable chicken a la king in round pastry shells and the Peabody's famous small vanilla muffins to the two dozen impeccably dressed women gathered to fete the bride and her mother. The guests all seemed to talk at the same time, asking each other questions and then hurrying to answer their own inquiries, letting everybody know they had the inside track. The most interesting comments, however, usually came out of earshot of the bride and her mother, often in the powder room:

"Of course, we know the wedding will be at 8 p.m. when it is cooler outside and the men will wear white jackets. Will the bride wear the English veil from her father's family, or will she wear that tacky old thing that looks like a lace window curtain that her mother wore?"

"Oh, I know she'll be pretty. I just hope they don't have children in the wedding like the English do. Why, the little dears just steal the whole show. That is, if they don't cry and refuse to take part."

"Well, nothing can top what happened at our last social wedding. You know, where the bride's old nurse was instructed to straighten the train just before the bride walked down the aisle. She took this responsibility so seriously that she proudly held the bride's train all the way to the altar."

"Speaking of brides, did you hear Nora Lou had her baby early? A little boy—eight pounds, seven-ounces – born two months premature. Her mother insisted the doctor put him in an incubator. The doctor said, 'Lady, I'll be glad to, if you can find an incubator big enough.'"

After coffee, mints and goodbyes said over a table decorated with a centerpiece of ferns and carnations big enough to drape a small casket, we took the express elevator down. We strolled through the lobby to the music coming from the Peabody's magical player piano.

In the main lobby, people streamed through the doors loaded with shopping bags, dress bags and hat boxes. All this enterprise happened because of cotton money. Farmers borrowed money from Front Street to make a crop and then Front Street made money buying and selling the cotton. It all poured back into the economy as the money was spent in Memphis shops and the Peabody Hotel.

Before leaving, we stopped by the Peabody bakery and now had a big bag of pastry to take to the farm. If you're from Mississippi, no matter if you're dressed to the hilt and your hat and handbag match, you still end up carrying home a paper bag.

I was in a hurry to find Wallie, my dog, a Sealyham mix that was going with us on the trip to Mississippi. Tied safely to the parking attendant's bench, Wallie looked at me with her one brown and one blue eye. I named her after Wallis Simpson, the Duchess of York. I had heard two neighbor ladies say that Mrs. Simpson was a bitch, and since Wallie was part English, I innocently thought it would be a good name for her.

Mother joked with the parking lot attendant as she gave him an extra tip for looking after Wallie. "Here's something for you to give your preacher," she said.

Wages were low and tips meant a lot to people in those lean, hard years. Once Grandmother Withers asked the plantation hostler, who had saddled the horses and handled the bird dogs for some visiting hunters at OK, if any of the guests had tipped him. With a downcast eye, the hostler replied, "Yes ma'am, one gent'man done give me a three-cent stamp."

This struck Grandmother as a ludicrous thing to give someone who could neither read nor write, but I remember her saying, "But I wager that if that man had been dancing on the Peabody roof, he would have tipped much more to impress his friends and the employees."

I thought of this story as Mother and I left the fantastic world of the Peabody, where Memphians and many others went to escape the reality of the Depression. Soon we would be going to the Delta world where poverty was evident from the minute we crossed the Mississippi state line. But we would find sanctuary at OK Plantation, with Grandmother, Aunt Camilla, and Tennessee, Grandmother's housekeeper and top cook, whom we called "Tennie". Well did these Southern women play the parts that the Depression had cast for them, and they would mold me as a young woman.

Soon Wallie and I were crowding into Mother's big Packard, packed as tight as a grocery bag for the trip to OK. On one trip to the farm, Mother had to miss a party in Mississippi because she did not have the right dress. From then on she packed as though we were going on a long sea voyage. We also took lots of special fancy foods that Uncle Sterling liked but could not get at the plantation commissary.

We pulled the car out of the parking lot, turned the corner on Third Street and headed south, leaving behind a world where many lived off the fat of the very land we were driving towards. When I was a child, the incomes of most of the wealthy Memphians I knew came from Mississippi, Arkansas, and Tennessee cotton and lumber, either directly or indirectly.

A few minutes and a few miles down Third Street, the road becomes Highway 61, the longest stretch of straight, flat highway in our part of the country. The road was lined with ominous black signs bearing skull and crossbones to mark each location of a fatal accident. Near Walls, Mississippi, a few miles south of Memphis, the road begins a gentle slope toward the Delta. Here, we passed the monument to Major Dabney, a relative on my mother's side known as "The Father of the Great Mississippi River Levee."

As we continued the trip south, Mother drove slowly, looking at the crops. She was so Delta-born that she could hardly drive a car for "road farming." As far as real farming, though, unlike my Aunt Camilla who ran plantations, lumber yards, and country stores on her own, I don't think Mother really understood the difference between buckshot soil and sandy loam. She knew the land where she was raised; that is, she knew which fields made the most cotton. More importantly, she understood our family's deep ties to the earth and the dependency on it for income, and that the land that stayed in families for generations was most likely near the river.

On the east side of Highway 61, just north of the town of Lake

Cormorant stands the house where my Uncle Tom Withers, whom my mother called "Br'er Tom," lived. Mother and I spent 2 nights with Uncle Tom on our way to Grandmothers. Uncle Tom's one-story house was comfortable, with fireplaces in each room, high ceilings, and a big, screened porch. This was the same farm where mother and her siblings had grown up in a large, columned, two-story home on "Wilson Hill," overlooking the flat, sweeping delta. Mother calling her brothers "br'er" did not seem strange to me, for in her youth, this usage was very common, made famous by the story "Br'er Rabbit."

When we arrived at Uncle Tom's, Aunt Camilla was waiting for us. Near dusk, the setting Delta sun resembled a candle nearly burned to a stump, the heat finally beginning to subside. We entered Uncle Tom's house from the back door. I don't suppose anyone in the country really ever uses a front door, except for company or salesmen. It never took but a honk or two before Uncle Tom's trusted houseman, Lorman, appeared at the back door of the large, screened back porch, hollering a hearty welcome.

Good old Lorman. I never had known what Lorman was supposed to do except keep himself warm by the kitchen stove in the winter. And yet, come to think of it, I can't think of anything Lorman couldn't do. He was not a big man, and his nappy black hair was turning gray at the temples. Perhaps he didn't call me princess like the bell captain did at the Peabody, but Lorman was cheerful, and I was glad to be with a real friend.

Lorman told us that Uncle Tom and his manager were out looking at the crops. The Delta was so hot, and before air-conditioning, that planters usually waited until around sundown to survey the fields, either on horseback or driving very slowly in the car. I had ridden with Uncle Tom before and had heard the men talk as they took a peek at other people's crops. You could shut your eyes, and except for the masculine voices, you would think you were with a crowd of ladies at a sewing circle, the way those farmers talked about each other: "I don't know why he keeps putting the corn over on that field. Never did do anything." Planters could tell how well the others were doing by their mules, barns and tenant houses.

Back on the farm, Mother, Aunt Camilla, and I lingered on the screened porch where we could see the lightning bugs twinkling in the yard. Mother was edgy because she did not want to offend her sister, a Mississippi Methodist, by having her drink or evening cigarette. She so revered her family that she even waited until after my grandmother's death to divorce my father.

Further irritating her, I kept asking Mother questions about the families, who married whom, who lived where, and how they made their living. Having spent a tiring day with me, she turned the history lesson over to her sister. Aunt Camilla carefully explained that the Carruthers had bought the first land for this farm in 1832, that Emily Carruthers married Sterling Withers, and that is how Aunt Camilla's father ended up owning the farm then called "The Carruthers Place." Their business, besides cotton farming, included shingle mills and lumber yards.

At one time, it was such a large lumber community that some of the workers' pay would be in wooden tokens to use at the commissary or the company store. My mother had three or four of the tokens. Then she told me how the family came to have this place at Lake Cormorant. I realized that I had opened up a subject very dear to Aunt Camilla. With pride, she recounted how her parents, Ada Byron Thompson and John Paxton Withers, had lived in Hernando, but after two years they moved to this farm in Lake Cormorant.

The more research I do, the less I can argue with Mr. Stadiem; the Carruthers and Withers lines do indeed trace back to the first families of the colonies. Among the papers I inherited from Grandmother's big cedar chest are the original deeds to Carruthers land in Virginia along the James River that was in still the family until the early 1900s, and copies of the enlistment papers of Sterling Adolphus Withers, who fought in the War of 1812 before moving to Marshall County, Mississippi.

Though she was a young woman when Sterling Adolphus Withers died, Emily Carruthers Withers was forever afterward known simply as "Widow Withers." In the 1850s, the young widow moved her two sons, John Paxton and young Sterling, from Marshall County to Tunica County, where she lived with her father John Paxton Carruthers at Commerce, just five miles south of the town now known as Lake Cormorant.

During my grandfather's boyhood, Commerce was a deep port river town competitive with Memphis. According to county records, two Carruthers brothers—John Paxton Carruthers and Robert White Carruthers—were among the first white settlers in the area and were engaged in the business, politics, and economy of this busy Tunica County river port from their arrival in the early 1830s. When an attempt to establish a railroad between Hernando and Commerce failed in 1837, John Paxton Carruthers and two other businessmen devised a way to turn the railroad failure into a financial success. They received a franchise from the state for a turnpike and turned the unfinished railroad bed into a plank road that was used throughout the Civil War. Nathan Bedford Forrest crossed this plank road when he made his famous raid into Memphis near the end of the Civil War.

Though settlers like the Carruthers brothers had been in the area since the 1830s, the town site now known as Lake Cormorant was not founded until 1850. Named "Blytheville" for the Blythe family on whose land the site was established, the town was renamed "Lake Cormorant" in 1903, and for a time was a summer resort that attracted young people from Memphis with its dancing, boating, sandy beach and its boardwalk made from the abundant cypress trees native to the area. The "new" town derived its name from the many cormorants that once thrived near the ancient ox-bow lake formed by the Mississippi River. A cormorant is a water bird that catches fish under the water.

Lake Cormorant flourished as a resort town in the 1920s, but by the 1930s the timber and the tourists were gone, and the lake was drained to create more farmland. There are still cormorants in some areas of Mississippi, but not at Lake Cormorant.

Mother's parents, John and Ada Withers, were married in 1874 in Hernando, Mississippi. Following the marriage ceremony, they traveled by train on a long wedding trip to Washington, D.C., Philadelphia, Boston and New York. Their first stop was Buntyn Station in Memphis, where they spent their wedding night in the home of my grandfather's maternal uncle, Colonel John C. White, who hailed from Holly Springs. White had purchased the home that stood on the Geraldus Buntyn property and which later became the first clubhouse of the Memphis County Club. The White name continues in our family through my mother, Mary White Withers Seabrook, and my daughter, Mary White Leatherman Carr.

Mother (born 1891) was the youngest Withers child. There was also my dear, sweet Aunt Camilla (Camilla Grissom, born 1875), and two brothers, Sterling (Sterling Adolphus, born 1877), and Tom (Frank Thompson, born 1880). A daughter, Emily Carruthers (born 1883), and a son, John

Paxton Withers (born 1889), died as toddlers and are buried at the Hernando Baptist Cemetery near their maternal grandparents, the Thompsons.

Mother described what Lake Cormorant was like when she was a young girl. She talked about the lake, the parties, and especially about dancing on the town's wooden railroad platform when W.C. Handy and his band came to play. Mother said the Memphis crowd would board the train known as the Cannonball at ten at night, disembark on the platform, now decorated with fancy Japanese lanterns, and dance with the Deltans all night long to Handy's mix of old-style blues and trumpet-blaring jazz. At five in the morning, the Cannonball loaded up its patrons and musicians and headed back to Memphis.

Mother said the house where she grew up had a huge center hall that ran from front door to back door, an architectural leftover from "dog-trot" log houses. When she was a child, they hung a hammock in the hallway so Captain Withers could nap after lunch and catch the breeze that was drawn through the long passage. Grandmother called her husband "Captain Withers" and never by his first name John, though his children called him "Papa." Captain and Mrs. Withers' 50-year marriage was private, and they would take long rides in the buggy when they wanted to discuss family affairs. It took Mother years to figure out why her mother and father would take drives with none of the children.

The house on Wilson Hill at Lake Cormorant burned when my mother was a young woman, and I've never seen a picture of it. But I could imagine it well from Mother's descriptions.

Mother's brother Sterling moved from the family home on Wilson Hill to Austin, Mississippi in Tunica County, south of Commerce Landing, about 1898, and there he rented land for the first year or two, living with a Mr. Bagley. Then, and I am certain he had help from his father, Uncle Sterling began to acquire land in Tunica County, Mississippi. After several years, Sterling had acquired the 5,000 acres or more that comprises the farm we call OK Plantation, which is the family farm today.

* * * *

There were no ceiling fans in Uncle Tom's farmhouse, so we relied on our unwieldy—though appreciated—oscillating fans. At night, we would lie in bed in a pool of sweat, anxiously awaiting the next short wave of cool air from the fan. I thought of one of our cousins who put her sheets in the icebox in order to cope with the heat. Just before she retired for the night, she would ask the help, who turned down the beds in those days, to get the cold sheets and lay them down seconds before she slipped in. I was always told that all of the Withers slept with one foot out from under the covers, and I am a witness that they did. My feet must be Seabrooks, because they stay under the sheets.

Winter or summer, at Uncle Tom's there was always an awakening rap on the bedroom door, and we would be brought a tray with juice, ice water, mush melon, and iced coffee. My coffee was mostly cream and sugar.

We were going on an excursion that morning to Hernando, and Uncle Tom, though he didn't want to go one bit, was going to drive us. Now Hernando isn't too far from Lake Cormorant—about 15 miles east—but the heat made it seem much farther.

When we arrived at Hernando, we went to the courthouse that sits in the middle of court square. It was the prettiest place, with a big, circular staircase with marble steps worn down from years of use. On the walls are beautiful paintings of Hernando DeSoto discovering the Mississippi River, rising all the way up the double height of the ceiling.

After that, we visited the cemetery, as usual. The last thing we did in Hernando was to stop and have tea at Miss Nellie White's. Miss Nellie, a Withers cousin, "received" on Saturday afternoon. As late as the 1940s in small country towns, a few ladies, even some in Memphis, received visitors at home on certain afternoons. You would be met at the door by a servant or a younger relative, and then you would wait on a settee or sofa in the main hall until received in the parlor by the hostess. Usually the visits lasted 15 to 30 minutes. This day old Miss Nellie was sharp as a tack and amused her guests with tales of bygone days. I remember her telling me that she could tell whether young men were light or heavy drinkers by the amount of sugar they took in their tea. Light drinkers, she said, take sugar; heavy drinkers don't, because alcohol is full of sugar.

I was glad of the custom of staying a short time because I have never known when to say goodbye. I learned at an early age most customs and good manners stem from being thoughtful. We left the big, white-columned house that sat down in a small valley and headed back to Lake

Cormorant full of conversation but weary from a long, hot summer day.

Late that afternoon, Lorman took LuLu and me, the farm cook's daughter exactly my age, fishing, and we played the rest of the day without history lessons and just enjoyed being children. It might have been the last carefree day for either of us, for the next morning, I was awakened by screams coming from the kitchen. When Uncle Tom went to the kitchen to see what all the screaming was about, he found Mabel, the cook, sitting in the corner with my friend LuLu pulled closely to her side.

She wailed out, "Mr. Tom, I done killed Jake. He done beat me for the last time. I told that no-good man to stop gettin' drunk and whuppin' me. Well, he won't whup me no more. Yesterday he said he'd chop me some stove wood if I'd pleasure him. Well, he got his pleasure all right, but there wa'nt no wood choppin'. He just beat me. When he fell on the bed and started snoring, I just went out to that woodpile, picked up that ax, and come in the house and chopped his mean old 'haid' off. Now, Mr. Tom, who's going to take care of them chil'ren? Right now all I can think about is me finally stoppin' him from givin' me those beat'ns. I ain't sorry yet, Mr. Tom. No sir, I ain't sorry a bit."

After that, all I remember was Uncle Tom walking fast down the hall to phone the sheriff. I lay in bed and pulled the cover over my head, and I kept thinking of Lorman, LuLu, and me fishing and riding yesterday and even doing silly things like smelling gas out of the gas tank and feeling funny. Now Jake was dead and cut in two pieces, and I wished I was back at Betty's house in Memphis where she and her Daddy would be getting ready to go horseback riding in the cool morning.

It was then I climbed out of bed and ran and threw up. I took a cold rag and wiped my face, and I took a rag out to Mother, because I knew this would bring on one of her headaches. Why had this happened to LuLu and her mother, and where was God, who was supposed to take care of all of us? Why did God let there be homemade whiskey in fruit jars and mean men who beat women and why did He let little Emily die at a young age and lie over there in the graveyard all alone? Right then I longed to be with Miss Lee and the school, the smell of chalk, and stories with happy endings. How could I tell Miss Lee about this awful thing next fall when school started, and what would Miss Lee say? Not even Miss Lee could have an answer for this mess.

At that moment in time in my young life, it came to me in a sickening, jolting way that for some things there just were no answers, and people who said there were answers were either lying or God had shown them things he had not shown me. I had grown up. My young heart pounded with confusion. Mother consoled me by saying Mabel would likely serve little or no time. In those days, an influential planter could get his labor out of the penitentiary with just a phone call if it was planting or picking season, and they were needed on the farm.

* * * *

Before we climbed in the car to leave Lake Cormorant, there stood LuLu by the gas tank. I whispered to her that Mother had said Uncle Tom would talk to the sheriff and try to take care of things. I crawled in the backseat and looked at my feet as the car pulled out, listening to the gravel hit the floorboard – I couldn't look out at LuLu. Tears ran down my face and I wiped my nose with the tail of my blouse, hanging out of my shorts.

Only last Christmas had I gone to the spooky funeral of my friend Helen's mother, where they played the funeral dirge. I haven't heard it played since at any service. And now the sheriff was coming for my friend Lulu's mother. As the gravel road finally came to old Highway 61, I pulled the shade down on the car window and ached to be back home, if not riding horseback with Betty, at least in Mother's bedroom with the curtains drawn and only the drone of her fan to keep me company.

Strong women that they were, Mother and Aunt Camilla chatted away in the front seat. I saw first hand why Southern ladies talk so much: it's not that they don't care about others, it's that they care too much. Perhaps for that reason, trying to take my young mind off the morning's shock, they stopped by Commerce, the oldest town in Tunica County, to show me where the Carruthers family had come from Virginia to build the railroad.

Mother told me that in its prime, Commerce rivaled Memphis for river traffic, shipped more cotton than any other Mississippi port except Natchez and Vicksburg, and had a population of 5,000. In the early 1840s the Mississippi River suddenly changed its course and violently flooded the business district of Commerce. Officials quickly moved the county seat south to Austin, and the bustling town of Commerce, now hundreds of acres smaller, almost overnight lapsed back into quiet, shady farm and pastures. Life is as wild and unpredictable as the powerful Mississippi river. A matter of minutes changed Lulu's entire future just as easily as it had wiped out the potential of an entire town.

Along the old Commerce road, I spotted a rambling white clapboard house nestled among native pecan trees.

"That's Ethel Leatherman-Andrews' place, isn't it?" Mother asked.

Aunt Camilla replied, "Yes."

Aunt Camilla, who had attended boarding school with her, told us that one weekend Ethel returned to school dressed in mourning clothes. No one in her family had died—she just liked black. Also, she didn't like the name her parents had given her at birth, Sarah Emma, so she changed it to one that suited her, Ethel. I sat back in the seat and wondered how she worked up the nerve to stand up to people and just change her name. Oh, how I wished people wouldn't call me "Sugsie."

We had gone from murder to the demise of Commerce, on to a lady who only wore black and then changed her name, and finally we were about to arrive at our destination, OK Plantation. But first we had to pass through a dark morass filled with deep mud and murky water. Tall cypress trees, with ugly warts, blocked the sun from the road, and the air reeked of the stagnant water. As I crouched in the backseat of the car, this scene reminded me of what Miss Lee had read to us from John Bunyan's *The Pilgrim's Progress*. "The Slough of Despond," as it is described in the book, is so depressing that people abandon all hope of salvation in its swamps.

To a child it was even worse than Bunyan had described, because sometimes in winter, the dirty water would rise above the road, and we could not travel through at all. When this happened, we had to take a longer, more tortuous route.

As my mind raced through these horrors, our car slid off the road, as often happened with Mother or Aunt Camilla driving. An elderly man who had been fishing in the slough came up the bank to help us. My mother called elderly black men, no matter if she knew them or not, "Uncle," and thanks to "Uncle," we made it past the slough. I would soon be in Grandmother's loving arms. Just as in Bunyan's famous allegory, we had to cross the slough of despond to reach heaven, and that's exactly what Grandmother's was for me.

[1] *Memphis Press-Scimitar*, October 28, 1980

Collection of Old Capital Museum, Mississippi Department of
Archives and History

Top row, left to right: Frank M. Norfleet, Company C, 18th
Mississippi Regiment/Forrest Cavalry; Emile Q. Withers,
Company G, 17th Mississippi Infantry
Bottom row, left to right: Captain James Dinkins, Aide de Camp to
General Chalmers 1st Division Forrest's Cavalry; Brig. Gen. A.J.
Vaughn, Preston Smith's Brigade; Hy C. Myers, Company E, 2nd
Missouri Regiment/Forrest Cavalry

My grandparents on my father's side, William Henry Seabrook and Katherine Carroll Seabrook.

Katherine Carroll (Mrs. W. H. Seabrook) was the daughter of Confederate Brigadier General William Henry Carroll and grand-daughter of six-term Tennessee Gov. William Carroll, a hero of the War of 1812. She is shown second from left in the polka dot dress with Willie Seabrook (far left); Mrs. Sam Coward (third from right); and Sam Coward (far right), all identified in a 1997 letter from Carlisle Page, who writes, "One of the other women is Mollie Carroll (Mrs. Vance), Elise Norfleet's mother."

Grandmother-Ada Byron Thompson Withers, the Ole Miss of OK Plantation in Tunica County.

John Paxton Withers, called Captain Withers by his wife and known as Papa to the rest of his family.

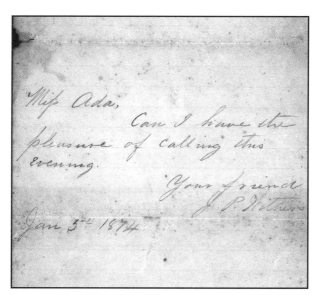

The note Captain Withers wrote to his future bride on January 5, 1874, asking permission to call on her. The two married later that year in Hernando. The note and one of Ada's calling cards, found in a wooden box in one of Grandmother's trunks, were labeled the "most cherished possessions" of their daughter Camilla Grissom Withers. Grandmother's father fought the entire Civil War under the wizard of the saddle, Nathan Bedford Forest.

Four children of Captain John Paxton Withers and Ada Thompson Withers survived to adulthood.

Camilla Grissom Withers was a capable farm manager and businesswoman in her own right and ran OK Plantation with the straw boss Boots after her brother's death.

Sterling Adolphus Withers has been called the premier citizen of Tunica County. He launched Tunica's first industry, Planters Oil Mill, and fought off flood waters of the Mississippi River, keeping the county high and dry through the devastating flood of 1927 and other high-water emergencies, including the near-disaster of 1937.

My aunt Ada Withers, who married Sid Dabney and died one year later in 1918, and my mother Mary White Withers, as children.

My father Carroll Breathitt
Seabrook

Mother in a lace dress.

Mother and her
children Jack, Sterling,
and me, of course, in
her garden on Court
Street.

The "star" of the Cotton Carnival Parade in 1941 gave the Miss America wave to her father from the float representing Miss Lee's School.

My chestnut gaited gelding Love was stabled at the Fairgrounds in Memphis for $2 a day.

I had the Veronica Lake look when I graduated from Miss Harris' School in Miami in 1945.

William Henry Seabrook, my half brother, at a young age.

My oldest brother John William "Jack" Seabrook ran OK Plantation and enjoyed the outdoor life, hunting and fishing alongside his guide Colonel, often accompanied by legendary outdoor writer Nash Buckingham.

Older brother Sterling Withers Seabrook served with distinction in the Mississippi House of Representatives and as a Tunica County supervisor. Here he is pictured as a 19-year-old in Officer's Candidate School in 1944; later he was shipped to the Pacific theater and seriously wounded in Guam.

Elsie Walker Seabrook married my brother Sterling when he returned from the Pacific area in World War II and they were married over 50 years at the time of his death.

Voted by wounded Air Force veterans as "The Body" on the beach in Miami during World War II.

My friend Martha's father Cole Early visited us in New York during the summer of 1946, when Mother was so ill. This photograph was made at the "New Yorkiest place on earth," the Stork Club.

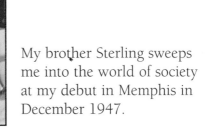

My brother Sterling sweeps me into the world of society at my debut in Memphis in December 1947.

Chapter 4

Childhood at Grandmother's on "OK"

Childhood at Grandmother's on OK

Nowhere in William Faulkner or *Gone With The Wind* can I find my grandmother. Her personality fit no single characterization of the Southern woman, so often portrayed in literature. A happy, busy woman, Grandmother owned enough diamonds and rubies to be presented to the Court of St. James, but rose each morning out of her high-backed bed, fell to her knees to say her prayers, and then put on her very simple, flowered house dress and piled her thick, white hair on top of her head with tortoiseshell hair pins. In her old age she seemed small, but her posture was perfect and her hands, beautifully shaped, were never idle. Unlike Miss Nellie White in Hernando, Grandmother never stopped to receive visitors or patronize social clubs. After a large breakfast, she raced from one activity to another: feeding chickens, beating cake batter, rooting cape jasmines in the garden, and even making wine from the elderberries. I never saw her without a handkerchief tucked handily under her belt or without her spectacles attached by a thin chain to a button on her dress. Having lived through the Civil War, this true Southern Belle was undeniably the "Ole Miss" of OK Plantation.

Although I was only 6 years old, memories of my summer at Grandmother's are etched in my mind like dates on a tombstone. Grandmother's house was also inhabited by her single, adult children (my Aunt Camilla and Uncle Sterling) and my brother Jack, it was always just

"Grandmother's" to me. The house would never have been included in an historical tour of grand-columned plantation mansions like those in Natchez, Mississippi, for it had been added onto so many times that some rooms stood almost a foot higher than the next. It would be labeled an architectural abomination by any good designer, but it was a splendid place for a child, and it certainly suited Grandmother.

The house was divided by a center hallway that led from the living room at the front, followed by the step-down dining room with its huge oval table, to a large kitchen and huge back porch. While there were four bedrooms with high ceilings and lots of windows, there was but a single bathroom in the center of the house, so large that it was furnished with dressers and chairs.

Mother and I always stayed in the front guest room. On one long visit, Grandmother had the farm carpenter, Swifty, build me a porch off this bedroom so I could play outdoors when the ground was wet. It was a simple, open deck with no railing, where I could ride my tricycle or bounce a ball.

The bedrooms were big and comfortable, and several windows would occasionally provide a precious breeze. Closets were nonexistent; enormous chifforobes held all of our outfits. Every bedroom had an old-fashioned marble-top washstand with a pitcher of water and bowl, which we used to wash our faces or wet a towel to put on the back of our necks to relieve the misery of the muggy, buggy summer nights.

In the summer—mosquito season—we climbed into oversized double beds covered by mosquito bar nets. Because we were so near the river, not only did we have these bloodsuckers, but we had bugs so tiny they were called "no-see-ums." On certain nights these bugs came in off the river by the thousands and flew right through the screens. The insects were so bad sometimes that supper was fixed and eaten by candle glow to minimize the light so attractive to the "cain't sees."

The guest room had a large fireplace. On winter nights the fire would be banked to ensure a continued low burning. Early in the morning, Coot, one of the housemen, would come in to stir the fire and lay on wood in order to heat up the room before we had to leave the warmth of the heavy covers. Once Coot had accidentally disturbed a rather playful young couple by entering unannounced, and from then on Coot would always peek through the keyhole before coming in.

Grandmother's ancient upright piano stood in the hallway right out-side the guest room, and from time to time I would practice my one-song repertoire of "Silent Night." One afternoon, I talked two of the young houseboys, playmates of mine, into pulling the piano away from the wall enough for me to peek inside and try to fix some of the keys that were stuck. Much to my surprise, I found a heavy drawstring bag made from an old flour sack wedged inside the piano. I hurriedly undid the string and found several dozen sterling silver dollars! Having never seen such riches in one place before, the bright, brown eyes of my two cohorts grew wide with the discovery. Though the thought of borrowing a few coins was mighty tempting, we carefully replaced the bag intact and pushed the piano back into place before getting caught. We made a pact between the three of us never to tell of our secret, but the promise didn't keep us from checking on the stash from time to time.

Tennie ran the kitchen, which was far and away the busiest room not only in the house, but maybe on the whole plantation, given the impor-tance the Withers side of the family placed on food. Tennie's territory also included the back porch, which was larger than most living rooms. It needed to be with all of the many things stored there on the oilcloth-cov-ered wooden tables that lined the walls. Always with a dog to flush out the snakes, we would gather pounds and pounds of vegetables from the gar-den to store on the back porch. Sometimes there were so many fresh veg-etables harvested every day that the mounds of produce smelled a tad too ripe for me, a city girl.

Like all Southern women, Grandmother kept two or three milk cows. We did whatever we could to keep the cows from grazing on the onion grass, because the resulting milk was of a particularly unpleasant flavor. I never learned the art of milking the cows myself, but we all enjoyed the dairy products that came out of the wooden churns on the back porch.

The long handles looked like a broomstick with an "x" on the end, which you plunged up and down to churn milk into butter and byprod-ucts. The cloddy lumps of butter would be taken out, churned again, and then rinsed until the water washed off clear. This hunk then went into the one-pound wooden mold, and Grandmother's butter came out with a four-leaf clover shape on top. The thick, rich cream and milk would be skimmed off, leaving clabber, or buttermilk; the very watery milk called "Blue John" was at the bottom of the churn. Many a poor Southerner's country supper featured homemade cornbread, doused in buttermilk or cream.

Tennie also oversaw the smokehouse, where ham, bacon and sausage hung from the ceiling. A sharp, razor-like ledge also went completely around the wall and over the door. That was to keep mice (or if you want to know the truth, grown Delta rats) from running up the wall and getting at the meats that were being cured.

Meals were served in the dining room on an enormous claw-foot table. A snow-white Damask cloth covered the many different leaves added to the table in order to accommodate crowded family get-togethers. If Grandmother was having company, we used two napkins a day; otherwise, we used the same napkin for all three meals, identified by monogrammed, silver napkin rings. I was especially proud of mine because it was engraved not with my name, but with "Emily." Emily Carruthers Withers, Grandmother's little daughter, who had died of a fever at age two.

At each meal, everything that could be harvested from the garden or picked that day was served in Haviland china dishes with matching Gorham Lily serving spoons. Highbrows today would have been more impressed by Grandmother's kitchen flatware, a mismatched collection of coin silver! After grace was said and the meat carved—both extremely important duties bestowed upon the male head of the household—the meal was served. Two young boys wearing starched white coats brought in the meat and bread, but after that, everyone ate "boarding house style." Meals at Grandmother's tables were always joyful, loquacious affairs. Not wanting to interrupt our conversations even for a moment, we would just point to what delicious item we wanted. I can close my eyes and see us talking, pointing, and passing food, with the man of the house seated at the head of the table and the other men, women, and children seated around him.

Every midday meal would consist of at least two meats, six or seven vegetables and always two kinds of breads. A typical Sunday breakfast at Grandmother's would be salted Spanish mackerel, calves liver, brains and eggs, sausage, ham, bacon, biscuits, eggs, fruit and butter. The Withers clearly were robust eaters. This differed greatly from my father's side in

Memphis, where dinners were merely "diet" versions of what we ate in the Delta (though maybe this accounts for the fact that several of the Withers family died young, while the Seabrook kin lived until their 90s). There was a great contrast not only in food, but also in attitude. I began to wonder as a child if the happy atmosphere at Grandmother's table was because they didn't drink before and during the meal. After the long cocktail hours at our house in Memphis, the dinner table talk could get ugly, and we would go on and on about things that didn't matter, for Mother and Daddy had begun to argue frequently. When this happened, I would sit outside on the kitchen steps, put my fingers in my ears, and cry.

At Grandmother's, we ate "dinner" in the middle of the day and "supper" at night. Supper wasn't the enormous meal that dinner was. Supper was usually something like a whole leg of lamb or potato salad with sliced tomatoes.

Occasionally Grandmother bought barrels of oysters off the riverboats. The barrels would sit on the back porch off Tennie's kitchen, and if we did not eat the oysters the first day or two, we poured cold salt water over them and fed them crackers to keep them alive for a few days. To my knowledge, no one ever died of eating a bad oyster at OK Plantation.

For dessert Grandmother might dish up boiled custard, rice pudding, bread pudding, Charlotte Russe, ambrosia, a pound cake, or on special occasions, a Lady Baltimore Cake – white cake with raisins and nuts, topped with meringue icing and shredded coconut.

A nice thing that Grandmother did, though most unusual, was to have one of the housemen pass a large, hand-painted French finger bowl around the table after we had finished eating. Draped across his arm he carried a fresh white towel for us to dry our hands. No individual bowls with a slice of lemon for Grandmother; she was an original.

The talking and eating continued in the living room, where there were always glass-lined silver bowls full of perfectly toasted, salted pecans. My Aunt Camilla was the best in the family at picking out whole, perfect pecans. They came from our orchard of 200 pecan trees, stately and tall, planted by my aunt in precisely measured rows. Being of a sentimental nature, she named each tree in the orchard after various families on the plantation. If it was a large family, she would give them two trees, but all the families had at least one tree that they could pick on shares. Aunt

Camilla divided the nuts with the various families fifty-fifty. This put a lot of responsibility and strain on the sharecroppers, because as they gathered nuts, they would certainly be tempted to eat a few. It was also tempting to gather nuts from under someone else's tree, which sometimes led to squabbles. Due to good shooting and skillets, squirrels were no problem in the orchard.

Pecan trees weren't the only things growing near the house. Grandmother and I kept a small garden on the side of the house facing the lake. I remember putting gardenia or "cape jasmine" cuttings in glass bottles to get them started, and being glad in early March to see the big yellow blooms of the wild buttercups, the first true sign of spring. Grandmother could root just about anything, including avocados, which we called "alligator pears." Split barrels brimming with petunias and ivy lined the garden. The garden was a mass of purple because of the multitude of violets, and to this day, I think of violet as "Grandmother purple." Once I heard my father say the garden was tacky. "Violets," he claimed, "should be pulled up like any other weed." Not surprisingly, Grandmother didn't care a lick what he had to say.

On long, rainy days when we couldn't work out in the garden, Grandmother saw to it that there was plenty to do indoors. There was always a jig-saw puzzle set out on a card table in the living room, and board games like Chinese checkers were kept in a large mahogany bookshelf.

Grandmother, an excellent speller, was determined to make me one, too. One day I had to sit in a chair, and she would not let me up until I spelled "Mississippi" correctly. What really taught me to spell was listening to Grandmother, Aunt Camilla and Mother gossip. When they reached the most interesting parts of their conversation, they spelled so I wouldn't understand what was being said. This did more to motivate me than a spelling bee.

After spelling lessons, Grandmother tried to train me to memorize George Washington's 110 rules of civility. I dare not try to repeat all of them, but I do remember a few. Standing up, if a grownup came into a room, was one; taking off your coat and carefully putting it out of your hostess' way, two; and thanking people was three.

Both my grandmother and Aunt Camilla were Methodists, so *The Upper*

Room, a Methodist book of daily devotionals, was never out of arm's reach. Grandmother also had a stereopticon, which was the most fascinating thing to a child. You would put pictures of exotic places or animals in the device, and it would make them look almost three-dimensional. I can remember sitting in her living room swapping out picture after picture. We also spent hours going over the Sears & Roebuck catalogue, page by page. You could even buy a house from Sears & Roebuck, and at least one in Tunica survives today. If there was one thing Grandmother could not resist, it was a young, good-looking man selling magazines to go to college. We sat together, mystified by the strange people and creatures in *National Geographic.*

Grandmother had a few records that we could play on the gramophone. One of our favorites was a male chorale's version of "General Order Number 9," Robert E. Lee's epic surrender order that Miss Lee had spoken so often about. One of Grandmother's fondest interests was opera, and every Caruso record ever made filled her shelves. She had studied voice as a young woman. As the years went by, Grandmother's recollection of her own talent increased, so by the time I came along, I almost believed she could have sung at the Met herself. The accomplishments of ancestors seem to grow especially after their death. One of my relatives only acted in a Southern amateur theater, but her obituary claimed that she had been a rising national actress who selflessly gave up her promising career in order to marry.

On Saturday afternoons at 2 o'clock, we listened to the Metropolitan Opera on the radio show introduced by the "Texaco Fire Chief." Always included in our small audience was Polly, Aunt Camilla's parrot. Polly would be taken from her cage in the kitchen and delivered to the living room, where she would sit on the back of a rocking chair, bobbing and rocking, and occasionally bursting into a hearty rendition of two lines of "God Bless America"–the only song she knew.

Polly's cage was kept out on the back porch or in the kitchen where every morning she drank coffee with sugar and cream. She ate sunflower seeds and occasionally an apple or slice of pear. Polly had to be nearly 100 when I was a child, for she was not a young bird when given to Aunt Camilla. She died about a year after Aunt Camilla.

Polly came from a riverboat captain, and having spent a good deal of her life among river men, Polly had a stout repertoire of cuss words. She was an ornery old bird. Her favorite trick was to call Uncle Sterling's hunting dogs, mimicking Uncle Sterling's whistle and calling them by name: "Hey, Bob!" "Here, Bill" "Here, Sue," and the poor dogs thought they were being called to eat their standard fare, huge pans of cornbread with pot licker (the juice cooked out of turnip greens) poured over it. When the dogs came running only to find an empty pan, Polly would cock her head to one side and cackle, knowing that she had played a huge joke on them.

Once, Mother arranged for a male parrot to visit Polly at OK. When Polly saw her potential suitor, she hollered, "Help, Milla, help!" Milla was what she called Aunt Camilla. We decided that Polly, like Aunt Camilla, was born an old maid; however, while Aunt Camilla did like men, Polly would have nothing to do with them.

Even if Polly didn't care for them, the Withers men were treated like princes at home. They were served first, they always claimed the best chairs, the best beds, and the best food—the whole house revolved around them. And even if a woman did work, like my Aunt Camilla, it still was the man who received the praise.

Some Southern women keep their talents in the background and learn to be cunning and manipulative to survive and get what they need from men, but the Withers women were not this underhanded—I think they liked being a little subservient. The whole atmosphere changed when a man entered the room.

Grandmother and I played game after game of solitaire and double solitaire to help pass time if Uncle Sterling or Jack was out late. Until they came home, Grandmother and Aunt Camilla were as nervous as if the men had gone off to war.

I had almost given up on solitaire one night at dusk, when we heard a gunshot from the front porch. The front door swung open and my brother Jack stumbled in, covered in blood. He had carelessly shot a gun without first examining it. A dirt dauber's nest in the barrel of the gun caused it to split, practically destroying Jack's left wrist. As soon as it happened, Jack wiped his hand across his face, smearing blood all over his head. Horrified, Grandmother and I thought he had shot himself in the head. Aunt Camilla just started crying.

Aunt Camilla had no use for sedatives or psychiatrists, because she knew how to cry. She would get the "vapors" and weep when things went wrong. She would cry without shame, and shake, and sniff smelling salts at funerals. Even as a child I thought, "You know, Aunt Camilla never is able to do what she wants to do," for most of her time was spent being nice to her mother and her brother Sterling, and to Mother and me and all the workers on the farms.

Early in life, this red-headed beauty vowed that she would take care of her mother and father. She had lovely skin, beautiful neck and shoulders, arms, hands and nails. Sterling remained a bachelor and also helped take care of his parents and sisters.

When my Uncle Sterling entered a room, even if he said not one word, the gathering knew he was the dominant male. He was about six feet tall, and just like his sister, had dark red hair which had since turned stark white. Big, handsome, a bit overweight, Sterling was a heavy eater, enjoyed a straight shot of bourbon chased by a Coca-Cola, and loved dogs and hunting, and he could dance all night. All Withers had barrel chests, and this trait, passed down from Grandmother's family, made for some surprisingly good tenor voices.

"I only light one cigarette a day," Uncle Sterling truthfully boasted, but this was because he never let a cigarette go out before he had used it to light the next one. This habit replaced his tenor voice with one as deep and raspy as a bullfrog in a grassy ditch.

He was best man in 17 weddings—he had women here and women there, but none were ever brought home or invited to family affairs. He soon took the place of my father as far as Mother's social life went. Since Daddy's politics, or maybe his attitude, stopped all mixed social life for Mother, "Uncle Saw"(his initials), as I called him, took her to the Kentucky Derby, Hot Springs, Mexico and Europe as governor of Rotary, and escorted her to other gatherings of planters (now called farmers). He loved horse races, but Mother did not, for like me, she would rather spend money than lose it.

Uncle Sterling has been described by Tunica historian John Dulaney as "the premier citizen of Tunica" in his day. As a young man of 22, he began farming at Austin next to the Mississippi levee, later becoming president of the Planters Oil Mill and serving in the State Senate. He was active in the local levee board and dealt successfully with several instances of high water on the river, beginning in 1913. With this experience, Uncle Sterling was put in charge of the Tunica levees during the 1922 Mississippi River flood and lead the locals at Devil's Hole when the levee held, even after two-thirds of it had caved in. He was called to this leadership again in 1927 when the Big Bertha boil arose at Commerce and also during the 1937 flood that was so devastating to the South Delta, miles below Tunica County. Uncle Sterling was given the title of Colonel for his service to the levee board.

Why would two of the most physically beautiful and outstanding personalities of the South decide to stay single? You would have to share a breakfast at the Withers' dining room table to understand the love and protection these people gave to each other. They seemed thoroughly content with each other, and because they did not marry and have children of their own, at their deaths the farm was not split like an atom as in so many Delta families. I was the lucky beneficiary not only of their love, but of their land.

Although I only knew my grandfather Withers through his children, he was apparently beloved by both his family and all who lived on his farms. When he died in 1925, a newspaper in Marshall County published a telling obituary.

It reads in part:

> "Never was the little church more beautiful with flowers, the flowers he liked, piled high from altar to choir, never were the hearts of a congregation fuller of love and sympathy, when with the church packed to overflowing some stood outside their heads bowed, mingling their tears with the tears of the faithful old negroes, former slaves of his family, who had traveled far to bid Mars John God speed on his journey. These old slaves had been freed of body by the Emancipation Proclamation but at heart they were still enslaved to their old Master, their old gray heads uncovered in grief and respect, as their tear dimmed eyes attested."

Small wonder that my mother did not smoke or drink in front of her parents and waited to divorce my father until after their deaths. Or that a generation after her, I chose to keep my Southern accent rather than fade into no-man's land.

It was through the Withers clan that I inherited the attitude that life is to be enjoyed to the fullest. Beautiful horses, magnificent gardens and dancing were the essence of life. Sterling Withers was the first one in Tunica County to own a car, and my brother, Jack, had the first central air-conditioned home. They might not have been nearly as wealthy as some of my Memphis relatives, but they managed to live a far more glamorous, exciting and comfortable life.

This lifestyle would not have been possible without the black people who were our caretakers and best friends. Besides Tennie, there were several young black girls who would help with the housework and cooking, and young boys who would help with the serving. Other employees on the plantation at that time were "Boots," Aunt Camilla's overseer; "Coot" and "Rooster," two top hands who supervised crews in the field; and "Swifty" the carpenter. There was a blacksmith, and hands to take care of the garden and chickens and farm equipment, and a hostler who was in charge of all the plantation mules, hogs and sheep.

We had an expression for someone who ran errands on the farm, which was a "go-for." Rather than being a term for someone low on the totem pole, a go-for was an important person on the farm, for we all depended on him.

I spent days tagging along with Tennie, often walking with her to services at the black church near Grandmother's house. It was a very simple white clapboard church with a steeple and bell and adjoining graveyard. The church was about a mile down the road, so Tennie and I wore our walking shoes for the trip. In a paper sack we carried our clean Sunday shoes to put on before we entered the "church house," as Tennie called it, and at the church door, we were handed one of the paper fans the undertakers in the county always gave out at funerals. If the preacher's make-you-tremble sermon stirred the congregation enough, the entire church would stand up and start singing loud, soulful spirituals.

The church year culminated in the baptisms held in the lake right in front of Grandmother's house. Singing all the way, the congregation marched from the church house to the lake. One Sunday with Tennie, I proudly watched and listened to this soul-saving musical drama, with its songs born of hundreds of years of back-breaking poverty. The participants, dressed in clean white robes, were led into the waist-high water and then completely immersed. They rose from the water to shouts of jubilation from all the churchgoers.

The sharecroppers and their families were a vital part of OK Plantation's existence. With the help of their families, sharecroppers provided the labor to cultivate about ten acres of cotton each and sometimes a few acres of corn, and they could have a garden. In return for their labor, the plantation owner provided a tenant house for the year. The tenant houses at OK were spaced about a half-mile apart. Every morning the sharecropper would go to the plantation barn and get a mule or a pair of mules, and farming tools. All supplies to make the crop were given to the sharecroppers by the owner from the commissary. Sharecroppers depended on the plantation owners, and the plantation owners depended on the sharecroppers completely to plant and harvest the crop. After the harvest, they would settle up. In later years, the sharecropper usually paid half the cost of various supplies. At the end of the year, he would be paid for half of the cotton, and he would keep half of the corn.

If they liked the owners, most families would stay to work on the plantation for many years. They would have children, and their children would live on the plantation. It was not unheard of for there to be three generations of a family on the plantation. I don't remember seeing many black babies on our farm as a child. I later found out the reason. Before World War II and the advent of penicillin, syphilis was so rampant in the Delta that the birthrate among the sharecroppers was surprisingly low.

There was usually a schoolhouse on the farm, though most were only in session about five months of the year. Many of the farm schools had fair teachers–usually volunteer churchwomen. They taught the basics, but most who learned to read learned from the Bible. Many of the farm people had Biblical names.

If the sharecropper didn't make anything, the owners usually cleared the sharecropper's debt. Sadly, families were often traded from one farm to another like you would trade horses. If a family didn't work out and another plantation owner you knew needed another family, then a trade might be negotiated. You might equate this practice with trading major league ball players. And sometimes families in debt just left in the night. No one ever chased them. It was the Delta version of filing bankruptcy—

they just moved and started over.

Most of the black laborers on the farms in the Mid-South belonged to an organization called "The Sir Knights and Daughters," basically a health and burial insurance program that could be purchased for a weekly premium of as little as a quarter. There were agents all over the area who collected the premiums. The health insurance maintained a black hospital at Mound Bayou, Mississippi. All members who used the health insurance had to travel all the way to Mound Bayou. A quiet knock on Grandmother's door and a request to call the doctor meant that the situation couldn't wait for Mound Bayou.

Early in the morning, the hostler would ring the bell and the sharecroppers would arrive to receive the mule or pair of mules he selected for them. There seemed to be a great bond between mules and the labor. The shuffling of mules' hooves and sharecroppers' feet signaled the start of another day's work. It was the custom to ride the mule side saddle-style rather than to sit astride. Each sharecropper carried a shiny tin lunch bucket, usually filled with side meat, a biscuit and lots of syrup. Going out for the day, they were in high spirits and would call back and forth to each other and sing.

Out in the cotton crop the mules, with their drivers walking behind, went up and down through the fields, turning at the ends of the rows in a dusty clearing that ran between the fields, giving rise to the farm expression "turn rows." Women field hands were brought in wagons or trucks to chop weeds and later pick the cotton, and in between this back-breaking labor, there has been more than one "turn-row baby" conceived.

At the end of the day, the sharecroppers would deliver the mules back to the barn. Up the road they came, dust rising beneath the mules' legs, singing and walking toward the mule barn and then home. But what I remember most are the joking and the expressive songs that told more of a black laborers' lives and feelings than the average person could comprehend.

Sometimes the mules would "founder." This happened when the mule ate something that upset his stomach. A side effect of this was that it made the blood vessels in his hooves swell. The hooves were hard and had no room for the swelling vessels. It was very painful to the mule, and he neither would nor could walk. There was no remedy for this except to put the mules in Grandmother's lake. The water was generally cool and would reduce the swelling. Sometimes the mules would have to stand in the lake for a couple of days before the swelling went down enough for the mule to start walking again.

People had good years and people had bad years—it's the nature of farming. The sharecroppers' fiscal year began around March 1, when they received their credit or "furnish" at the commissary. This advance on the proceeds of their crop would stop when the crop was "laid by" (from about July to harvest time), and no money would be coming in again until the harvest began.

The first job was breaking the heavy, black soil. Because of this chocolate-like soil, created and nourished by the coursing Mississippi River, the Delta produced more cotton than any other spot in the world. Our family was lucky to have good sandy loam, and we always broke up the soil in early spring to avoid erosion from the winter rains.

In my childhood, only corn was planted behind the levee, because spring rains in the north could bring high water in an instant, ruining the crop and plunging the family into sudden poverty. Planting cotton behind the levee was as chancy as shooting craps, and planters read the river gauges and listened to the report on the radio for any news that the river was rising, but corn was a necessity for feeding the hundreds of mules it took to farm.

Cotton planting traditionally began around April 1st, but Delta farmers also relied on the Almanac. And there is an old expression that it's not time to plant until a woman fishing on a bank could pull her skirt up before she sat down, meaning the ground would be warm enough for bare flesh to be comfortable.

Using a two-row planter drawn by a pair of mules, laborers planted rows of "separate" cotton seed (seed from which the lint had been removed). About seven days after planting, little green cotton plants begin to appear.

In the middle of May, the laborers would chop out about half the cotton plants to give the remaining ones a better chance to grow. In June, "choppers" continually hoed the fields to remove the morning glory vines, and cockleburs that would infest and take over if not chopped. If there was a skip in the cotton when it first appeared, the women laborers dropped new seed and then pressed it into the black dirt with their bare feet.

From mid-July to mid-August there was a respite from the field work, when the crops were "laid by," as Southerners say. Sharecroppers had free time to tend their own livestock, gardens, repair equipment, cut firewood. In those times, many of the cotton gins ran on firewood, and keeping the gin operating was crucial to all concerned.

My brother Jack was learning to farm, and he rode his tall Tennessee walking horse through the crop to check its progress. I sat smugly on the front of his Buenavista saddle as the horse did his running walk, and my brother checked on the tenants. He gave them each a dollar after they had talked about the crop, the weather and plantation news.

When harvest began, the sharecroppers would begin to receive "seed" money, which was another advance based on money received for the seed ginned out of the cotton and sold to the oil mill.

Settling day was usually around Christmas. Certainly there were good and bad planters in the Mississippi Delta, and some owners were not good to their sharecroppers. Many, if not most, of the sharecroppers were illiterate, and an unscrupulous owner might try to throw a sharecropper off by telling him he had bought things from the commissary that he had not—like two barrels of sugar instead of one—but this was not the case at OK. Or at least I try to believe this, just as I try to remember some good out of what was no doubt a feudal system, one very like the Middle Ages. Uncle Sterling always gave a bottle of whiskey to every sharecropper to celebrate the occasion. To make their settling day whiskey stretch farther, many of the old sharecroppers would put one stingy teaspoon in their morning coffee.

All cotton farmers love a good, dry summer with light rain, but of course, they seldom get what they want, which leads to much complaining, speculation and worry. Grandmother used to tell a story about Captain Withers complaining to visitors about the usual poor cotton crop. Mother, then a little girl, said, "Papa, don't worry about it. We do perfectly alright and we've never made a good crop yet." What Mother meant was our family had all it needed and more.

To hear the farmers in the Mississippi Delta, they never *did* make a crop. There is probably no other profession that generates the degree of complaints, dissatisfaction and disappointment of farming, for what happened in the field affected their whole cotton-driven economy.

Cotton is graded by color, strength, length and size of fiber and trash. This is called "classing" the cotton. You depended on the cotton factors on Front Street in Memphis to class and sell the cotton. Not only do you need a lot of cotton, you need good cotton to receive the best price. If the cotton is too plentiful, the price goes down; if it's a short crop, there might not be enough money to make expenses.

There is a bronze plaque on Front Street between McCall Street and Union Avenue that reads, "Nothing happened at this spot 1897." Well, maybe nothing happened at *that* spot, but just read the chattel mortgage books of Tunica County and the South, and you'll see that a lot happened at other spots. No doubt Front Street life was more sophisticated than Delta farming; it was a gamble, but the stakes were even higher. To ease the pace and cut the boredom during the off season, Front Street men played jokes on each other, like putting Roquefort cheese in a colleague's hat band. Card games and whiskey drinking flourished, and there was even a Front Street shooting over someone who hated his nickname more than I mine.

This poem by William Britton perhaps says it best:

FRONT STREET

On Front Street lives the cotton buyer,
He's called a thief; he's called a liar,
He says if he should have to pay
The price you ask for cotton today
He might as well his business sell
And spend his days in darkest hell.

On Front Street lives the cotton seller,
In some respects a decent fellow,
He says the mills don't pay enough
To keep his customers in snuff,
He says the profits mills are making
From downtrodden farmers they are taking.

From other sections come the spinners
Who say they often skip their dinners
In order to economize
Which sounds to me like a lot of lies.

But statistics show the farmer planting
Still more cotton, tho' still he's ranting
About the awful cost of labor
And accusing him of profits stopping
Because he pays so much for chopping
And in the fall when things are clicking,
He cusses about the cost of picking.

The laborer says he cannot live
On what the farmers want to give
As daily wages for the toil
Of this poor tiller of the soil.

But every year the crop is made,
And every year the game is played
And most all of them are satisfied
Tho' bound to admit that they have lied,
And their satisfaction only lacks
The getting by on income tax.[1]

Since the first time I ever visited OK, uppermost in my child mind was being big enough and strong enough to go to the cotton field and pick cotton with Tennie. It had been a long time since my dear friend had been a picker, having been promoted to house help several years before. But in these days, being a good cotton picker was a high honor, and just like fishing and hunting, the pounds of cotton picked by one person in one day were often exaggerated. Having cleared our plan with Grandmother and Boots, the straw boss (who wore a wide-brimmed straw hat that signified his position), I was ready to hit the fields.

Tennie had fashioned me a small cotton sack more my size, for there was no way a child could pull what the real pickers used: cotton bags that ranged from six to nine feet long. Then my dear friend helped me make some "snuff" out of cocoa and sugar for me to carry around in a silver tin can. Tennie kept her real snuff in a soiled brown bottle that had attached to it an old toothbrush wrapped with a rag. She, like most of the workers would take the brush, dip it in the snuff, and then paint the inside of her bottom lip. This gave the user a quick high, although some preferred chewing tobacco like Red Mule to the powdered snuff.

Cotton picking leaves the back aching and the fingers throbbing; I didn't last a single row. Trucks with scales waited at the ends of the fields so that the heavy bags of cotton could be weighed. Feet dangling, I sat on the end of one of these trucks and talked to Boots about the fields. We talked and laughed until Boots lifted his thick, brown finger towards the fields and said, "Listen." One lone voice started up in a tired, melodic cry, and the entire field began to hum. Then they just took off singing. High voices and low voices wove in and out of the song. Pickers across the field straightened their backs and turned their sore necks to the deep orange sunset. It was the end of the day. One by one, the voices grew quiet, and a single, deep voice bellowed, "Looky, looky yonder, where the sun done gone."

[1] *Front Street – A Book of Poems.* William Johnstone Britton, Memphis, Tennessee, 1948

Chapter 5

Life Behind The Levee

Life Behind The Levee

One of my favorite pastimes was to climb in the buggy with Grandmother and Coot or Rooster, and ride to the west "unprotected" side of the levee, where the Mississippi River could wreak instant havoc with its rushing waters. The levee divided OK Plantation into two parts. I loved the part behind the levee the best…because of my love for the river.

To me, behind the levee was a completely different world. For one thing, there were about 2,000 acres of woods still left. Most of the lakes on the plantation were behind the levee, and there was the big Flower Lake that came to an end up on our plantation. It was as if we had two farms; one that was on the front and that was the regular farm with the big pecan orchard, all the barns, all the headquarters, and Grandmother's house and many, many tenant houses; the other was behind the levee, with its trees, lakes, the river, the sorghum press and tenant houses built on stilts, with a boat tied up outside.

Silage was made behind the levee. Silage, a feed that Grandmother, Aunt Camilla, and Brother Jack would fix for the cattle to eat, smelled sour and bad. It was made from green grass crop, usually corn or sorghum. The first time Grandmother said corn was a grass, I looked rather puzzled, but then if Grandmother said corn was grass, corn was grass.

I enjoyed watching the making of sorghum molasses. Sorghum was a kind of sugar made from a grass-like sugar cane. The cane was put in between two large rollers, to extract two kinds of sap. The sap from the center of the stalk was where the molasses came from. All the sap would be boiled in huge pots. You separated what would rise to the top and threw this away, keeping the remaining sugary syrup.

In order to squeeze the good sugar juice out of the cane, the rollers were hooked on gears, and the gears were pulled by mules that walked in a circle around the gear and roller mechanism. When you finished you put the bottom syrup into barrels or jars. This was known as sorghum molasses.

One of my favorite recipes for big country breakfasts was when Tennie let her biscuits get stale. Then she would put them in a deep pan with butter and sorghum and bake them slowly in the oven. There has never been anything better than what we called "Tennie's Sticky Biscuits." With these sticky biscuits, we would have scrambled eggs, sausage, ham that had come from the smokehouse, grits, Spanish mackerel, and brains and eggs. Every meal at Grandmother's really was a buffet.

With Coot or Rooster driving the buggy, Grandmother and I would head back over the levee. Having never seen this plantation without a levee, I could hardly picture it as it must have been. I could not imagine that all the land would have been flat all the way to the river and where we were then had, at one time, been the village of Peyton, a town with houses, a cistern and a cemetery that we could still see. At one time Peyton was the county seat.

Not too far distant was the "mystery earthwork," as Uncle Sterling and Grandmother called it. A mile long and at least 16 feet high, this levee, dike, Indian mound, or whatever it was, lay between Flower Lake and the river in Harbert's Bend, in the middle of an uncut forest. Large trees grew right out of this ancient landmark. In appearance it looked like a short length of levee, but Uncle Sterling talked to old-timers and determined that it pre-dated Tunica's first levee, built 1849, which had been lost during high water in the Civil War. Later Uncle Sterling had some timber cut on the earthwork and found "grape shot" in an old tree, 45 feet from the butt. He knew very well that the shot was a relic of shelling of the county by Yankee gunboats, and its position in the tree was proof to any timber man that the tree was a large one by the time the grape shot was fired during the Civil War.[1] Uncle Sterling came to believe the mysterious earthwork pre-dated the Tunicas and Chickasaws, though this has not been confirmed by archeologists.

Another favorite spot behind the levee was the enormous tree where the paddlewheels had docked at OK Landing. I loved to step down out of the buggy and walk over to that tree. I could imagine deckhands and roustabouts winding the big chains around the huge tree, as the calliope played and the riverboats' whistles sounded. We could still see where the chains had dug two to four inches into its bark. The tree finally fell down in a storm a few years ago.

Not far from the old tree was our hunting camp, whose Faulknerian-type dwelling was really a huge tent with wooden floors. It was nothing like the fancy-pants duck lodges of today, where people pay huge sums to shoot in the Arkansas rice fields.

The famous outdoor writer Nash Buckingham once wrote, "Few places in the world are better fixed for hunting and fishing as OK Landing Plantation in Tunica County, Mississippi. Not only does the plantation boast Beaver Dam and about one-third of Flower Lake, but also a very special place in my heart called 'Blue Hole.'"[2] It usually looked blacker to me than blue, so I do not really understand the name. But a lot of people must have been confused, because most lakes in Mississippi near the levee are called blue holes.

Levees were built to keep the Mississippi River from flooding the farm land as the levees followed the course of the river. When the river was at flood height, it would flow along close to the levee. When the current was fast enough going around one of the curves in the levee, it would form a whirlpool. The whirlpools excavated dirt and left a hole. After each high water, the hole would be made deeper and larger. When these "blue holes" became deep enough, the water would stay in them permanently. These holes eventually became excellent fishing places all along the Mississippi River delta.

Whenever the water rose on the river side of the levee, it created a downward pressure. The water was pressed through the sand strata and came up out of the ground on the protected side of the levee. These were called boils. If this water flowed long enough, it would carry dirt from under the levee, causing the levee to collapse. Water would flow through sandy land, but if the soil was clay, the water didn't flow and therefore did not create boils.

You might say the river is like a paddling duck–calm by all appearances as he glides across the water, but paddling furiously underneath. That helps explain how a whole town might suddenly disappear into the river, as Commerce Landing did. Unbeknownst to its citizens, the bank at Commerce was being eaten away by the relentless forces under the seemingly serene surface of the river. And one day, the bank finally gave way to this force, and Commerce was no more. The river was ever whimsical; Austin, Tunica's second county seat, was a small but thriving port during the Civil War, but the fickle river changed course and left Austin high and dry.

As we would head back toward the house, Grandmother, who was the most natural teacher I have ever known besides Miss Lee, would give me my first lessons on the Civil War. She explained that a scalawag was a white Southerner acting in support of the reconstruction governments for private gain, and a carpetbagger was a Northerner in the South seeking private gain. Since she had lived through the Civil War, Grandmother was forever biased against anyone she considered a carpetbagger.

Maybe the memories were too painful to volunteer the information, but she replied to my questions concerning the old uniforms and medals in her cedar chest when I pried the answers from her. The last newspaper of the Confederacy intrigued me. Grandmother had a copy of this edition, which had been printed in Vicksburg on wallpaper – the only paper available the day it was published. Grandmother and my Uncle Sterling always felt, however, that the South was punished in hidden ways. She felt it was unfair to charge higher freight rates from the Delta to Chicago than from Chicago to the Delta. Now whether this had anything to do with the Civil War, I know not, but Grandmother thought it did.

She was proud of her father, Benjamin Franklin Thompson, who was in the cavalry for four years under General Nathan Bedford Forest, who was called "the wizard of the saddle".

Benjamin Franklin Thompson was a first lieutenant in the 18th Cavalry Company G. He served the entire war under Forrest, the most daring general by some opinions. He was not hurt or injured and returned to Hernando following his release from a Yankee prison in Memphis. I am puzzled that my great grandfather B.F. Thompson's rank was only first lieutenant. I would have thought with his length of service and the mortality rate of the war, he would have made major. Perhaps he was not a pet among his contemporaries, because I have learned that officers below the rank of major were elected by their own men.

It is another uncanny coincidence that General Forrest and his wife, Mary Ann, once owned the land behind the levee where our hunting camp sits. In a 1859 sale handled by the Union Bank of Memphis, Forrest sold this land and 28 slaves, most in their twenties, for $38,000 to a Henry C. Chambers from Coahoma County. Forrest also owned land in Tunica County near today's community of Hollywood.

While her father was serving in the Civil War under General Forrest, Grandmother stayed with her mother and sister in the town of Hernando and attended school there. She graduated with many honors from the Gwynne Place and Baptist Female College in Hernando, Mississippi. I have several beautiful gold medals awarded to Grandmother when she was valedictorian of her class and a senior thesis she wrote on astronomy and architecture.

One consequence of the Civil War was a plus for Grandmother. Mary Tate Pope founded a small school at Calvary Episcopal Church in Memphis, Tennessee, in 1840 and was headmistress in the 1860s. During the Civil War, she was banished from Memphis for her loyalty to the Confederacy. She moved her school to Hernando, and named it the Gwynne Place and Baptist Female College. In 1868, she returned to 350 Poplar Avenue in Memphis. Grandmother would have been proud to know that both of my daughters attended St. Mary's.

Grandmother told me the story of General Forrest and his Uncle Jonathan Forrest, who had a livestock business in Hernando, and how Jonathan Forrest had been killed in a pistol duel in Hernando Public Square. At this point, Nathan Bedford Forrest left Hernando. The house in which the general had lived carelessly slipped through the fingers of the community, and a man from South Mississippi very quietly bought it several years ago.

From the Bibles of family members I learned the names of family members who served for the Confederacy: Emile Q. Withers, 17th Infantry, Company G; First Lieutenant Benjamin Franklin Thompson, 18th Cavalry, Company G.; Edward Seabrook, First Lieutenant, D Company, Sixth Infantry; John Seabrook, Private, Company A, Fourth

Infantry, in the Confederacy; Colonel Charles M. Carroll, 15th Infantry; and Colonel William Henry Carroll, 37th Infantry (later Brigadier General). On my husband's side, were three great-grandfathers who served: Robert Clell Irwin, Louis Bond, and Dr. George Washington Leatherman, a surgeon.

One of the saddest stories told to me about the Civil War in Tunica County was the story of the burning of Austin in May 1863. Austin, located one mile from Grandmother's OK Plantation, was the county seat for Tunica County, Mississippi, after it was moved from Commerce. For a short time, the county seat also stood at the village of Peyton, which today is the site of the OK Hunting Club. Riverboats could land there easily, and it was a natural as far as location on the river went, but because it was low and swampy, the county seat was moved back to Commerce. It did not stay at Commerce very long before it was moved back to Austin, and then after a vote, moved where it stands today, in Tunica.

Grandmother read me an account from the cedar chest written by the captain of the U.S. Steamer *Diana*, a Union vessel on its way to Helena, Arkansas, May 26, 1863. Grandmother and I would sit on the leather settee stuffed with horsehair, and I turned the pages as she read to me.

> On the east bank of the Mississippi, a part of OK Landing Plantation, about midway between Memphis and Helena, Arkansas, laid the little town of Austin. Its population was scarcely one hundred when the men were at home, but now that it had linked its fate with that of the Confederacy, it had valiantly sent every man and boy to war leaving their homes in the hands of fifty women and children. Austin was a clean, little town right on the river.
>
> On a Saturday afternoon, May 23, 1863, a fleet left Memphis. This Yankee fleet of nine boats was going to make a run of ninety miles. On board was a regiment of infantry, four squadrons of cavalry, a battery of six rifle guns, and two pieces of mountain howitzers used for field service. These boats were casemated from lower deck to the hurricane roof, pierced at suitable distance with

loopholes for musketry and artillery, and each provided with one or more twenty-pounder palate guns. Amphibious in its character, fitted out for operation, both marine and on-land, it was at once formidable and fully effective in its many trying adventures.

The fleet left for Helena with the *Fairchild* as the quartermaster and a commissary boat taking on supplies to follow. Nothing occurred as they reached their destination about sunset. But the *Fairchild* had no such good fortune. Her officers reported being fired into by a Confederate battery of two guns on a point in the river, where a fine academic school was located about a half mile above Austin. On receipt of this information, the commanding general of the fleet at once issued orders for the return of the entire fleet to Austin.

We took an easterly course along the thoroughfare of the town, which beyond it, stretched away into a country road about a mile and a half away. There was a primitive forest with much underbrush which now is OK Plantation. When the cavalry reached this branch in the road, they halted, and intended to remain there until the infantry came before moving on to the academy, where they supposed the Rebels still were stationed in their positions of the day before. In this supposition they were correct, but the Rebels had formed their own plans.

Having witnessed the debarkation of the cavalry, they reckoned upon this being all of the forces of the Yankees, so they laid a plot to decoy the cavalry to the woods, where capture would be easy. They placed a few mounted men on the edge of the woods. They opened up a scattering of fire on the cavalry. The whole Rebel force consisted of one regiment and two six-pounder guns. The battle got so confused that the Rebels were so sandwiched in between the Yankee cavalry in their advance, and the infantry in their rear. The battle finally ended by the infantry having a very confused and terrible battle in the woods. Two Yankees were killed and six Rebels. But, because of this, the general made a very harsh decision. He decided to punish the Southerners by burning the town of Austin to the ground.

In Austin there were just women and children, but they were told they had to be out of their houses by four o'clock that afternoon. They could take things with them if they dared. The women decided it would do no good to take things, because with no home to go to and the academy having been burned, and no roof over their heads, their few possessions would be stolen. Most of them at four o'clock, when the bells rang on the boats, simply left their houses, holding their children's hands, and stood as they saw their houses burned to the ground."[3]

But one house survived, apparently because it carried a Masonic symbol over the door, and still stands today.

Yankee troops even chased a scattered remnant of Rebels east to White Oak Bayou, where slaves were hidden out. Relics from this scrimmage have been found there in the last twenty years.

The Yankee captain who entered this story in the ship's log was very chagrined, embarrassed, and humiliated by such an action and Austin's cruel fate. He wrote beautifully, and as a child, I can remember fighting back tears as Grandmother read to me. I was not only hurt for the women and children, but I was impressed and very moved that an enemy officer could be so appalled by the horrors of war. He ended by saying one would never forget that sad scene of women and children left alone with their burning houses slowly eating away all hope of shelter. "We may cease to think of a Nero, but one never forgets to pity Rome."

Austin in Tunica County was a rough and tumble river town in the year 1874 and had an unfortunate uprising. A white doctor had a dispute with a black man and shot at the man, missing him but killing a young black girl watching the fight. Although the doctor was arrested and charged with the girl's murder, the magistrate let the doctor go free on bail.

Outraged Tunica County blacks formed a posse, re-captured the doctor and returned him to jail. The doctor was once again freed, and this enraged the blacks to the point that Sheriff Vannoy Manning, followed by other whites, left Austin. There was looting of stores, and several hundred blacks surrounded the town of Austin. A telegram was sent to Memphis, Tennessee by the remaining whites of Austin that they needed support at once.

A newspaper article from the time read:

> A full blown race war is taking shape at Austin, Mississippi … A mob of some 800 Negroes have surrounded the town, which is protected by about 250 white citizens within. A desperate appeal was received over the wire last night asking for armed assistance. Tennessee cannot send armed troops into another sovereign state, but all private citizens who wish may go."

> The call went out and in a few hours' time over 250 citizens had gathered at the Cotton Exchange on Front under the command of Col. John B. Morgan. Rifles belonging to the Chickasaw guards were taken aboard the steamer *A.J. White*. As they departed, thousands of citizens, black and white, gathered on the bluffs to see them off. The Negroes did not seem very pleased with the proceedings, but they said nothing.[4]

Despite the fact that the Carruthers were early settlers in Tunica County, Grandmother and Aunt Camilla preferred to talk about the family's earlier roots. As recently as Reconstruction, much of Tunica County, except towns like Austin and Commerce along the river, had not even been cleared and was overgrown with trees. People from the hill towns of Hernando and Holly Springs considered Tunica County little more than a swamp and Austin just a wild river town. So even though our Carruthers family had played such a big role in the early history of Tunica County, they spoke more about the Carruthers land in Hernando and Marshall County, where our family settled when they left Virginia shortly after the War of 1812.

Grandmother, who was a proper Mississippi Methodist, would continue her Civil War tales by telling me, "Mary Carroll, the Bible says there are bad women in this world. During the war General Hooker let these bad women follow his men. To this day, these bad women are called 'hook-ers.'"

And she told me about Samuel Fletcher, a part Indian man who ran the blockade at Vicksburg, Mississippi. Fletcher was a member of the Sanders' Scouts, who were started right next to our farm at Austin. Not nearly enough people know how wonderful the Sanders' Scouts were. They knew how to get down the mighty river as silently and coolly as any of their Indian ancestors. They could float undaunted past watching federal gunboats right into the city. This was only one of the tasks performed by the Sanders men.

No duty was too hazardous, no adventure too desperate to be performed in the service of their beloved Mississippi.[5] Sanders, though he really fought under Nathan Bedford Forrest, was not considered a real part of the Confederate Army. The reason was he had as one of his scouts a deaf mute, who was one of the best men on the river. He was famous for his ability to be a spy and a blockade-runner, but the Confederacy would not accept a deaf mute as a soldier.

Even as a child, I was proud that this poor deaf mute, raised by his uncle, did find a place in life where he excelled and was respected. There are no records of the Sanders' Scouts, because when Austin was burned, all the records went with it.

Very few of Grandmother's good soldiers came home at the end of the war. Many were missing before Lee surrendered, and lots of fine men of the North and of the South, lay in the trenches of Franklin, Atlanta, Shiloh, and the Wilderness. Only the real students of the Civil War know how many good men were lost in small scrimmages, like that at Austin.

Then Grandmother would start on other things. She would tell me that there were only a few Civil War soldiers alive that she knew of. Almost with tears, we would go back to the old times. Grandmother enjoyed reliving her life for me. Because she had told these stories before to her children, Grandmother appreciated me as a new audience. Grandmother, proud to be from Hernando in DeSoto County, told me when the Confederacy started, Tunica County was real pioneer territory.

"It's true," said Grandmother, "there were plantations, and great plantations, but the majority of the places were only partially cleared, and the rest was a virgin forest, where bears and panthers made their dens.

Through plantations roamed herds of wild turkey, while overhead the very air was gay with the flaunting colors and shrill cries of ducks and geese."

Grandmother talked about hunting in order to exist in the early pioneer days in Tunica County, where animals were abundant. There were bear, foxes, wolves, panthers, raccoons, possums, and rabbits that ran through the woods. The people lived off this game, and venison haunches and bear steak were common fare to the pioneers. At the establishment of the county, the board of police ordered a bounty on panthers and wolves. This bounty of three dollars for each animal could be collected by presenting the scalp to the clerk of the board who paid it. Many presented the scalps to the tax collector when taxes were paid. This order was enforced as late as 1860 and had not been repealed as stated in a history book written in 1941. Fact is, there was a bounty on beavers in DeSoto County up until the late twentieth century, when it was repealed.

Grandmother told me one of the greatest ship disasters occurred immediately after the Civil War. Early on the morning of April 27, 1865, the side-wheel steamboat *Sultana* exploded and sank nine miles north of Memphis, Tennessee. Equipped with four big tubular boilers and designed for the lower Mississippi trade, the *Sultana* had a legal limit of 376 people–including crew. But when it left Vicksburg, Mississippi, on the evening of April 24, it carried the biggest shipload of humanity ever carried on the Mississippi.

Most were Yankees returning north from a Confederate prison camp. The steamer's clerk estimated a passenger load of "more than twenty-four hundred soldiers, about one hundred civilian passengers and a crew of eighty." For a few hours, loading officers tried to keep them in line. Then the half-starved soldiers shoved past them and swarmed aboard. After a leaking boiler was repaired, the Sultana chugged toward the debarkation point in Cairo, Illinois.

About seven p.m. on April 26 – eighteen hours after leaving Vicksburg – the *Sultana* docked at Memphis. Weeks earlier, a Creole member of the crew had warned Captain J.C. Mason that trouble would come because a nine and one-half foot alligator had been taken aboard as the ship's mascot. This caused great unrest on board because there was a superstition about alligators.

Whether the 'gator had anything to do with it is doubtful, but about two a.m. on April 27 one of the *Sultana's* big boilers blew up, tearing the ship apart and instantly killing many passengers. Fire and hot metal showered down on the half of the ship that didn't disintegrate.

Many of the men suddenly thrown into the water couldn't swim. Those who could were seized by comrades. Often they went under in clusters.

An estimated two hundred men crowded together on the bow of the drifting hulk. Then the two big smoke stacks crashed down, the wind changed and blew flames directly toward the survivors.

Lieutenant George B. McCord rode a plank to safety. Private Otto Bardon floated away in a trunk. Seaman William Lugenbeal found a bayonet, killed the ship's alligator, and drifted to shore clinging to the crate in which the pet had been kept. Some men were saved by clinging to the tails of mules. A few drifted as far as Memphis on bits of debris. Fifteen men in Union blue rode to safety in a dugout canoe brought to the scene by a Confederate soldier.

Bodies continued to surface and float in the river, and some were entangled in tree roots for more than a week following the explosion.

The investigation into the tragedy that took more lives than the *Titanic* turned into a whitewash of the officers involved. The *Titanic* went down in 1912 with a loss of 1,517 lives as compared to the *Sultana's* 1,700 casualties.

The incident received scant newspaper coverage because it was overshadowed by other events, including General Joseph E. Johnston's surrender to General Sherman and the aftermath of President Lincoln's assassination.

But the soldiers and civilians who lived through it held reunions for years afterward. As for the *Sultana*, what was left of her vanished into the mud and sand of the Mississippi.[6]

Around 1940, I was told never to ride my pony behind the levee where camps had been set up, when the Corps of Engineers was making the last cut-off called Tunica Cut-off. I did see these tent cities, though, in the company of my uncle. I remember seeing the tents, which though large, had rough wooden floors and no plumbing. There would be large pots in front of the tents for boiling water to bathe, drink, cook, and wash. People looked very thin and very poor and seemed to be sad like people you see in movies about the Irish potato famine, which brought many Irish immigrants to the United States.

I don't think Grandmother wanted me to see how depressing the tent city was, but she was quick to tell me that it was a vast improvement over the way the people who built the Irish Ditch in Tunica County lived before the Civil War.

"At the beginning of the Civil War, camped near McKinney Lake were over three hundred Irish laborers that started building a canal that was to drain Lake Basin into White Oak Bayou. They were in the charge of Mr. John Saffarons of Memphis, Tennessee, the contracting engineer.

"Briefly, the first call for volunteers for the Confederate army found many classes of people in Tunica County; the planters and their managers, the professional men and merchants in the few tiny towns, the contractors and carpenters employed on the new plantations, the 'Deadeners,' and John Saffarons' Irish.

"At first call for troops, Mr. Saffarons paid off his men, telling them he was going to Memphis to defend his home from the Northern invasion. They left their tools in heaps and followed him to form the nucleus of an Irish regiment Colonel Saffarons raised in Memphis. Perhaps it is only fair that the glory of the Fighting Tenth should belong to Tennessee, but at least Tunica holds as a memorial to the part her Irish played in a half completed canal, overgrown with the tangled undergrowth of a half century, that is today known as the Irish Ditch.

The "Deadeners," as they were known, had come to Tunica County before the Civil War to help clear the land. Because the trees were so abundant and so large, this being an untouched forest, men would "girdle" the tree, cutting a ring in its bark around the whole circumference. This would so damage the tree that it would die, making it easier to come back later, and chop it down.

The Deadeners enlisted, and many went back to their original homes to fight beside their kin, but the greater part enlisted in the companies organized at Austin. They were young men, rough in many ways and uncouth when contrasted with the polished planters but loyal, truthful, unafraid, they formed a romantic group in Tunica's past well worth the admiration accorded all pioneers."[7]

The history of the Corps of Engineers describes the people who built the Irish Ditch as living in three tents: workers, all men, would sleep in one tent, eat in one tent, and have one tent for entertainment. This tent would provide female companions and gambling. In later years, the entertainment tent was outlawed as one could only guess the superintendent would profit from such a setup.

Throughout my childhood, I saw dread poverty in every race. Through my visits to Tunica, I also heard about mixed marriages. Before 1900, the South may not have been as backward in attitude as perceived. My Uncle Sterling Withers bought a large farm, house, and a cotton gin from the widow of a mixed marriage. She was the executor of her late husband's estate, and to my knowledge they had no heirs. This lady was respected both in business and our families' close relationship. I have since learned that this may have been a common-law marriage, because "miscegenation," (interracial marriage) was illegal in Mississippi at that time.

Grandmother's OK Landing life, stories, and dreams were passed to this child, so that they could be passed on to future children. My grandmother shared with me–her only granddaughter–many extraordinary dreams. Often this was in her garden near the levee that protected Grandmother and me from the Mississippi, or as Grandmother told me the Indians called it, "Meh-I-sepe."

I add my own dreams, but I cannot tell you where Grandmother's dreams end and mine started.

I am a part of my grandmother. More than once I have known things I should not have known for my age, and I can even describe rooms and places that have long since disappeared or been destroyed. I can tell you where furniture was placed in rooms that I have never been in or ever seen a picture of or read about in letters. So strong are some genes that I believe we possess part of our ancestors' minds and emotions. We like the colors they liked, the music they played, the food they ate and above all, love the men that were as close as possible in character and charm as the men who were their fathers, husbands, brothers, and sons.

As a child I was made to think about death at times. One cold, cloudy winter day at OK, Tennie and I stopped to see an old, sick sharecropper. There is no way I can describe the smell of the decayed cabin heated by a small, potbellied stove and insulated with newspaper on the wall. This broken and bowed old fellow, riddled with aching bones, was in a simple cane straight-back chair and had pulled it up close to the stove.

Tennie and I had brought him a jar of snuff. Not knowing the man's name I called him "Uncle." He worked and lived a long way from the headquarters, and he was a relative of Tennie's. He had a rusty coffee can he used as a spittoon. As time passed and Tennie and Uncle talked about his old age and grave condition, I all at once realized there was no anger, or better still, no fear in the old guy.

Such faith, I have never seen since. He looked at Tennie and me, for now I was as close as I could get to the old man and the potbellied stove. This creature of God simply said, "Tennie, I is goin' home."

As we left Uncle's house, Tennie and I walked slowly up the gravel road to Grandmother's. I hated sad things and Uncle's belief in going home might have suited him, but it scared me. I started to cough and sneeze, and Tennie handed me an old red bandanna handkerchief to blow my nose. Tennie kept two red bandannas stuffed in her bosom, one to blow her nose and the other to keep her money tied up in a large bow knot.

What had been a troubling day turned into a more upsetting night. At supper, I was told that Grandmother, Uncle Sterling, Aunt Camilla and Jack were moving to Tunica to a big bungalow near the Planters Oil Mill.

"Why just think, Mary Carroll, you and Grandmother can go to the movies every night," Mother told me.

Pooh, I had movies or what the country people called picture shows, in Memphis. In town, there wouldn't be big eagles that nested near the lake and frogs to croak all night, even if I was able to go to the farm with Aunt Camilla every day.

After dinner, I was so sick I spent the night in bed with Grandmother. We pulled the mosquito netting around us. Grandmother fixed me a cut glass tumbler with paregoric and sugar water, a common home remedy of the day. Such a concoction would sometimes be put it in a cloth pouch, so that a baby could suck on it for relief of colic or teething pains. People called these pouches "sugar tits."

I drank the concoction slowly; to me it tasted of licorice like they sold at the commissary. But it wasn't the taste I remember, it was the feeling I had soon after I drank it. Things didn't seem nearly so bad. Maybe Uncle was right not to be scared of dying and maybe moving to Tunica would be alright as long as I could come to OK in the daytime. I looked out the window and saw a full moon. A feeling came over me, and I had found comfort.

[1] From an unpublished portion of Miss Ellen Farrell's WPA history of Tunica County

[2] *Game Bag* by Nash Buckingham, 1945, G.P. Putnam Sons, New York, New York

[3] *Journal of United States Steamer Diana*, pg 67, "On Board U.S. Steamer, Diana, Helena, Ark. May 26th 1863, Chapter IX, Guerrilla Warfare and Burning of Austin, May 1863.

[4] *Commercial Appeal*, July 28, 1974, "100 Years Ago

[5] Tunica County History, "The Civil War" Genealogy: Tunica County, Mississippi

[6] *National Enquirer*, 1970, by Webb Garrison

[7] Genealogy: Tunica County History "Civil War", Mississippi

Chapter 6

Tunica Town

Tunica Town

Tunica County lies in a shallow soup bowl of earth on the flood plains of the Mississippi created by millions of years of silt deposited in the flood plains of the mighty river. While the soil of Tunica County is spectacularly rich and fertile, its county seat, the town of Tunica, always seemed so plain and unremarkable in its architecture and so nondescript in its character that it looked to me like a Monopoly board town. Unlike the Mississippi hill towns just a few miles inland, it didn't have the country charm of a town square, and except for three or four old two-story homes, its landscape lacked even the historical appeal of a Confederate statue or an ancient oak that shaded the ghosts of the Chickasaw Indians beneath its branches.

Yet in this plain-as-vanilla-pudding town, I spent many happy childhood hours visiting Grandmother and Aunt Camilla and sharing the last two years of Grandmother's life.

Just to drive through its sleepy, straight main street that followed the railroad track, you would never guess that this flat North Mississippi county was criss-crossed with bayous and lakes, including two famous ones—Lake McKinney (named for a prominent Chickasaw family) and White Oak Bayou, in the 1930s called the "Irish Ditch."

Founded in 1836, Tunica County is one of ten counties formed from the Chickasaw Cession of 1832 resulting from the Treaty of Pontotoc. The county and town are named for the Tunica Indians. Tunica means "the people." The Tunicas had once lived in the southwest part of the county near OK Plantation but were run out of the area by the Chickasaws in 1763. In time, white European settlers and their appetite for more cotton land pushed the Chickasaws out, and by the 1830s the Chickasaws had joined other tribes in western Indian Territory.

The Chickasaws of this area were sophisticated for their time and were considered one of the "Five Civilized Tribes." They left few, if any, of the customs of their race as a heritage to the people who now live on the lands, with the notable exception of the Mississippi law which gives a woman complete control of her property and keeps her from being responsible for her husband's debts.

When the railroad was built in 1885, an "official" town of Tunica was soon established. In 1888 the citizens of Tunica County voted to move the county seat from Austin (near OK Plantation) north to Tunica. This had the disadvantage of losing the seat on the scenic Mississippi, but the advantage of gaining one that was in the center of the county. The rule of thumb for selecting a site for a county seat was that a person should be able to ride there by horse or buggy, tend to business, and ride back home in a day.

You can't talk about Tunica without talking about mules. In the days before mechanized farming, mules (and the weather) could make or break a farmer. Large plantations had hundreds of mules and hands to train and manage them and grow their food. Mules were bought when they were four or five years old and with proper care, they would live to be about 25. Most of the mules used in farming were males, because they were cheaper.

Mule traders were a Southern institution, and a good one would be well known and sought after throughout the region. In Tunica County, there was a gypsy family of mule dealers named Costello. Mr. Jim Costello brought mules from Columbia, Tennessee, where they were raised. Almost all of the gypsy mule dealers in the Mississippi and Arkansas Delta were related to the Costellos or the Rileys.

As far as other local commerce, with the exception of a few stores, there was little industry in Tunica until the 1900s, when a group of local businessmen that included my uncle, Sterling Withers, established the Planters Oil Mill.

On one of my first trips to visit Grandmother at OK, I remember smelling the unmistakable aroma of a cooking bone-in ham. I wanted to track down the scent like a dog to get a sandwich, but Mother explained that the hearty smell came from the cottonseed being pressed at the mill.

The Planters Oil Mill was the largest building in town. It was the pride of the county and was the first mill in the South to crush soybeans as well as cottonseed. After picking, the seed is ginned out of the cotton and then pressed into several byproducts, including an edible cooking oil. This boon brought valuable extra income to the farmers.

The mill was also the center of business and social activity in Tunica. It was the Peabody Hotel lobby of North Mississippi; that is, just about anybody with business in this part of the world dropped in.

The railroad track that ran through the middle of town also went right by the oil mill. Several times a day a train's ear-splitting whistle and clanking boxcars interrupted conversations and the flow of business. In fact, the late night train was blamed for waking many a couple, who nine months later would be changing the diapers on the newest addition to the family.

The main office of this big cement structure was just off old Highway 61. Beside it was a small grocery store where people bought peach or vanilla soda; sundries like hair pomade, Red Mule chewing tobacco, cigarette paper and Bull Durham loose tobacco in pouches; or Southern delicacies like pickled pigs' feet and pickled hard boiled eggs, sardines, smoked sausage and stage-planks, cakes made with ginger and sprinkled with purple and pink sugar.

Across from the store and backed up to the tracks was the town's ice house, from which deliverymen filled their trucks and made deliveries throughout the county. Ice was a precious commodity in every household in the days before refrigeration. The ice house, with its close proximity to the oil mill, also made a convenient place for Uncle Sterling to cool watermelons that he gave out to his customers and friends.

The ugly front office of the oil mill was the scene of important political deals and high-stakes gambling. Just inside the front door was an enormous Coke-box full of soft drinks and cold beer. The opposite wall had a large window, behind which sat one of the toughest, most able women I have ever met, Miss B. She was my uncle's right hand and ran the mill with an iron fist. It was her job to make sure the loads of seed were properly weighed—no one put anything over on Miss B. Few sailors could cuss any better, and she dealt with the mule-drawn wagon drivers like a drill sergeant. Miss B was a large woman, and not pretty, but her strong personality made you forget her lack of good looks. My Uncle Sterling sure did. All the Withers women disliked Miss B's relationship with Sterling. They intensely resented his dependence on her to run the large, influential oil mill operation. They thought he might be dependent on her for more than her business acumen, too.

I'll never forget sitting in wicker rocking chairs on the screened front porch in Tunica with Mother, Aunt Camilla and Grandmother and watching their reaction when they spotted Uncle Sterling and Miss B driving by in his black Cadillac on their way to look at the crops. The chairs began to rock as fast as a child's brand new hobbyhorse on Christmas morning. Disapproving glances flew from lady to lady as plenty of bad words were spelled out loud. But their disapproval changed nothing, and Uncle Sterling and Miss B remained life-long friends and business associates.

Uncle Sterling enjoyed presiding over the mill. He and the locals always had a bridge game in progress, along with poker and craps. The mill was also the scene of an annual ritual of manhood and major political event—the Fourth of July Barbeque. The night before, men stayed up all night smoking the meat and icing down the watermelons for the next day. The melons weren't cut in mere slices, they were handed out in halves so everyone could have the juicy "heart." There simply was nothing more refreshing on a hot summer day than the heart of an ice-cold, sweet, drippy Mississippi-grown watermelon.

The crap games started early and lasted late, and more than a few players went home "over-served" and broke. No fireworks could surpass the excitement of grown men on their knees on the cement floor, rolling the bones. Crap games were just another metaphor for Delta farming, for even the most church-going man was a gambler if he had chosen the life of a farmer.

During the year, my uncle and his partner Scrap Woolfork kept a suite of rooms at the King Edward Hotel in Jackson, Mississippi, where any friend was welcome to stay in order to seek the ear of politicians who frequented the place. Then, in the summer, these same campaigners would come to the barbeque at Tunica. No Northern Mississippi politician would dare miss the Planter's Mill Fourth and the chance to press the flesh, especially in an election year.

At noon the pork shoulder and ribs were served to the throng of visitors who came to town for the feast. This was no family barbeque, though; children and ladies were not encouraged to attend. As a matter of fact, children were warned *never* to go near a gin, and for good reason. Many years before, the town founder's grandson had his leg cut off when he fell into the gin machinery while playing with other small boys.

His young friends were so frightened that they abandoned the little tow-headed lad as he screamed frantically for help. Tunica old-timers will tell you that an angel appeared to help the pitiful child. Bob Mangum, the victim, said a man walking down the railroad track heard his cries and called out, "I'm coming."

This stranger–never seen before or after–pulled the boy loose and picked up his small leather shoe. The "railroad angel" carried the boy and his leg and shoe to the mill and from there the boy was rushed first to a local doctor and then to Memphis. No one ever met or talked to the stranger, or angel, and he vanished, only to become a town legend. The small leather shoe is still in the boy's family. Bob became my brother's best friend, and lived in Tunica until his death in the early 1950s.

Not all of my time was spent listening to angel stories. At family and friends' dining tables, the children were brought into all conversations, if it was not "graveyard talk," as Aunt Camilla called gossip, since you should carry some things to your grave.

An interesting thing about Tunica County was that by 1900, two-thirds of the region's farm owners were black, not white. The acreages were mostly parcels of 60 and 80 acres purchased in the 1870s and 1880s by former slaves. The 1890 federal census reported 1,559 whites and nearly 15,000 blacks in Tunica County. After 1900, the number of black landowners began to decrease, as farming methods changed and costs increased, causing many to become tenant farmers instead of land owners. It became harder and harder for a family to support itself on a small acreage.

Even white sharecroppers began to leave Tunica County as farming became mechanized. This trend continued into the late 1960s, when desegregation of the schools sent many whites into the surrounding hill counties forever. For all practical purposes, the public schools then became all-black, as the children of the remaining whites began to attend a newly-established private school.

The whole county was poor and the town was plain, but the people were colorful and some boasted of fine farms on the outskirts of town. Like the two-block main street that faced the tracks, the community's church buildings were also unadorned, and only the Gothic-style Episcopal church lent visual interest to the landscape. Even the gravestones in the cemetery were modern and unremarkable. There wasn't much political diversity either. There was only one registered Republican in the county when I was a little girl!

But this place called Tunica provided me with some of the happiest days of my childhood. It was in these plain clapboard houses that I heard some of the most titillating gossip and loved with all my heart the people who lived in them. It was here that I met one of my mentors and best friends, Liz Farmer.

When I was nine, Aunt Camilla, Grandmother and Uncle Sterling moved to a comfortable bungalow near the end of the Tunica's main street, about 20 minutes north of OK Plantation. Uncle Sterling backed a friend in the purchase of a local movie theater so Grandmother could go to the picture show every night. If she liked the movie, we saw it three or four times.

Our beloved Tennie and her husband, Nelse, lived in an apartment over the garage. In the South, even modest homes in those days had servants' quarters.

Though I wasn't all that happy about Grandmother's move, living in town proved to be not all bad. For one thing, my brother Jack and his new bride lived in a cottage on Main Street, and I was able to spend time with them. He and Aunt Camilla drove out to OK Plantation every day, where they kept a small house across from the commissary for a headquarters that had a bedroom, kitchen and bathroom, and I could go with them whenever I wanted. Lots of days, Liz and I went to OK to ride horses, to fish, and to spend hours reading under a huge willow tree. Aunt Camilla kept a good cook, and we lunched on farm vegetables.

Liz's parents lived in Washington, D.C., where her father worked for the government. Her mother was too ill to care for her, so Liz stayed in Tunica with her aunt and uncle and two first cousins in a small house that faced the railroad tracks. Like the men in her family, who were lawyers, Liz was a reader and grew up in a home where the walls were lined with so many bookcases that there was no room for wallpaper. If Liz did not understand a word, she never failed to look it up. Though she was my age, I consider her one of the best teachers I ever had.

We played paper dolls and listened to daytime dramas like *Stella Dallas* on a small brown radio. When other children played with us, they would stop what they were doing and just listen to our dolls live out their often-confused and amusing lives, thanks to our imaginations. Our storylines became even more titillating after a friend invited a group of girls to her home one Saturday morning for the sole purpose of educating us about "hygiene." With much drama she led us to her father's bureau, opened its top drawer and showed us a small paper package marked "Trojan" hidden beneath her father's socks. With haughty superiority she then enlightened us about its purpose and use. Armed with this information, our paper dolls soon began to "copulate", which made our dolls' dramas much more interesting.

Living in a small town without museums, zoos, swimming pools or amusements spurred our creativity. We spent hours writing plays and casting the neighborhood children into the supporting roles. Sometimes our "creativity" went astray. We sneaked out to an abandoned car in a weedy lot to smoke cigarette butts that Liz had collected from her aunt's ashtray. At age nine, we would take a drag off the lipstick-stained butts and plan our day. First we would drop by to see if a certain clergyman was making a house call on a female choir member of his church. This sneaky preacher bought a car just like his lady friend's husband's car and would back in the driveway so it faced the street and no one could tell if it was the husband's car or the preacher's! We girls would walk around the car to read the license plate and then peep in the window to see if we could catch the preacher and lady making out. Once we got caught by the preacher. Oh, did we run!

Sometimes we visited with a lovely older woman with an unusual name. Miss "Peekie Boo" welcomed us, along with friends and family who stopped by for daily morning coffee. Liz and I would sip iced tea that made see-through beads on the tall, cool glass while the ceiling fan stirred the hot Delta air. Lounging out on the porch swing, we made like we were cooling off, all the while listening to the grownups. It was there that we would hear the really interesting talk.

We knew who was about to lose their land if they had one more bad crop. We knew who married whom in order to save the farm, and we heard about mysterious accidental deaths that provided insurance money just in time to keep so-and-so from going under. We became pretty good detectives and could tell you who was bad to drink on the weekend, and who (besides us) was a peeping Tom.

Liz and I once went to visit a new child in town and returned home to tell Grandmother the new child would be our new best friend.

"Why, Grandmother," I said, "everything in her house is big and works and is beautiful."

To that, Grandmother looked over her glasses and up from her knitting and answered in a most self-confident tone, "Yes, and all just bought."

Grandmother didn't understand why anyone would go buy someone else's second-hand furniture. To Grandmother it wasn't an antique unless you inherited it.

After supper in Tunica town, the men would go to the veranda to smoke. Grandmother said that the women went to the parlor to have intercourse. When we heart that word, Liz and I were shocked. Liz looked up the word in the dictionary and found that intercourse also meant an exchange of ideas. Once again, Grandmother did not have all of those scholastic gold medals she won at the Female Academy for naught.

Liz and I thought Delta boys were dumb because they couldn't even read the Bible well (though they did seem to understand math better than we did). During this time from age 9 to 12, I went to church often, as it was one of the only local diversions available. I went to the Methodist Sunday School with Aunt Camilla and then attended church services with Liz at the Episcopal Church just a few steps down on the next block, where I would sing in the choir. I went to church so much in Tunica that I sometimes forgot myself and said, "Amen," instead of "Goodbye" at the end of phone conversations.

One Sunday at about age 12, I was singing with Liz in the Episcopal Church choir, when we watched a young, handsome boy being confirmed. I later learned that he was Richard Leatherman. This was the first time I saw the man would become my husband of 53 years.

Blacks and whites were, as they say in today's world, totally co-dependent. The blacks helped raise the white child in most families I knew. They loved the children, and we loved back. The servants taught us to cook, sew, fish, hunt, play cards, make home brew, and even gamble, and yet there was still racial discrimination, as only it could be played out in the South.

One Easter, our Sunday school teacher announced that the mite boxes full of our nickels and dimes were being sent to help the poor in Africa. I stood up and asked, "Why Africa? Why can't we give the money to the people living here in the alley?" What we called "the alley" was the poorest section of Tunica. It ran along a drainage ditch on the backside of downtown. In the 1980s Jesse Jackson dubbed Tunica's alley "Sugar Ditch" and made it infamous. The answer my Sunday School teacher gave wasn't satisfying, but it was the way people thought in those days.

"The people in the alley," she said, "have their own churches, and the money we collected will go to Africa for the people who have not yet received the Word."

On Saturdays in the early 1940s, black farm laborers would come in droves to the streets of Tunica to spend their hard-earned money—sometimes foolishly—on things that were irresistible to them. These people would arrive in old, beat up third- or fourth-hand cars, making the main street so crowded that one would have to turn sideways to pass.

One such Saturday, I saw a slim black teenager wearing a dark red Tunica High School sweater. Two well-built football heroes from the all-white public school stopped the boy and ordered him to take off the sweater and to never wear it again. The black boy didn't say a word, but Liz and I guessed that a family had cleaned out their closets and given clothes to the family of the household maid.

Racial prejudice wasn't the only cruelty on the streets of Tunica. I remember that a young girl had a child out of wedlock. Of course, the family wanted to keep it quiet, because in those days, it was ruinous for a girl to have an illegitimate child. The local druggist found out about the baby and cruelly spelled out in blue crepe paper in the front window of the store for all to see, "It's a boy."

It was above this same drugstore that Grandmother and I often climbed the iron stairs to have tea with Mrs. Leatherman-Andrews in the upstairs apartment she kept to entertain her sisters and friends in town. It was there I saw my first ostrich egg, and guess who it belonged to? When I picked up the huge egg to look at it, she told me to be careful, it belonged to her grandson, the good-looking Richard Leatherman.

Occasionally when I was vacationing with Grandmother, I visited the Tunica Public School with Liz. Once, in the middle of the class, in burst this great big, tough-looking woman in a nurse's uniform, and she called two children out of the classroom. I wrote a note to Liz: "What is that woman doing with those two children?"

Liz wrote back, "She's taking them out to bathe them for lice." There were poor whites as well as poor blacks in Tunica, and as I have mentioned, there were many white sharecroppers in the Delta, too.

But most of our adventures were happy. After school, Liz and I had a route we took on the way home. Our first stop was the drugstore. One day, we saw a box of candy with a key and punchboard next to it. For a nickel, you could buy a chance or a "punch" on the $3 box. Liz and I figured there were only five punches left and ran as fast as we could to borrow five dirty nickels from Grandmother. So for 25-cents we won a big box of Whitman's chocolates and headed to our abandoned car, where we ate every piece.

The drugstore was only two stores from the barbershop, the place for gossip, checkers, and haircuts. One old-timer, as he had his precious few strands snipped, told the shop about a contemporary of his who was notorious for posting "Keep Out" and "No Trespassing" signs all over his vast property to keep out hunters. So *many* posted signs on so *much* land just seemed un-neighborly. The property owner had even been known to pull a gun on hunters he found on his land. The old-timer joked, "If I die before him, I'll go to Hell for sure. But if he dies first, I'll be safe, because I know he will have Hell posted before I get there."

If talk didn't pass through the Planters Oil Mill or the barbershop, it went through the Blue and White Café on Highway 61, a legend in the Mississippi Delta. If you had no connection to the Planters Oil Mill, you could still be in the swim if you stopped at the Blue and White. Anyone passing through the Delta slowed down for at least a cola or a cup of coffee.

In my childhood years, the Blue and White had slot machines called one-armed bandits, though they were later removed. But we were allowed, even as children, to play the slots there.

You met people going and coming to Memphis to shop, go to movies or to eat at Britling's, one of the first cafeterias in the South. All the hunters–and there were plenty of those–met at the Blue and White. They might have had breakfast already at the hunting camp, but they had to stop by to meet up with the other hunters and brag or complain about their day's shoot. Farmers arose as early as 5 a.m., and many of them went for a cup of coffee at the Blue and White before the day started on the old plantation. Sitting at the counter, they could talk of boll weevils, insecticide, and what kind of crop they were going to have.

Of course there was small town gossip. Such gossip makes good conversation but is seldom validated, and truth often stands in the way of a tall tale. One story goes that a prominent lawyer and another politician got into a scrape after an election. The lawyer's opponent was headed down Main Street with a gun, and spectators thought he was going to see the lawyer. Word goes that the lawyer was handed a gun to defend himself, for he was–according to biased account–one of few men who did not carry a pistol in the early days of Tunica County. The lawyer shot his opponent as the man entered his office. More of the saga has it that the dead man's daughter, when she found out about her father's death, armed herself with a gun and shot the lawyer. The lawyer never served a day in prison and practiced law from a wheelchair until his death. For several generations neither family spoke to the other. Years later, descendants from both sides of the Tunica shooting saga–both pretty females–married brothers, and then all was forgotten–forgotten except for a few old-timers who would tell and spell the tale. Liz and I felt lucky that for once neither of our families were in that mess, and we could speak to everyone on both sides of the street.

There have been some enormous deals made at the Blue and White over the years. When the casinos came to Tunica in the early 1990s, you never knew if while waiting on your turnip greens and blue plate special you would be sitting next to Donald Trump, down to look over the casino scene.

Even though it "had a face only a mother could love," I am sometimes homesick for Tunica with its loud train that switched cars in the middle of the night and where the biggest event of the week was the Friday night football game. How simple times were there. And yet as I write about Tunica, I find the plot of every great novel ever written.

My plain, country, Tunica town seems too simple and uncomplicated for million-dollar talk about casinos and fancy resorts For me, gambling meant borrowing a dirty buffalo nickel from Uncle Sterling and sliding it into the slot machine by the Blue and White's front door. This door opened up to Highway 61, and either way you turned—left or right—you were leaving Tunica town.

Chapter 7

High School and The War

High School and The War

During Mother and Daddy's bad marriage years, Mother and I spent most weekends and much of the summer at Grandmother's. As a child I could feel the tension, and I would ask Daddy why he did not ride with us to Tunica or go with us for a swim. One weekend when we returned from the farm, Daddy's things were gone. Shortly after that, my parents were divorced. With my father gone, and my brother, Sterling, in military school, Mother and I became closer than ever. Grandmother had died, and we traveled to Tunica less frequently, partly because of World War II gas rationing, but mostly because I was now a teenager and in a new school.

"Good morning, girls," said Miss Hutchison after she walked into study hall each morning, standing there with her "skeet feet" (her nickname) angled so that her heels were together like a ballerina in first position. We all stood up next to our desks, took a bow and said, "Good morning, Miss Hutchison."

It was 1942 and the war was in full swing when I entered Miss Hutchison's School in Memphis. Now over 100 years old, "Miss Hutchison's" as we called it in those days, has changed tremendously since I attended there. Then, all the girls came from virtually the same backgrounds, and we shared the same interests. This does not mean that some were not better students than others. Some girls were better athletes than others, and some were just plain better looking and more popular. No Jewish girls attended Miss Hutchison's then, although Jewish students attended another prestigious Memphis girls' school called Lausanne.

Miss Hutchison's was located in what had been a very grand home on Union Avenue. It suited beautifully as a place for high education. Where Miss Lee's had fun and adventure, Miss Hutchison's School focused on academics, and the standards were high, with little emphasis on arts and sports.

With dignity, Miss Lee had always called me "Mary Carroll," but my school identity changed the day I arrived at Miss Hutchison's, because with me came my nickname, Sugsie. Thanks to an older girl from my neighborhood who attended Hutchison, I carried into my new life the household name given to me by my brothers that I so hated, but everyone else found cute.

However, being friends with this neighbor girl turned out to be an advantage for me as far as meeting other girls, and I had another break as well because a certain young man in my dancing class had a crush on me. His sister was in my very grade, and whether she liked it or not, because of her brother's urging, I soon had to be her new best friend.

I was asked to spend each Friday night with this particular beautiful and able leader of our class. Others might not know their plans for the weekend, but I knew mine. All was going well until one day in the crowded lunchroom, where we had the same menu each week–Monday, roast beef and mashed potatoes; Tuesday, spaghetti–I overheard much twitter. A certain girl was going to give a huge, elaborate party and boys would be invited. Naturally, I thought I would be included and even went so far as to persuade my mother to buy me a beautiful party dress. I rushed home from school every day to look in the mailbox, but my invitation never came.

Having been the "star" at Miss Lee's, this snub came as a real shock to me. Like a true Southern damsel, I handled the affair with as much grace as I could muster–between screaming fits, crying, and threats to jump from the window. To protect my reputation, I told everyone I was going to visit my Aunt Camilla in Mississippi, where there was going to be the biggest, most unforgettable party in the history of the Delta.

Of course, there really was no big party at Aunt Camilla's. By this time

Grandmother and Uncle Sterling had died, and Aunt Camilla had moved from Grandmother's bungalow to a small duplex. Jack had moved from Tunica back to OK, where my mother and aunt had built a fine house for him and his wife. But once again, Aunt Camilla was there for me.

My Hutchison classmates and I soon graduated from Friday night sleepovers to co-ed dancing class at Diana Day's dancing school in mid-town. I was standing by the wall in my black Mary Jane pumps and white ankle socks at one Friday dancing class when in walked a beautiful, tall, older girl. She even wore stockings, since she must have been at least 16. I soon learned that this beauty was not only my age, but also the younger sister of my big crush, Richard Leatherman!

The girls in the class above seemed to adopt me, and I was soon making new friends and even was asked a year early to join an elite girl's club. Because none of us could drive at this age, on most weekends we Hutchison girls walked down to the Number 2 Streetcar track. There we climbed aboard the old, rattling, swaying car that stopped at every other corner and headed for what we thought was paradise—downtown Memphis.

Though many stores had bare shelves because of World War II and rationing, the trip was still exciting. It seems strange today that shoes were rationed, but we had shoe stamps that allowed us to have a few pairs of shoes a year. For this reason, we spent entire afternoons carefully choosing our favorite footwear.

After shopping, we ate lunch in the department store. It would usually be what I term a "drugstore" sandwich—two thin pieces of toast with either tuna fish or chicken salad—and on a toothpick, two stuffed olives served with four or five potato chips. With this we had orange floats made from orange sherbet and soda water. Our group then strutted into one of the glamorous movie theaters, with huge lobbies, grand red-carpeted stairs leading up to the balcony, and luxurious ladies' rooms. The theater was one of the first buildings in Memphis to be air-conditioned, so we didn't mind at all going to see the same show three or four times a week. Once we were finally seated, a panel in the floor rose to bring up a man playing an organ. A little ball jumped from word to word on the screen so that we could sing along. Newsreels, showing the latest advances of the troops and close-ups of some of the soldiers, were of the utmost importance during wartime and would come before the previews of coming attractions and then the feature film.

Horseback riding seemed to be a great sport, even during the war, and many of us Hutchison girls took riding lessons. Those of us who could afford it each owned our own horse. Boarding my fine chestnut gelding, "Love" at Miss Burbank's stable at the fairgrounds cost $2 a day. Even in wartime we had horse shows, and it seemed to be a good occupation for the girls during pre-dating days.

Before we officially dated, boys would try to attract our attention by playing in our front yards. They pretended to play a serious game of football, all the while keeping a close eye on the house. We girls slowly opened the door, trying to look very casual, and wandered out in the yard to start up a conversation. Three of these young men who used to play touch football in my yard went off to fine boarding schools. I told them all goodbye one afternoon, but within two days, two of them were back out in my front yard, playing ball again. I do not think they even bothered to depart the train at their fancy prep schools up East.

To put our dancing lessons to practice, we were beginning to attend dances, where our mothers would drive us to the Saddle and Spur Club next to the stables at the fairgrounds. Here, we learned to do the "Big Apple."

The Saddle and Spur Club was the site of a tragic accident. My favorite pediatrician, Dr. Rosemond, was playing poker there one Saturday afternoon, when he was shot by a robber. A young man came in to hold up the poker game, and when one of the gentlemen reached for his wallet, the robber thought he was reaching for a gun. The thief shot at the man and missed him, but the bullet hit my doctor, paralyzing him from the neck down.

Mother and I often visited Dr. Rosemond, who sat tragically in his home, where before the accident, he had energetically cared for his breathtaking rose garden of almost a hundred bushes. While I pushed the wheelchair, Dr. Rosemond would tell his faithful gardener in a slurred voice exactly which roses to prune or fertilize. Next to this garden was a plain swimming pool, one of the few private ones of that era. On special occasions, Dr. Rosemond would invite friends and their families over for swimming and Mother's spaghetti and hot dogs. Since it cost $60 worth of water to fill the pool, this was a real treat during the hot summer.

These cookouts were a welcome rest for our mothers too, for they stayed very busy volunteering at military hospitals and officer's clubs and USO's. During the height of World War II, patriotism was blazing through the city, so Mother and I thought it would be a great idea to rent our upstairs to two young brides of officers stationed at the Navy base in near-by Millington. The only drawback to our patriotic duty was that I had to move down to the guest room, meaning Mother and I had to share a bath. Like most houses, we only had one kitchen, and this caused a great deal of camaraderie, confusion, and near combat in the culinary war.

With all the military activity, my father, as Chief of Police was very busy, but I saw him regularly for lunch, though I never spent time in his home with his new wife and family. Between the time of her divorce and before my brother Sterling graduated from his military training academy, Mother's health and spirits seemed to be plunging. After one serious operation of Mother's, I stayed several weeks in the grand estate of the grandmother of my cousin Peter—the good childhood friend with the snake farm.

Having never had a daughter of her own, Peter's grandmother was intrigued by all the boys who came to visit me, wearing zoot-suits, pompadours and driving cars with the mufflers taken off. One night I would go to a fraternity party at the Peabody, and the next to a football game at Crump stadium. Most of the boys that drove me around went to either the best public school of the day, Central High School, or the Catholic high school, then called Christian Brothers College, known as "CBC". These boys were not only rivals for my attention, but on the football field as well.

There was a coach at Central High named Glass. As the story goes, before the big CBC-Central High game, Coach Glass had spies go over to CBC to learn their plays so Central would be ready for them. Well, as I remember the story, Central won the first game and the Coach was given the nickname of "Spyglass."

Boss Crump didn't stay out of much of anything in Memphis, and when he heard the rumor that a team had cheated, especially in a game played at Crump Stadium (named for him, naturally), he demanded a rematch. The city was thrown into a frenzy of anticipation. Every teenager in Memphis dressed up to watch the great Central-CBC replay. Boss Crump made a grand entrance. With his shock-white hair down to his shoulders, double-breasted camelhair overcoat, velour hat and cane, he strolled into the stadium like he was a British prime minister. He took off his hat and bowed to the cheering crowd, side to side. The entire spectacle was so grand, I don't even remember who won that night.

When Mother recovered enough and we had saved up enough gas ration stamps to drive to Columbia Military Academy in Columbia, Tennessee, we packed the car full of beautiful young girls eager to visit the handsome cadets. Military schools were quite the rage in the South, and Columbia was a town that could stand on its own without an academy, because it was the home of President James K. Polk and the site of a famous Civil War battle. We were traveling to see Sterling before he was shipped off to Officers Candidate School in Fort Benning, Georgia, where if you passed muster, you were an officer known as a "90-day wonder." June Week at Annapolis and West Point pale in comparison to the festivities at CMA. Girls came from all over the region to the Columbia dances, wearing elegant antebellum dresses. Dance cards filled up weeks in advance.

I had one problem: my best friend Martha, who though shorter than me, was one of the most beautiful and popular girls in the Mid-South. Martha had an irritating habit of claiming every boy as her own, even if she had only just met them. This meant that these boys were off limits to me. At the end of only one day and night, I could see we were in for a second famous battle at Columbia. I announced to Martha that we could solve our dispute by splitting the corps, Martha taking companies A and B and me, companies C and D. Guests of the graduates stayed in a hotel so old that our fire escape was a rope hanging by the window, and my mother was not pleased at finding Martha sliding down the rope. As for me, I was tempted to cut it!

Perhaps knowing the mortality rate of young officers in the service, Sterling bought me a charming aquamarine ring the day he graduated from CMA in 1942.

Although Sterling stirred up a bit of trouble arriving at OCS driving a brand-new, pale blue Buick convertible, he passed with flying colors and fell in love with a Georgia peach. One day a letter arrived from Sterling, written from the Pacific, asking Mother to invite his peach from Georgia for a visit to Memphis, and even more startling, to present her with an engagement ring. Thank goodness for Grandmother's almost inexhaustible supply of diamond rings in the cedar chest, where she used to keep her taffy. As a child, I used to think she would rather give away a diamond than a piece of candy.

For someone who didn't live through WWII, this type of proposal might seem odd, but for those who lived through this disastrous time, it was not unusual in the least. Elsie accepted Sterling's proposal, but as wartime fate would have it, it was not too long before the dreaded phone call came, telling Mother that Sterling, though alive, had been seriously wounded in Guam and was being transported to a hospital in Honolulu.

War, though inconvenient, was not affecting my young life in such a harsh way. In fact, my life was so good during these years, it is almost indescribable.

Back in Memphis, I felt that having a little bait to get the attention of young men wouldn't hurt. Certainly cosmetic surgery was out of the question in our youth, so we used socks to pad our brassieres to look like we were more voluptuous. Some even used eyeliner to emphasize cleavage. We couldn't get silk stockings during the war, so I actually used a cream that you painted on your legs to look like you had on hose. There were plenty of other ways to attract boys. First, I talked my mother into buying me a bicycle built for two, known as a tandem, so my dates and I could ride together. When beaus stopped coming by for bicycle rides, my best friend and I talked our mothers into letting us buy a Model-A Ford for $125. Neither of us was old enough to drive the car, but that was not the purpose. Every young boy who liked to fiddle with an old car came by on Saturday afternoons to work on our Model-A, that we had christened "Miss Carriage."

Very few people went "steady," as we called it in those days. The more popular girls had dates with two and three boys a week, and if it was summer, six and seven different boys a week, though they might have their favorite.

I ran into Richard by chance at a fraternity hayride. In fact, it was the only fraternity party that he had ever attended. When he saw me with my date, a fraternity pledge, he sent the boy off to do some errand for him and climbed on the hay truck with me. Just seeing Richard again was a special occasion, because he was always off either in Michigan, where his family spent summers, or at St. Paul's, a preparatory school in Concord, New Hampshire—much too far away from Miss Hutchison's.

Towards the end of the year at Hutchison, all the girls took part in the May Day celebration. We actually did the maypole dance, but this was no simple reenactment of the fertility dance done in early times in England. We practiced for weeks to make our beautiful colored satin ribbons to intertwine perfectly. There wasn't much emphasis on the artistic side of education at Hutchison, but the maypole dance was one art performed perfectly.

After the end of my ninth grade year at Hutchison, I heard that two of my good friends were going off to an Eastern boarding school. It was August, and there was certainly no way I could get accepted, wartime or not, in a good Eastern boarding school at that late date. Miss Harris,' a very good school in Miami, Florida, was suggested to me. I asked my mother if I could go off to school if I was accepted, and my sweet Aunt Camilla said she would be happy to help pay for this great opportunity.

Through my friends, I found the number of Miss Harris' School. After two or three reference calls to Hutchison, Miss Harris' accepted me. At the end of the ninth grade, my braces had finally come off, I had grown to my long legs, and with the help of a little peroxide, my thin, mousy hair became a shoulder-length Veronica Lake "do," and I was off to school as a glamour girl.

I had enjoyed my time in Memphis, and certainly I had been popular enough, but the sound of going off to school excited me beyond my shell. Never will I forget my mother and my sister-in-law driving me to Jackson, Tennessee, in the fall of 1944 to catch the late night train to Miami. My only companion was a white teddy bear. There I was, in my pale green gabardine suit with a cloche hat, matching bag and shoes that I had bought with one of Aunt Camilla's shoe stamps, not knowing where I was going, whom I would meet, or what I would do.

When the train pulled into Miami, servicemen were everywhere. Never have I seen so many good-looking young officers. And there I was to be picked up and taken to a strict all-girls school. A nice lady came up and introduced herself, and before I knew it, I was being driven through the gates of a school whose big columns made it look more like it belonged in Charleston, South Carolina, than in Miami.

I was introduced to a completely different world than OK Plantation, Tunica town, or Memphis. For one, the Navy and the Army and the Air Corps seemed to be every place. Most of the nice hotels on Miami Beach were turned into hospitals during the war, but my mother managed to find a hotel room so she could visit me during the winters of my two years in Miami.

The weather was glorious year long. That Christmas in 1944, I returned to Memphis not with as high an education as some of my Eastern boarding school friends, but with a perfect golden tan. I think I majored in sun tanning. I also had managed to go around Miami, where I bought a complete white wardrobe, with the exception of one or two baby blue (called "pushover" blue), clingy dresses. One night when I was squeezing into one of these, I could see the line of my underpants. Remember, there was no such thing as panty hose in the late 1940s. It would be out of the question for me not to wear underpants, but I was saved by remembering that Aunt Camilla wore undies that came to the knee, called "step-ins." These worked beautifully, and I only smiled when I heard the jealous cats whispering in the Peabody's powder room, "You know, there's no way she could have pants on underneath that dress." When I returned that Christmas, I felt downright sorry for the girls who had gone East and come home pale and a bit overweight.

Richard had invited me that Christmas holiday to visit him. We had been exchanging letters, and he had graduated from St. Paul's. After four years of school, he was accepted in a government program called the Victory-12 (V-12). An eligible student would go to college and be prepared to graduate as an ensign in the Navy.

He was sent to Millsaps College in Jackson, Mississippi. I could tell from Richard's letters that after four years at St. Paul's with only one weekend free as a senior, he thought he had gone to heaven at Millsaps. He wrote that nothing would please him more than having me come to visit after Christmas Day. My only problem was how to go to Millsaps in December 1944 with gas rationing in effect.

My brother Jack came to the rescue by sending up an old Ford, full of gas, from my dear OK Plantation. When it arrived, I acted a teenage brat and told Mother I could not dare be seen at Millsaps in a drab car that did not even have a radio in the dashboard. Later I learned how lucky I was to have a car with tires, gas and a wonderful mother who would chaperone Richard's sister Kate and me down to Jackson, Mississippi.

When I returned to Miss Harris' in Florida, I received a letter from Richard that read:

> *Dear Sweetheart, I am writing by the light of my radio since it is lights out. Thank you for coming to Millsaps. Your mother was nice to come and find a car with tires and gas. I think I am in love with you, but Daddy says I am too young. I have your picture in your white Lastex bathing suit taped to the top of my book. No wonder those poor shot-up Air Force service men at the hospital voted you "The Body." Keep warm and tan. Love, Richard.*

The hospital he referred to was a huge, gaudy Miami Beach hotel next to the inconspicuous hotel where Mother always stayed. I remember seeing a sign on the desk there, "Gentiles only." And the bathing suit Richard talks about was one of two, both so tight that it took both my Mother and my roommate to squeeze me in them.

But in World War II, even glamour and honors have a downside. For out of vision of the camera is a box of Kleenex where Mother and I had cried when I saw the wounded young men who had made me feel so important and special.

As the picture was being snapped, a poor creature whose injuries made his limbs look like a spider ran to the water and plunged in smiling. I guessed he had once been some high school's biggest football hero. But the distraction of many happy times in Florida soon healed those memories. For down in Florida at school, we had a rip-roaring good time. While in Miami, I visited a great many people. There were important admirals and politicians in Key West. Some officers even took us on a tour of a submarine. I had the privilege of having lunch with Winston Churchill when they gave him an honorary degree at the University of Miami, where my friend's father was president. On one of our chaperoned jaunts to Havana, Cuba, we saw Ernest Hemingway in Harry's Bar. We watched World War II being wrapped up like the Cuban cigars at the Hotel Nationale.

VE Day occurred on May 8, 1945, and Japan surrendered in August of that year. So my last year at Miss Harris' was war free. The whole world thought that we were out of war—perhaps forever, but certainly for our lifetime. Except for the empty chairs at family dinners where some young men had not returned, our spirits were high, and everyone thought we were in for a long, long stretch of nothing but better times.

The spring of 1946, I asked Miss Harris if I might skip a grade and go to New York to attend another all-girl school called Finch Junior College. Since it wasn't an academically demanding place, Miss Harris told me if I took the college board and passed, then I could go. I took the exam and was accepted at Finch, the garden spot of the world for the debutantes of the South, East, the North and any place else.

Having been voted "The Body" by the Air Corps, visited Cuba, bone-fished in the Florida Keys and even discovered a love for Eudora Welty's "Delta Wedding" (which could have been a letter from Aunt Camilla), I had done more than many girls who had finished four years of college, much less high school. I had made it through high school without smoking or drinking, so I knew one could have a good time without doing either, but life in New York would bring surprises.

Chapter 8

Finch

Finch

Finch Junior College was known across the country for its attractive and wealthy girls, but the school was frowned upon by those more interested in serious academics. For me, a girl who had gone to Southern private schools in Memphis and had two unbelievable years at school in Miami, Florida, it was a perfect choice. Nowhere else in the world could I have been so enlightened. More might be taught in classrooms tucked away on rural campuses, but no place but New York could expose a young lady to art, music, theater, politics and the beating pulse of energy of the literary and business worlds, with the United Nations thrown in as a mere extra.

The day I arrived in New York City as a student at Finch I was assigned to live at 903 Park Avenue, an impressive address. But one look at the school made me know that instead of Park Avenue, I wanted to live at 61 East 77th Street, a building for boarders that was across the street from the prestigious Carlyle Hotel. Not only was this building connected directly to Finch's academic quarters, but also my best friend from Memphis was assigned there. Four of us ended up living that first year in a big room on the top floor, next to the badminton court.

Behind Finch's entrance hall with the elevator and check-in room for our housemother was a beautiful drawing room where tea was served each afternoon. More importantly, it was also the place where we would meet our dates who would escort us to fancy French restaurants, debut parties, jazz clubs, concerts, ice hockey games, and once even a flea circus. When we did not meet our young friends in Finch's fancy parlor, we met them under the clock at the Biltmore Hotel adjacent to the Pennsylvania railroad station, which inspired the song "PN Six Five Thousand."

Finch's dress code differed from the bobby socks, saddle oxford, sweater-and-skirt uniform of rural campuses. Our dress code was so sophisticated that we could have left class and gone straight to lunch at 21. Once a naïve Southern girl, because it was spring, made the mistake of wearing white shoes in late May and was laughed out of the student lounge.

In the fall of 1946 what was called the "new look" was the rage in high fashion. Skirts dropped almost overnight from an inch above the knee to ankle-length. Three trunks of clothes I brought with me from Memphis were immediately relegated to the school basement. Instead, I bought two black ankle-length skirts, a wide belt with a big brass buckle and a few sweaters and blouses. One long, black cashmere coat, a few silk scarves, and the must-have basic, black cocktail dress had me fixed for the "City," as New Yorkers call it.

Finch girls paid half rates to Michael, the hairdresser at the Carlyle. For some reason, I did not want to be the flashy blonde with the perfect suntan up East and had Michael darken my hair. In the East there is a very fine line as to how far to push it if you are beautiful, without being cheap or baby-doll looking. I was light-haired, but not as light as peroxide combed in with a toothbrush. I knew to tone it down a little bit in New York. Later I wore French heels, silk stoles, and one or several gold bracelets.

Mr. Post, a dean in Finch's drama department, thought I had a future in television. Not only did he want me to go into a brand new medium with an uncertain future, he wanted me to drop my Southern accent and leave my part of the world. But he has to be given his just due, for at this very time, my "look alike", Grace Kelly, did exactly what Mr. Post wanted me to do. After Grace Kelly became famous, I was often mistaken for her — until I spoke. To be frank, even I see a resemblance.

I did not want to drop my Southern accent, which I could have done, with a great deal of voice training from Mrs. Hall, a "Professor Higgins," who was interested in me going into at least the theater. Not that I am saying Mrs. Hall wanted me to acquire the "Long Island Lockjaw" (talking like your jaws are wired together), but she did want me to have a strong, clear, theatrical voice.

However, all aspects of my life were at a standstill because of my mother's illness, which I learned about in January 1947, following my first and only carefree semester. My whole life changed when Mother called to tell me she was coming to Sloan Kettering Hospital in New York; she had been diagnosed with cancer of the throat. She had found out just before I arrived home for my Christmas holidays but had selflessly kept it a secret so I could enjoy myself. It was so like Mother.

At 18 I became responsible for my mother's care, since my eldest brother, Jack, was slipping deeper and deeper into his problem drinking, and brother Sterling was still in veterans' hospitals recuperating from wounds received as a 19-year-old officer during World War II. There were many days when I could have pinched my father for leaving me in this situation, but in all fairness, he did not know my mother was going to get sick and die.

Maybe I was not on the stage Mr. Post or Mrs. Hall envisioned, but I became an actress, pretending to be the typical Finch girl, when inside I was a frightened, 18-year-old caretaker.

When I was not at the hospital, I was wearing a mask, dashing from college to college on weekends, going to New York nightclubs, attending concerts, visiting art galleries, and doing community service. It seemed to bring Mother great pleasure that I did these things; her eyes lit up as I shared with her my escapades. For the first few months, Mother and I really held out hope for her recovery. After that, we both were actresses.

If a Finch girl was in town, the weekend was not complete if we did not stop by the famous Stork Club, America's most famous nightclub and the "lost world of cafe society," located at 3 East 53rd Street. Sherman Billingsley, a former Oklahoma bootlegger who arrived in New York right after Prohibition, founded the Stork as a jazz-age speakeasy. The club was at its zenith in the 1940s, when I attended Finch.

It was referred to as "the New Yorkiest spot" in New York. Billingsley was so proud that his daughter had gone to Finch, that each year before Christmas holidays he gave his Finch, preppy "jelly beans" a spectacular cocktail dinner dance. There was a solid gold chain at the Stork Club's bar to keep people out, but it was let down on sight of a good-looking Finch girl with ivy league college boys, rich fathers and out-of-town uncles in tow. Billingsley liked the Finch girls to be the first thing you saw on entering the club.

For some reason Sherman (but I never called him that to his face) took a shine to me, and his second in command, Larry, held my favored table at all times. My second year at Finch, my good friend, Larry, presented somewhat of a problem. I was dating a handsome ensign from Clarksdale, Mississippi, an Annapolis graduate who at that time was commuting on the U.S.S. Wisconsin from Havana, Cuba to New York harbor, where he kept a snappy red convertible. Being a sheltered Southern girl, it took me several weekends to figure out that my friend Larry was more interested in my ensign than in me. He kept suggesting that my date stay at his apartment when in New York. This was my first awakening to the gay world on a personal level. Little did my friend, Larry, know that my ensign was one of the most notorious ladies men in the South.

There were many things I learned at the nightclubs. There was a lot of talk that went on in the powder room. When I arrived at Finch, my roommate, who thought she knew everything because she had been at an Eastern prep school and to New York a few times, wrote me out a list of dos and don'ts , so I wouldn't ask for "sweet milk" or call a lowly bus boy a maitre'd. She even told me where the Larue and Copa Cabana ladies rooms were so I could act like an old salt. In high, high heels and long, ankle-length dresses, my hair pulled back with a big solid gold barrette, I knew where to go to powder my nose at just about any of the better places in New York.

It was then that I learned if a man had a date with a call girl, he handed her money to go to the ladies room "to tip the attendant." Hundreds of dollars would be discreetly counted by the girls as they pretended to primp, and a small amount – if any – left in the tip jar.

The Stork Club played such a part of my life in New York that a book called *The Stork Club*, authored by *New York Times* writer Ralph Blumenthal, has me immortalized on its cover. Of course, Orson Welles is the *central* figure, but there I am, sitting on a banquette in the background.

Looking at this smiling photo, one would never guess that I often went to the powder room, tipsy and in tears, worrying about my mother, while the ladies of easy virtue counted their nightly stash. I had learned to deaden my feelings with a drink. I didn't know how to step out of the circus parade at Finch – we had to be free, gay-spirited girls. Drinking gave me the same ease and comfort as Grandmother's paregoric and sugar water back at OK. I drank to forget that a portion of my 52-year-old mother's face had been removed.

It was very likely that the next morning I would awake with a hangover to the screech of a violin played by a desperate street musician needing money for a fix. I would open the window and throw out coins, hoping he would stop, then pull down the shades and grab the aspirin bottle.

Other clubs we frequented were Larue, 21, the Versailles, Café Pierre, and the St. Regis bar, where the Finch girls gave our own cocktail parties at least once or twice a year. The first TV set I ever saw was over the bar at the 21 Club, where a Yalie had taken me to watch an ice hockey game. After dinner we were taken to the wine cellar, where the swells kept a collection of their own wines. Being country come to town, I blurted out, "I know that man," when I saw the name of a Memphian over his resting wine bottles. This very man, who drank nothing but the best, years later gave himself a party where he served his Memphis guests some of his finest. The next morning, he went to the garage and killed himself over financial difficulties.

We also use to frequent the jazz clubs on 52nd Street, where Birdie Parker and others played, or to the German-American Club to drink beer so our dates could stretch their allowances. There was a reason for this, because more than once after an elegant French dinner, I had to slip my date my entire allowance to cover the bill. Of course, the next day I was compensated with a dozen red roses, charged to his mother's floral account, but there was no way I could buy train tickets and pay for hotel rooms on college weekends with flowers.

My first year at Finch, Princeton was my favorite college to visit, and I dated the captain of the tennis team. My first weekend at his club, I came out of a bathroom designated for the dates to use as a powder room and announced loudly in my Southern drawl, "Why, you Princeton athletes just have everything, even little foot baths!" They didn't have urinals and bidets on OK Plantation!

During my second year at Finch, I dated a boy from Yale. My roommate's beau (later her husband) was his good friend and they belonged to the same club. Her future husband played on the baseball team, whose captain was George Herbert Walker Bush, later our president.

Throughout all of these glamorous affairs it never entered my mind to pursue a wealthy or influential Eastern marriage, I only went out with men who were attractive to me. Mother and Aunt Camilla never told me I should marry money, power or prestige. However, both my mother and father felt strongly that I not marry a Catholic, or "Roman," as they were called by some in the Deep South. This feeling had not a thing to do with most Catholics in Memphis being Irish or Italian. No one can say there was a snob bone on either side of my immediate family (although there were some who thought they were top drawer on Daddy's side), nor did the Withers side of the family (all Methodists) worry about me losing my figure having children, since Grandmother Withers bore seven. No, the rub was the idea that I would have had to sign papers before marriage committing my children to be raised in the Catholic church. The idea that I would be told what to do galled and appalled my family. They were democratic to the core. For some odd reason though I dated many Catholic boys, I was never serious about one, and so luckily never had to jump through that hoop, for I had more than my share of problems in life already.

There was definitely another side to life at Finch. For two years my favorite course was community service. The first day I learned to read *The New York Times*. This was no small feat for a girl from a city of 350,000. We were taken to Welfare Island where we saw immigrants take their first steps on American soil; we studied Tammany Hall. Our teacher, Mrs. Smith, took us to New York courtrooms to watch trials. She showed us the ethnic cultures of New York. We spent Chinese New Year in Chinatown, and one of the best, fried domestic duck dinners I have ever had was served at a Czechoslovakian restaurant. We also went to as many different types of religious venues and events as time allowed.

My most vivid lesson was at a day nursery in the bowels of poverty in the giant city. It was here for the first time, I was called a mother fucker by a frightened, hungry boy around age four, who had an open sore on his face where he had been bitten by a rat. Poverty knows no boundaries, and I saw that the South had no lock or claim on the cruelties of life.

Escapism was my middle name, and I found another way to run from

Mother's illness. Every night after dinner a limousine arrived to take students to operas, ballets, concerts or plays, and I was the first name on the list on any weeknight.

Most girls my age in 1946 dated several boys, though might, like me, have a favorite. There were many men in my life, but Richard Leatherman was not one of them at this stage. I had lost touch with him after my visit to Millsaps College during the war, because he was sent to the University of South Carolina and then on to the University of Virginia. We had simply gone our separate ways.

Girls at Finch were great about helping each other with blind dates. Monday through Thursday we could not leave the building but could receive guests. Martha Buck, later Mrs. Charlie Bartlett, asked me to meet with a young man—one of Joe Kennedy's sons. Since I can't remember which one and I never heard from him, it must not have been a fatal attraction. Perhaps it's because we, for lack of anything else to do, played bridge. I have wondered what my Aunt Camilla would have thought of this Catholic boy because I think she would have favored our relationship partly because he was such a big Democrat. My Aunt truly believed Franklin D. Roosevelt saved the country and she loved the democratic party next to God.

Aunt Camilla loved the democratic party so dearly that she kept invitations to Roosevelt's inaugural balls next to the family wedding invitations.

At the end of my first year at Finch, one of my good girlfriends from a college in Virginia came to see me. We were still in New York a few days after Finch had closed and all of our Finch friends had gone home. Martha and I had tickets to fly home, but the flight was cancelled and like most college girls, we were flat broke. We wanted to come home on the train which left in a few hours, but we did not have time to wait for money to be wired to us. Then a light went on in my head. I would call my father and ask if he would call a good friend who was in the F.B.I. and had worked in Memphis during the war, but who was now in New York.

It was close to train departure time when a large black car with two powerful looking men like you see on T.V. came in the hotel and paged us as we sat in the bar drowning our troubles.

Out they whisked us like we had been arrested as spies, past the guests in the bar and the management. One flashed his big badge as crowds parted and we pushed through all obstacles and boarded the train as it pulled out.

Wonderful, I thought, except in our rush I had forgotten to borrow money for Martha and me to eat.

"Fret not," said Martha. I saw some guys playing pinochle. Martha played well, so we had no problem, for any man I have ever known was no problem for Martha in her day. Martha had the face of a Michelangelo angel. She had huge eyes well set three fingers apart, just like the make-up artists and photographers say they should be, and a perfect nose. She had a toothpaste smile with dimples so deep on each side of her mouth that they could hold water like a puddle.

In no time, Martha had a drink and was in the card game. The strange tough-looking group played most of the night with time out for dinner. The next morning after breakfast, bought by Martha since she had won lots of money, the card game began again. As I watched, I also listened. Finally one rough-looking guy from that group of people asked if I wanted to come see him fight the next night.

"Oh, you fight," I said, and not too surprised because he could have been cast as the fighter in a play.

"Don't you know who I am, Dolly?" he asked. (Martha and I were dollies, not dolls, the whole ride to Memphis.)

He was Rocky Graciano, the lightweight champion of the world.

In the East there were many people who did not try or care to understand the South. A few had been in service during World War II in Southern states and had unfortunate experiences. I didn't know then how to either defend or explain the South, but I never apologized for being a Southerner. Once a Yankee asked if we had libraries in the South, and I told him about Liz Farmer's house in Tunica so crowded with books that there was no need for wallpaper.

Southerners still seem to have a constant that if they are a Troy from Troy, Mississippi, they are as good as anybody who ever lived. Apparently we have an inner confidence that if your grandfather had a little land in Mississippi or had been in the state legislature, there isn't a living soul any better than you. Southern mamas always sent their children off to a new life at school or wherever with this reminder, "Now just be sure you to tell them who you are!"

That first year of school I learned a lot besides academics.

* * * *

We still had an elevator attendant at Finch, Peter, who would often bring us food sent from the Carlyle Hotel across the street. And we had a friend whose mother was the very famous Claire Booth Luce. Whenever she entertained, her son would send over her leftovers. Once, this young man promised my roommate a mink. Thinking he meant a coat, she didn't know how she was going to handle that. We had more of a problem when the gift arrived, because it was a real-live little mink.

There I was with some of the richest men in the country, and some of them rather enamored of me, but no one had ever told me that it would be nice to marry money. It just never dawned on me to think like that then. Instead I dated men I found attractive.

By the fall of 1947, mother's condition had worsened, and her doctor, with mercy, let her return home to the care of her family, friends, and a local physician. The previous summer, Mother and I received a call in New York City from the Memphis debutante committee urging me to join the 1947 group. Though mother was desperately ill, the family insisted that I make my debut in Memphis at Christmas with twenty other girls, including two of my cousins and my best friend, Cecil Williams. Like so many choices in my life, I was not certain this was a wise one because of Mother's health, but it worked out well and gave my mother happy things to think about before her death in the spring of 1948.

Christmas holiday was the official debut season, with parties given morning, noon and night — luncheons, tea dances, brunches, any type of entertainment one could dream up. We all wore beautiful dresses and long kid gloves that were so fitted that we had to put talcum powder inside to put them on. I wore my hair in a long pageboy, the style of the day, and endured waist pinchers that made my middle so small I could have worn a dog collar for a belt. It was well worth the pain when I saw the radiant look on Mother's disfigured face that had once been so beautiful as I left for the parties.

Mother arranged for a friend who owned a dress shop to order my debut gown from New York. When the dress arrived, I was disappointed. Though an exquisite ball gown, it was not my dream dress. I drove as fast as I could to the home of the talented Lucy Dabney Walt, the cousin who

Mother and I sewed with when I was a child. She sent me downtown to buy magnificent white satin and French tulle. She added beautiful heirloom lace and created a "Cinderella" dress for me in two days and a night.

December 23rd was the official coming out party for our group. The J.P. Norfleets also gave a lavish dance for my cousins and me, and on New Year's Day, we stood in our long formals to receive the older people of Memphis society at a reception given by my cousins' grandmother, Mrs. R.O. Johnston. "Cousin Lizzy" as I called her, was so provincial that she did not have on her guest list anyone who was divorced. This, of course, excluded my father, her cousin. It was held in her ancestral home with family portraits on the wall and memorabilia from the past everywhere. I think Mr. Stadiem of *Town and* Country who writes about first families of the South would have given it a ten.

A friend of mine from the Midwest who'd had an enormous debut party that I had attended the year before came to Memphis for my party. The morning after her first night in Memphis and her first date with a Memphis boy, she walked into Mother's sick room and said, "I want to tell you, I'm engaged."

To this, Mother answered, "That's perfectly all right, Eleanor. You are only visiting for three days. Just don't tell anyone and have a good time."

Eleanor moved closer to mother, like she was whispering something in her ear. "You don't understand, Mrs. Seabrook, I'm engaged to the Memphis boy I had a date with last night. We fell in love and became engaged on our first date. My mother will be surprised to hear that she will be mother of the bride at a large wedding this summer, and of course, Sugsie will be a bridesmaid."

Not being in the room, I have never known what Mother's answer was, but I later heard that she was not only surprised, but concerned, since the whirlwind courtship had been on her watch.

After the holidays I returned to Finch worn out, but pleased, because I knew Mother had been happy with the debut, and though unable to attend any of the parties had enjoyed it vicariously.

Back at school in January of 1948, I tried to stay busy and live as normally as possible. Though it was no great honor, I had been chosen president of the house. This job was not of great importance, but it kept me in touch with anyone who broke a rule. These broken rules were not serious, and usually concerned a glamorous Texan who had signed in late because her father's private jet had been fogged in, or something as trivial as coming in after 1 a.m. because she had been "caught in traffic" with her movie star date.

However, there was one glaring problem when I was house president – theft. The college administration decided to bring in a detective to find the culprit. Once the detective became involved, it was no longer my problem, and I just shelved it in the back of my mind.

In early May I received the dreaded telephone call telling me that Mother was failing and that I should come home. The young ensign who had taken me to the Stork Club had returned to the South and was now farming, and he took good care of me at this very tragic time in my life. On the day of Mother's death, I remember sitting in the living room and watching as I saw Mother's first cousin, a typical Southern gentleman, cry unabashedly with his head held in his hands. I knew that cousin Pete and other men of the family would never leave my mother's body, from the time of death until the last clod of dirt had been thrown on her casket.

Of all things, my front door opened, and expecting one of Mother's friends or relative, in walked my Finch friend, Eleanor, whose large wedding I was to be in the following month. At first I could not find my voice, but I managed in a stutter to say, "Eleanor, what are you doing here?"

Of course, I was hoping she would answer that she had come down to see her fiancé and to discuss the wedding plans. Not so. Eleanor broke into sobs, telling me she had been expelled from Finch. I never asked any more questions, because at that very time my next door neighbor came out of Mother's room and told me that it was all over. The next time I saw Eleanor was at the cemetery after Mother's service. The morning after mother's burial, I was taken by the cemetery by my brother Sterling and then driven to the airport where I boarded a plane for New York.

Although Eleanor never returned to school, it was said that after treatment for her problems there would be a wedding. This never took place, and I never saw her again.

On the flight back to New York things went through my mind that I have never shared with anyone. Throughout my life, I hid my biggest secret from the world and from myself — the indescribable love I had for my mother. I loved Mother so much, and her death was so painful to me, that

I never told my own children much about her and I kept very few pictures of her out for display. Now, of course, I wish I had shared more about my Mother with my children and kept her pictures out and even read the letters she wrote me that I have never been able to take out of a box. Hopefully, this book might remedy what might have seemed to them indifference on my part and let them know how much I really cared.

Please do not misunderstand. Mother and I did not have an easy or smooth time of it in our short nineteen years. Great love is not always an easy love. It is more like being in a scary and terrible storm on the seashore. There are times in a storm when the rough waves beat against the beach and rain pours down. Later, the beach can be sunny, with a big, blue sky overhead and a view out to sea that goes on forever.

After Mother's death in May 1948, I went back to Finch for the end of the semester and graduated. It crossed my mind that I might return to Finch for a third year and try for theater with Mr. Post and Mrs. Hall.

At graduation, Finch gave me a charm inscribed "ineamus meliora" which means God knows what. Graduation went off very well. A Yale beau, who had proposed (telling me we did not have to live in his hometown in Connecticut but would move any place I liked), came for the celebration and gave me a lovely gift and treated me to a champagne lunch.

Driving to the airport by cab, I understood for the first time why many people call New York City, "the" City. How arrogant I had thought them only two years ago, and now fighting back tears, I turned to see the skyline. Memories of my time there was like looking in Grandmother's old stereopticon, and I saw visions of me lying in bed at Finch, chewing bubble gum and reading the *Daily Mirror,* or dashing over to the Carlyle drugstore for ice cream before ten o'clock, when the front door of Finch would be locked on weeknights. Imbedded in my mind would be Peter the elevator man and Mrs. Gurney, the school telephone operator, and our lenient housemother.

Funny that the Finch faculty would have asked for volunteers to take a psychological test. Since as the saying goes, I am an egomaniac with an inferiority complex, I volunteered. The critique that came back reported that I was a sane person who tried to be honest, but it was clear I'd had a very diverse childhood, as I say, half city-mouse, half country-mouse.

I knew that even if I were the one in a million to make it on the stage or TV, my heart would always yearn for the dark black soil of the Mississippi delta. I would return to the South and like Grandmother and Mother would make homemade Christmas wreaths of magnolia and holly berries and place them on the graves of my ancestors.

Chapter 9

My Two Single Years

My Two Single Years

Aunt Camilla, her night nurse, Mrs. Harmon, and Tennie were waiting when I returned to my childhood home in Memphis that my mother had left me. No question about it, before her death Mother had made arrangements making certain that I had a safety net. Although our household was a bit different, being an all-female establishment where the big meal was still served at noon like on the farm, Aunt Camilla had to be the most understanding woman in the world. Out-of-town friends visited by the dozens, and more than once I came in late, having had far too much to drink, and left the front door wide open. My precious old maid aunt should have written a book on how to live and let live. Come to think of it, Aunt Camilla could have written bestsellers on any subject, because any small talent I have in writing must be her genes.

As for the relationship between my ensign (now a farmer) and myself, it went from a short high to a plunging low in a matter of several months. It would have been impossible for me to be happy with any man, for I was not happy with myself. I had never really accepted Mother's death, because I had been away in New York City. If I had put on an act in New York, it was pale to the performance demanded by this suitor. Once that short affair was over, I began to travel and visit many classmates in different cities.

In the next two years, I visited friends in Birmingham, in New Orleans at Mardi Gras, and I returned to New York several times. Being home was of some comfort, but it was strange without Mother. Living in the South as a single woman was very different from New York, and I kept myself busy going to as many parties as possible.

I remember well going to an Ole Miss football game in 1948. Like the East, there were tailgate lunches in the famous Grove at Oxford, Mississippi. To compare tailgate parties at Princeton and Yale versus Ole Miss would be like a comparison of a scoop of vanilla ice cream compared to banana split. To me, everything at Ole Miss was more and better. Instead of entering the stadium from a field house like Eastern teams, the Rebel football players would run through the Grove between long lines of cheering fans. Southerners are naturally friendly, but people in the Grove greeted each other as if they were comrades from the same hometown who had met on a battlefield. Southerners also drank more before the game than Easterners. Unfortunately, whiskey and football do not always mix, and I witnessed several fights during and after the game.

I remember one poor beauty in the crowd who slipped her silver flask into the stadium. She started the game screaming, "Rah, rah, rah," loud as a drill sergeant. By halftime, her voice dropped an octave to "rah, rah," and by the end of the game, as she was carried out, she let out one whimpering "rah."

I had been warned that people would wear their new fall finery, so I was not dressed for comfort that warm fall afternoon. The young woman who sat in front of me at the game was typically dressed — wool suit, very high heels and a velour hat with a peacock feather as long as a TV antenna. Other ladies wore fur stoles of three or four little mink skins that still had their heads on them; they took their gloves off and put them in the mink's mouth, which had a spring behind it.

When at half-time the Ole Miss marching band entered the playing field covered by the world's largest Confederate flag, it was easy to forgive the hats, the outfits too early for the season, and the furs. All the excitement made me know that Southerners can have as much energy as the biggest hustler on Wall Street.

Leading the band was the drum major, along with the majorettes who twirled their batons. The star of the whole half time show was a little girl around five or six years old, dressed exactly like all the majorettes and almost as able as they were, she threw her baton in the air and strutted in perfect time to the music.

Because I was with an Ole Miss graduate, as well as my date, after the game we started hitting the fraternity houses. In 1948, everyone who was anyone at Ole Miss was in a fraternity or sorority. I've never seen such beautiful girls, and there is no wonder the college boasts several Miss Americas. The fraternity and sorority houses were well furnished, and I felt like I was a "pilgrim" on a house and garden tour in a Southern city. If I might choose one scene to portray the old South and its aristocrats, it would be Ole Miss, since one of the definitions of "aristocrat" is someone who has land and power.

After making a wearying round of the houses, I was finally driven back to Clarksdale, Mississippi, where I spent the night in a large tester bed, where I rolled over and thought, "You know, this staying home at Ole Miss wouldn't be so bad." I understood why so many Southern girls went off to the East to school for the first two years and then returned to Alabama or to Sophie Newcomb in New Orleans, or to Ole Miss. Why not have both sides of the coin if you were able to flip it?

It was always a treat to visit my date's Williamsburg-style home in Clarksdale. In the main hall, the traditional Martha and George Washington portraits painted by Frost hung by the front door. An antique early American sofa upholstered in petit point sat in the hall just as casually as one would leave a pair of hunting boots. This piece of furniture bought at auction by the lady of the house would easily be worth the value of the house in its plantation setting.

Seeing these fine things, I remembered Miss Birdie's decorative arts course at Finch. Miss Birdie would have been pleased that her lessons, though squeezed in between weekends on Long Island and Jersey, influenced my adult life back in the Mississippi delta.

I still favor good furniture polish and flowers from a Delta garden over some of the almost scary name-dropping art I viewed in New York apartments. And the Delta had more fine oriental rugs than any other part of the world, many purchased from an Armenian rug broker who used to call on Delta homes after the cotton harvest and roll out his wares on the driveway.

Off and on through the next two years I came back to the Delta for more house parties. Once, a very sad thing happened at an otherwise storybook Delta weekend. A young man who had come in a car with a friend asked me late one night if he could drive back to Memphis in my car, and I foolishly lent it to him.

The following morning I went, as was the custom, to my older hostess's bedroom for rich, black coffee and clotted cream, where I overheard a phone conversation. There had been a terrible accident the night before on Highway 61, the straightest highway in Mississippi. My young friend had gone to sleep at the wheel of my big, black Buick (formerly Mother's). He collided with a car carrying two teenagers coming home from a football game, killing them and almost killing himself. He lay in a full body cast for almost two years.

The accident sealed a very lasting relationship. I went to see my friend most days during his recovery at his stepfather's fine English house and came to call him "Willie Rabbit" after the oversized Easter bunny I brought him. Hal, one of my favorite male friends who still lived in the big house on top of the hill in our neighborhood, would often drive me to visit in his large, maroon Packard convertible. It is no surprise that a female friend once told me, "Tell me about yourself at lunch, because I don't talk to females after 6 p.m." She was smart, for I learned early in life that my closest friends are men. Sometimes our cocktail hour visits to our injured friend got a bit out of hand. To prove the point, when they cut the cast off Willie Rabbit's leg, they found a lady's earring.

Willie spent summers at his grandmother's home when his mother and stepfather went to Newport for the season. His grandmother, a real character who kept a radio tuned to the police band 24 hours a day, had a hairdresser come to her house to Marcel her hair. She loved parties, and her escort was usually a Catholic monsignor. The lady once told me that when she died, until the time she was buried, she wanted to be laid out on the chaise lounge instead of in her casket.

Later that year, I attended a lovely dinner in the Mississippi delta with the family of a beau. The hosts father ranted and raved that he had received a letter from the board of a prestigious Memphis club that his son had broken a rule by taking me as his guest to dinner there since I was not a member. Never before or since have I felt as embarrassed. The conversation seemed to go on and on, although my host were defending me. It was not long after that night that a bachelor influenced the board to change the rules. I can only hope that this ridiculous rule was a leftover from World War II when country clubs all but shut down. The incident left a mark on my pride. The whole business taught me tolerance for those shut out for no reason.

It was at this dining table that the lady of the house told us Depression stories. The family's kitchen maid suddenly quit, and when asked why, she replied, "Well, there is just too much shuffling of the dishes for the scarcity of food." My hostess had been born into a very fancy household in Memphis, where soup plates, salad plates, dinner plates and dessert plates were used at each meal – that meant five or six plates to serve instead of one. She also shared that when she first moved to the Delta, she lived in a farmhouse that was so primitive that the funnel of wind blowing under the house would actually lift her oriental rugs off the floor. Like so many, after the Depression when economic times improved in the South, she built a fine plantation home.

I was fast learning that just as there was a difference between the North and the South, and between Memphis and the Delta, there were also variations among Delta families. You would never have found my hostess on hunts. In most Southern families in 1948, women were not encouraged to hunt; however, my brother Jack included me in many of his trips to the OK woods and fields.

Hunting on OK Plantation was known far and wide as some of the finest in the Delta and the world, thanks in large part to the writings of famed outdoorsman Nash Buckingham. "Mr. Buck," as we called him, was a regular guest at Jack's hunting camp behind the levee.

Jack, Mr. Buck, and Jack's guide, Colonel, conducted many of the hunts immortalized in Buckingham's *Game Bag* [1] and other books. Colonel came to OK from Beaver Dam Ducking Club, where he had been understudy to the famous Horace, from Nash's story *De Shootinest Gent'man*.

A dozen or so men, mostly Memphians including my great-grandfather William Henry Carroll, had set up the Mid-South's oldest and the nation's second-oldest hunting club at Beaver Dam in Tunica County in 1881, before there were paved roads or even a railroad coming through the county. Instead, the men came down the river on the *Kate Adams* or another packet and were met at OK Landing by wagons to take them on to

Beaver Dam.

But the plentiful waterfowl and other game drew the men like nothing else could. Beaver Dam Ducking Club's treasurer described one early hunt this way: "Lake simply covered with ducks, geese, and swans that kept us awake nights." That hunt's three-day total was: 480 ducks, five swans and 22 geese [2].

The club continued until 1946, when the lease for the land went back to the owner "due to poor duck hunting, the loss of interest in the club by the members, and drinking problem of the caretaker...." [3]

Nash Buckingham died in 1971, just before a new Beaver Dam club was founded, still in existence today.

It should be noted that game was much more abundant then than it is now. In Buckingham's day, the ducks came by the millions and the hunters were few. Then the natural habitat of the waterfowl began to disappear, as more and more land was cleared, not only in the Delta but also in the North where the ducks began their winter migrations.

In *Game Bag*, Nash Buckingham describes returning to OK for a hunt. "This tent house of '44-'45 is homecoming to the river....I will gun hereabouts and well below, with Jack Seabrook and Paul Banks." Buckingham ends the story with Colonel saying, "Like ol' times, ain't it, Mist' Nash?" [4]

Even as late as 1949, when I hunted with Mr. Buck on OK, I remember the sky literally being black with squawking and squealing ducks and geese as they came in off the river to the corn fields Jack planted behind the levee. Many times they were so close that they almost landed on top of us as we crouched in Jack's pits, deliberately placed in long, narrow corn fields so we would be sure to get a good shot. This afternoon shoot would be icing on the cake after a grand shoot on the Mississippi River in flat boats that morning.

One opening day of duck season when I was visiting OK, my brother was in a full cast on the lower part of his body. We couldn't travel over the levee to the Mississippi River and put Jack in a boat. Even *we* knew that was impossible. By dern, if Jack didn't have his man Colonel and me put him on a makeshift stretcher and hoist him up into the back of Jack's pickup. It was the opening day of duck season, and Jack Seabrook was going to shoot some ducks.

In the back of the pickup, with Jack lying flat as a flounder, we drove just behind his house where there were some ponds and parked. We waited, and we waited, and we talked. I knew Jack was in severe pain, but suddenly, those ducks and geese came flying off the river. It looked as if they might flare off to the south, but they turned back towards us at the last minute. Jack, flat on his back, shot two of the most beautiful green heads that I ever saw, just as the sun in the winter Delta set an orange that no painting can capture.

Now, this is sounding like a Mississippi hunting tale, but I have the proof: a clipping of a story by Henry Reynolds that ran on the front of the Memphis *Commercial Appeal* sports page!

* * * *

One night while dancing at the Peabody, I met a young man who looked me square in the eye and said the very last thing I ever expected to hear from a Yale graduate who had helped break the Japanese code in World War II. J. Tunkie Saunders jumped right into my background. These are his exact words: "You are somebody. Why, your Uncle Sterling rode in a big black Cadillac, ran the only business other than farming in Tunica County and was head of the levee board during the floods. He was Mr. Tunica."

I was stunned. Tunkie and I talked as though we had been close friends all of our lives. I do not remember going near the dance floor. Nor do I remember with whom I had a date. All I remember was that at last I had met someone who spoke of my world, my people and my background.

For me to meet a Southern man who asked me questions and valued my answers was a culture shock. Tunkie and I discussed classical music and books, and the interesting people he knew, and to whom he introduced me later. My new mentor had grown up in my own Tunica town. He had even been a member of the tony Fence Club at Yale that I frequented more than any other club during my Finch years. I had even been given a treasured Fence Club charm by my serious beau.

Between marriages, Tunkie's mother had left him, at a young and impressionable age, with his grandparents in Tunica. They lived in one of a few two-story houses in the little Delta town, but later his mother made an amazing second marriage to a world-famous man, and Tunkie left his grandparents and joined his mother in Memphis. Like me, Tunkie understood the dark side of Delta life as well as the happy memories.

Tunkie shared with me that at Yale, he told everyone about his Mississippi background. And although his grandfather, Sam Houston, helped finance his Yale education by taking a county job, all his fancy admirers thought he was a direct descendant of *the* Sam Houston. Both Tunkie and I were amused that Easterners seem to want a Southern friend for a trophy. We laughed even more over the fact that they seem to think that all Southerners know each other, no matter what part of the South they come from.

Tunkie was very proud of our backgrounds and wanted me to be proud of my people and our Tunica County. He believed that people who came from the dirt – the landed gentry – were the backbone of the South.

Tunica just kept coming up in my life. One day, I walked into the First Tennessee Bank to buy travelers checks for a trip to New York, and there sat Richard Leatherman. Like so many Delta sons, he was apprenticed for a year before going to work on the farm. Naturally, he worked at First Tennessee, where his father was on the board.

Shortly after that, I began to see him at the social functions of our age group. This was a nice surprise, because the year I made my debut, Richard had come to only one party, because he spent so much time hunting on the farm at Commerce. Now working at the bank and living in Memphis, he began to socialize with his college crowd and others, and this included Tunkie, who was the leader of the social pack.

When I first met Tunkie, he was sharing a cottage in Germantown with a very eligible bachelor from Philadelphia who had moved to Memphis to work in one of his family's cotton brokerage firms. Mickey McFadden and Tunkie became my blood brothers, protectors, and stand-ins any time there was an empty spot on my calendar. Mickey had the distinction of being the first man in Memphis to wear khaki pants and a blue blazer to a cocktail party. Unfortunately Mickey's signature dress code lasted only one night. Soon every young man in Memphis was wearing what soon became the dress of the day. The McFaddens had the reputation of being fashion trailblazers. Mickey's uncle was the first man in Memphis to wear patent leather Brooks Brothers dancing pumps with no socks.

Tunkie picked out many classics for me to read and then along with a famous author of today, Shelby Foote, we would critique the book. Often we would read one author (Anthony Trollope, for example) for a full year. Though I had always appreciated music, he had me listen to everything from *Peter and the Wolf* to Wagner's *Ring*. When anything to do with the arts came to Memphis, he had great seats and I was asked. Because of Tunkie's tutelage, I did sound very smart on a local quiz show, when I could answer a question referring to the 1812 Overture.

Tunkie even advised me to wear simple silk dresses and had me order Lobb shoes like the clodhoppers the Queen of England wears. Now, I'll admit these $500 numbers that looked like golf shoes without cleats impressed no one but Tunkie.

Our pressed wild duck dinners were prepared in the style of the famous Parisian restaurant, Tour D'Argent. The ducks would be served with martinis, watercress and salt, and lots of conversation.

Instead of just listening to a mere symphony, Tunkie also made me listen to tapes of famous and temperamental conductors rehearsing their orchestras laboriously for hours. For parties, he hired some of Beale Street's best musicians, and on several occasions paid for musicians to come up from New Orleans.

Naturally, a dog or cat wasn't enough for Tunkie. He kept rare and exotic fish in a tank on his mantle. One night as we danced with fervor, his angelfish catapulted onto the floor where it was stomped into paté by a one of his glamorous guests.

No eggnog for Tunkie on Christmas morning. In a large silver loving cup he mixed an extraordinary drink called the "the green cup", made of crème d' menthe, brandy, and goodness knows what. It went down easy, but you didn't as you fell to the floor from its effect.

About 1949, Tunkie moved to a charming old stable in downtown Memphis in Victorian Village. Although wild stories were told about our crowd, we were all just young and fun loving. Dancing, drinking, and liberal conversation about politics, art, and reading occupied most of the time we spent at the stable. The only love affairs I noticed were those with the whiskey bottle. Young men were optimistic about business, and most had fine educations. With a loan and hard work, like Tunkie they could climb the ladder of success in the corporate and social world.

On the social side, Tunkie would issue an invitation to one of his affairs by announcing, "My guest list is very impressive, so don't forget to bring your ladder." Of course we all know Tunkie borrowed this line from a famous comedian, but like Tunkie, it was still entertaining.

Before Tunkie moved to the stable, in the spring of 1949, I had an accident at his Germantown home that changed my life. That day I had hosted a Sunday brunch at a private club. After the brunch, we continued the party at Tunkie and Mickey's. I walked by a gentleman sitting on a sofa who had been over-served since World War II. He stuck out his leg as a prank and tripped me. The fall broke my right arm and demolished my elbow. The next thing I knew they were cutting off the sleeve of my dress at the hospital because my arm had swollen that quickly. One of the most famous orthopedic physicians in the world came in and told me he could fix my right arm so it would bend again, but this surgery left a scar that goes completely down the back of my arm.

I had been tripped in two ways, for now I could not travel and visit out-of-town friends. First I lay in a hospital bed for weeks, and then in my own French gold-and-white bed at home. Maybe Daddy had no patience for me when I fell in the shower as a child, but dressed in flesh-colored satin nightgowns trimmed in lace, I found that a small army of sympathetic young men surrounded me. Since it was my right arm and I was helpless, I had a sexy young nurse who made a good bartender at the cocktail hour.

One Saturday night with my nurse serving drinks to three young bachelors in my upstairs bedroom, Richard, in his typical, direct, Richard way, simply asked the other young men to leave, that he had something he wanted to ask me. He then picked up the phone and called his aunt who lived up the street to ask if she had a bottle of champagne.

My other suitors went straight to the Memphis Country Club, where people in those days met every Saturday night for a nightcap, and announced, "Raise up your glasses and drink, and maybe soon we will know the answer to Richard Leatherman's proposal to Mary Carroll Seabrook known as Sugsie at this moment at her home."

The next day Richard's mother received a call from the aunt who had provided the champagne to Richard. She asked bluntly if he had proposed. Richard played it cool and said we were serious but had made no plans to marry. Our "engagement" was not announced at that time because of my social commitments.

I had promised to attend June week graduation activities at Annapolis to watch my very dearest of all male friends graduate. This young man had been my escort for most of my debut parties, and I had visited him at Annapolis many times. Except for Richard, there is no one that I thought more of then or now.

Also, I was to be in a wedding in East Orange, New Jersey in June 1949. It all seemed very glamorous to me, with the church ceremony followed by a dinner in a magnificent green-and-white striped tent. I was surprised that the flowers and all the decorations were beautiful, Southern gardenias, Grandmother's "cape jasmine". The next day I was driven to New York City by a most attractive one-armed man. I had watched him play tennis the day before and found that night at the reception that he was also a wonderful dancer. After a few days in New York, I went on to Charlevoix, Michigan, to visit Richard's family. If all went well in the Leatherman's summer home, where the whole family spent busy days and nights together, our romance would have passed the acid test and we would announce our engagement.

When I arrived in Charlevoix, I found myself in a magnificent resort town. This was Hemingway country, and I was often reminded of the Hemingway stories, particularly the Nick stories written after World War II. There are three lakes around the resort, Round Lake, Lake Charlevoix, and Lake Michigan. The Leatherman house sat on Round Lake. The Great Lakes looked awesome to an inland girl.

Each morning at the Leatherman cottage, we were allowed to sleep as long as we liked, unlike some resort cottages, where breakfast is served at eight sharp. At the Leatherman's, you could eat breakfast until noon. The maid brought up from the old plantation made a hundred biscuits every morning, and people came in from all over the resort to the Leatherman dining room to have homemade biscuits, Michigan berry preserves, and a second cup of coffee. The dining room was very long with a fireplace at one end. Even though it was summer, Charlevoix could be cold, and we had many fires, particularly at night. My first mistake with Mrs. Leatherman was saying I was cold one night there. For the rest of my marriage I was seated in front of the fireplace and Woodie, the houseman, was instructed to put another log on the fire because "Miss Sugsie is cold-natured."

The food and company were absolutely superb, but the activities were not for the faint of heart. Arriving with a cast on my arm, I was secretly pleased, because I did not have to play all the sports with those excellent athletes.

First, the whole cottage played tennis in the morning. Then after lunch at the golf club and 18 holes of golf, we rushed back to the cottage, dressed for water skiing and boarded the family's 1947 Chris Craft, "The Rebels," exactly like the one in *On Golden Pond*. We would have an enormous evening meal: plank white fish with whipped potatoes, broiled tomatoes, two or three kinds of vegetables and beautiful berries and cherries in season. The only food lacking in northern Michigan was a good vine-ripe Mississippi tomato. Several times a summer Mr. Leatherman would go back home to the plantation, and when he returned, he would always bring back two or three large boxes of homegrown tomatoes.

Tomatoes hold an esteemed rank in our family to this day. Once I heard a son-in-law tell a friend, "I married into a most unusual family. While other people talk politics and the stock market at dinner each night we have long, graphic discussions about tomatoes." It became such a joke that years later when other well-groomed ladies of the resort wore heirloom pendants and pearls, Mrs. Leatherman wore a painted wooden tomato necklace. Even the soap in the powder room was shaped like a tomato.

After a large, seated dinner each night, if there was any light left, we could work in a baffling game of croquet. Croquet was played on the side of the house, on a slope, and with any luck, when you hit someone's ball, you could send it right up under the cottage. There were enough holes in the latticework around the foundation that your ball could go through and end up under the house. That was the shot of the afternoon.

Occasionally we went to the movies in Charlevoix or nearby towns. Naturally there was no television in those days. Other nights, as if we hadn't had enough togetherness, we played parlor games. The Leathermans loved games. Their favorite trick was to work on a new game and perfect it, then invite some defenseless soul over to the house and beat the socks off them. Such competitiveness I had never seen. As the old comedian said, "I thought about taking exercise once, but I lay down until the thought passed." I shared his feelings by bedtime after a Leatherman day at Charlevoix.

Other nights we went out on a friend's sailboat that also had a motor on it. I tried with the cast on my arm to ski on a surf board, and I hung on for dear life. The suction of the water pulled my bathing suit down to my waist. I didn't care; I was just trying to stay alive.

My first visit, I could tell I was being sized up, for it was very important to be accepted in Charlevoix if you were going to visit often. As time passed, it became obvious that the pecking order was there–just as it was at the sorority house, just as it was with the snobs who read the most books, or the person who played the best game of golf. Wherever I went, I knew not to run from it. There is politics from the sewing circle to the United Nations.

After returning from my visit with the Leathermans at Charlevoix, I spent a great deal of time with a Finch friend in Alabama who had asked me to be a bridesmaid in her forthcoming wedding. More than once walking down Fifth Avenue in New York City, I had slipped into a church and sat in the very back row and watched perfect strangers get married, but this was the first Southern wedding I had ever been in. Peggy, an only child, had an extravagant dress designed and made in Hollywood.

Because of the summer heat, the ceremony took place at 8 p.m. in an awkward, double-aisle Methodist church. When the bride looked at her husband-to-be at the end of the aisle, I saw a stricken look appear on her face. Only the night before, the groom had been tall and handsome–with hair! But the day of the wedding he unwisely went to the hotel barber, who made him look like his head was shaved for brain surgery.

Instead of flowers, the reception at her lovely home on the side of a mountain was decorated with big bunches of grapes and oranges to match our unusual bridesmaid dresses in shades of "grape juice purple" and "Orange Crush". The beaming mother of the bride and the chattering florist were ecstatic with the results.

Because of Peggy's wedding, I started thinking of my own upcoming nuptials, and I decided that with Mother gone, I wanted a simple, small wedding and not a Hollywood extravaganza. Little did I know that what I wanted and what would happen were worlds apart.

When I returned home, secretly engaged, I looked up my mother's wedding pictures and read the description written by the newspaper. It was then that I realized I may have judged my friend's weddings a bit harshly and burst out laughing. Although Mother's picture was beautiful, I want to share with you the lavish description of her attire, in a double-aisle Methodist church no less.

Quoting from the newspaper article, dated October 2, 1912:

> "The bride, who is a petite blond, entered with her father, who gave her in marriage. She was never more beautiful than in her bridal robe of white charmeuse satin, veiled in Duchesse lace caught with chiffon and valley lilies, with garniture of bands of rhinestones. Her long court train was adjusted at the shoulders with rhinestones and was caught with chiffon and valley lilies. Her tulle veil, which fell in filmy folds that partly concealed the bridal shower bouquet of valley lilies, was arranged in a Juliet cap with real orange blossoms.
>
> "The bride's sister, Miss Ada Withers, was the maid of honor. She wore a gown of white satin entrain draped with cream Chantilly lace, and held a sheaf bouquet of yellow chrysanthemums tied with yellow tulle. She wore in her hair a bird of paradise held by a gold cord.
>
> "The bridesmaids were gowned alike in green satin entrain, veiled in green chiffon, with garniture of green chiffon roses. Instead of the conventional bouquets, they carried muffs of yellow chiffon with a shower of roses."[5]

* * * *

When Richard and I became officially and publicly engaged, it was announced with a half-page picture in the society section of the Sunday newspaper. This is quite a contrast to today, when engagement and wedding announcements must be paid for. In that day, newspaper accounts of nuptial events sometimes even omitted couple's last names, saying, "Supper given for Sugsie and Richard last evening...."

At the small wedding I envisioned, I wanted Aunt Camilla to act as my mother, and my oldest brother, Jack, to give me away, since he was my surrogate father.

As plans for the wedding snowballed, I missed Mother more and more. A cousin on my father's side offered to have it at her home, which would have been perfect in both size and setting, but this was *not* agreeable to my dearest of all people, Aunt Camilla, who had taken my mother's place in my life. It would mean my father would give me away. Since Aunt Camilla saw neither my father nor his second wife, that would be awkward. Two of Richard's aunts then offered their homes as a place for a reception.

That summer, my groom had refused to go on a trip around the world with his first cousin in order to stay home and work on the farm and marry me. However, Richard's family told us if we put the wedding off for six whole months and had a big wedding at Christmas, the first cousin and Richard's brother (who had taken Richard's place on the trip) would have returned. Also, Richard's sister would have had her second baby and could be in the wedding along her husband. Then it was suggested that it would be nice if we married on December 29th, my in-laws anniversary. My simple wedding suddenly had bridesmaids and groomsmen coming from all parts. And then there were parties that were going to be given…large parties…small parties…the rehearsal dinner. I sensed things were not going too well. Aunt Camilla and Tennie could feel it too.

To put an end to all the indecision, I finally took matters into my own hands. Remembering weddings I had attended in New York, I settled on a five o'clock ceremony, followed by a reception at the Peabody Hotel with dinner and dancing. As for the libation for the reception, brother Jack told me to go by the local bootlegger, or blind tiger in Tunica. The store sold liquor after hours and outside municipal boundaries, like many Chinese groceries did at that time, giving the name blind tiger to the taxing of illegal whiskey. This whiskey, made in Louisiana, entered the Delta over the river bridge at Vicksburg and proceeded up Highways 1 and 61, where there was a tax on the sale of illegal commodities. This practice continued until 1965. It is fortunate that I bought extra, because I began to have out-of-town visitors for the round of prenuptial parties that started that fall.

Being an avid hunter, my mother-in-law attended very few of my wedding parties, because she was off hunting in Arkansas or down in Mississippi most of the time. But she was great fun when she did come. One day she took me to go pick out silver, crystal, and china, and my Aunt Camilla asked her to stay for lunch, catching Tennie somewhat off guard.

We had our large meal in the middle of the day, so we certainly had ample amounts. But all through the meal, my future mother-in-law had a quizzical look on her face, though she was trying to be very polite to Aunt Camilla and me.

I had never told my mother-in-law that we had brought up our Polly parrot from Mississippi, and Polly lived in the kitchen. From time to time Polly would join in the conversation. Several weeks later when I mentioned the parrot to my mother-in-law, she said, "Thank goodness. I thought you all had some family idiot you kept in the kitchen, and no one had told me about it. Of course, you know, dear, it wouldn't have mattered, but then it is nice to know that it was a bird."

My wedding went anything but smoothly. Two of Richard's aunts and uncles hosted the rehearsal dinner the night before the wedding. It was held at the Memphis Hunt & Polo Club, a very special setting because the club was founded in the early 1920s at the Leatherman's dining room table by Mr. Hugh Fontaine, an uncle by marriage to my husband. The dinner was charming, with dolls dressed as the bridal party decorating the center of the table. This night could have been used as a movie script. For a starter, the two aunts had all of their nieces and nephews as guests, leaving no room for my out-of-town guests who were not in the wedding party. My husband-to-be and his parents noticed none of this.

A few other things went wrong, too. I learned that Jack, who was going to give me away, could not come to the dinner because he had been goose hunting with Nash Buckingham down on OK and had broken his rib climbing out of the goose pit. Then, a married friend ran off in the bushes with an old beau, upsetting her new husband. Another friend of mine was over-served and threw a big diamond ring that had been her grandmother's into the bushes because she said it was too heavy for her finger. We were all crawling around looking for the ring. Meanwhile, a bridesmaid took this opportunity to break her engagement, and her fiancé left the table and drove to Chattanooga. Naturally, everyone fussed over her, trying to console her. I somehow remembered there was a wedding the next day, and it was going to be mine.

On my wedding day, I awakened to read the morning newspaper brought to me with my breakfast tray. There on the front page I read that my stepmother had filed for divorce from my father. This must have been because she had not been asked to sit in Mother's place, because she reconciled with my father shortly after the wedding.

My favorite dog Wallie died on the day my wedding pictures were taken, so I looked very sad. My dress was a replay of my debut dress, with the addition of the Leatherman family rose-point lace veil and $300 worth of illusion to puff it out. My bridesmaids' wore stunning, strapless eggshell peach dresses and small capes of tulle. The attendants carried cabbage roses – a large version of a rose made from many rose petals. I carried a satin-bound *Book of Common Prayer* topped with a single orchid.

In 1949, people did not have professional wedding coordinators, but I certainly needed one. For the ceremony I had chosen hundreds of calla lilies to decorate the church. The florist failed to tell me there had to be a member of the altar guild present to take down the Christmas decorations and watch her glorify the church. After a call to my old friend the bishop who was marrying us, this problem was solved.

The wedding was to start at five o'clock at historic Calvary Episcopal Church where my great-grandparents, the William Henry Carrolls, had married in 1840. I was dressed beautifully, feeling fine and looking good, but I thought I must be the most anxious bride in the world. I couldn't understand why the wedding didn't start.

Then I overheard the minister say, "Flowers or no flowers, this ceremony is starting in five minutes." I was then told that the florist had stopped by the hotel to drop off some things and was running late.

Everyone kept telling me just to stay calm, that all brides got nervous. Beautiful Kate, Richard's sister, tried to distract me, telling me, "I have known Richard all of my life, but even I was taken aback when I walked in his room this afternoon and saw him polishing the soles of his black patent leather shoes. 'Really, Richard,' I asked, 'isn't that a bit much to polish the soles of your shoes?'"

"Wrong," he said in his almost Richard growl. "Several hundred people will see the soles of my shoes when I kneel down to pray during the wedding vows."

This story alone would give me insight into the whole character of the man I would live with for 53 years.

The flowers finally arrived, but there was one more holdup. Ahead of me was my future mother-in-law, who was to go down the aisle to be seated. She was in a stunning brown lace cocktail dress accented by a stylish pillbox hat with a brown demi-veil. Suddenly, everyone started slapping her in the face. She had taken one last drag on her cigarette and caught the veil on fire. Someone produced fingernail scissors and trimmed away the veil before she was escorted to her seat.

I turned to my brother, his broken ribs bound but still looking as handsome as any movie star, and told him to take out his chewing gum. He took me on his left arm and from that moment the wedding and the reception that followed went off with out a hitch.

As Richard and I left the church, Silas, the church handyman of many years, rang the wedding toll for us.

Though there had been one other engagement between the two oldest families in Tunica County – that of the Widow Emily Carruthers Withers to John Abbay (killed in the Civil War) – finally the Abbays, Irwins, and Leathermans were united with the Carruthers, Withers and Seabrooks,

While Richard was checking out of The Peabody the next morning, I was packing for a two-week trip to Nassau, Bahamas. Mind you, I had to express my desire for this trip instead of going with my husband's family to New Orleans for the Sugar Bowl. As I counted my bags, I remembered what an aunt of Richard's had told me: "Whatever you do in your marriage, get a bad back first. If you don't, you will always be carrying the luggage." Thank goodness we have luggage on rollers now.

From the lobby, I called Richard's parents to say good-bye. My mother-in-law had just talked to her cousin and wanted me to know what the cousin had to say about our wedding.

"Never have I seen a wedding so beautiful and one that went off without a single hitch," she said. "For a 21-year-old to accomplish this feat by herself is remarkable. At last our family has someone who is able and outstanding."

That was certainly news to me!

[1] *Game Bag,* Nash Buckingham, G.P. Putnam's Sons, New York, 1943, 1944, 1945.

[2] *The Golden Age of Waterfowling,* Wayne Capooth, M.D., Wayne Capooth, M.D., Germantown, Tennessee, 2001.

[3] *Ibid.*

[4] *Game Bag,* Nash Buckingham, G.P. Putnam's Sons, New York, 1943, 1944, 1945.

[?] *The World Book Encyclopedia,* 50th Anniversary Edition

[5] *The Commercial Appeal,* October 2, 1912

Chapter 10

Living and Learning The Commerce Life

Living and Learning The Commerce Life

When I was 10, my older brother Jack promised me a lovely playhouse to put in Grandmother's back yard in Tunica. Envisioning a storybook white, clapboard affair with shutters, you can imagine my disappointment when two weeks later, he blindfolded me and led me outside to unveil my playhouse – an ugly, discarded tenant house off OK Plantation.

At 21 and now engaged to the eldest son of a prominent farming family in the same Tunica County, I felt much the same, as my future father-in-law, Mr. Leatherman, Sr., drove me to see the house he had chosen for our first home. We stopped first at the Leatherman' imposing English house, so I could drop off my overnight bags. We then passed the charming home of my fiancée's aunt and uncle, right down the road. At one of our many wedding parties, Mr. Leatherman, Sr. (who was affectionately called "Mr. Big Richard" by the plantation staff), had told me that there was no need for us to build a nice house, since we would be inheriting the big English house one day. Of course, he was only 46 when he told me this, and I was 21. I should have realized it would be more likely that my *son* – not Richard – would live in the house. When he said not to build a nice house, I thought he meant not to build a grand plantation-type house that would be in competition with his. About two miles from his oak-lined driveway, we came upon the barn which housed 80 less-than-fragrant mules. Right across stood two tenant houses nailed together.

Mr. Leatherman introduced me to my new home.

The former tenant, I learned later, was a gin manager who had just been fired for striking a belligerent employee in the head with a crowbar. At best, when I looked at this three-room tenant shack, I thought he meant we would live there temporarily while we built a better house. Almost 20 years, six additions, and one tragic electrical fire later, I was still remodeling this "temporary" lean-to.

While the rest of America was being introduced to color TV that following year, I was moving into a house that had no telephone. When I finally did get my precious phone two years later, it was a wooden crank wall phone on a four-party line. First, I would pick up to see if somebody was using the line, and if the phone was free, I would turn one crank and Miss Happy, the telephone operator, would connect me with my party. Maybe I didn't have any TV, but some of the calls I heard on the party line were far more entertaining.

Mr. Post at Finch must have been right when he said I was born for the stage, because the day Mr. Leatherman introduced me to my first home on the plantation, he announced at dinner that I had been such a good sport when I saw the house in all its shocking plainness, that he intended to have the small house moved back from the road and to add on more rooms.

All at once, sheets of engraved stationery and pens appeared so that the three Leatherman ladies and three Leatherman men could take a stab at designing a decent and functional first house. We added a long hall, a spacious dining room, a breakfast room, and closets all over the place. Two brandies later, I had changed the kitchen into a bedroom. There was a plantation carpenter who was a very good cabinetmaker, and with my imagination and his patience, we would have a very serviceable country house. In the state of Virginia, they call houses of this nature "shed architecture," and I would like to agree that they are charming, comfortable, and full of happy memories. But for practical reasons, houses on plantations can be disasters: when needed they're not there, and when you need to sell them, there's no buyer, since they sit in the middle of a farm.

Young married couples often started their lives together in very simple rambling houses. When first married, Richard's parents themselves lived in a very old house on the river behind the levee, with rambling porches and arbors covered with wisteria. I have only seen this house in home movies from 1927, because it burned down. The only thing the farm labor managed to save from the flames was a cheap card table with the bridge hands still on it. My mother- and father-in-law then built the big English house on a tall manmade mound, because senior Mr. Leatherman's grandmother, an eccentric old lady who always dressed in black when not in bed with a migraine headache, refused to let her grandson build anything on the original Indian mound that stood on the property. The Mississippi Department of Archives named this Indian relic the DeSoto mound because it lies on the route taken by Hernando Desoto on his way to discovering the great river. The grandmother believed that the spirits of the Indian dead resided on the mound. Having spent many restless nights there, I believed her emphatically. One night while I was in my in-laws' house alone, I saw a doorknob on a closed door turn, and when Richard returned home from playing donkey baseball, he found me locked in the bathroom reading a book in the tub. I don't know whether the mound was truly haunted or if the presence of Keva, an old woman with a huge goiter on her neck, only made it seem so. Keva, who lived in rooms adjoining the wash house, never left the premises and kept a radio blaring 24 hours a day. I only know that no one living on the plantation except for the household help would come near the big house. I once went so far as to have my Episcopal priest read out of the Book of Common Prayer the petitions for the peace of the souls that go knock, knock in the night.

There surely were sad spirits that inhabited the plantation, for when Richard and I returned to Commerce from our honeymoon, we learned that a child of Richard's aunt and uncle had been badly burned drying her gown in front of a free-standing heater we called a chill chaser. The little girl lived only a couple of weeks after the accident.

While our house was under construction, Richard and I became sort of permanent houseguests of my in-laws, who were away much of the time anyway. This dark and foreboding house was a dismal place on rainy winter days.

Bleak or not, the pitter patter of servants' feet made this otherwise dysfunctional house one of the most comfortable homes I have ever visited. The way of life for this plantation family included freshly washed and folded laundry brought on covered trays from the laundry room, separate from the house. Beds were turned down every night before you retired, and a tumbler of water always sat on the bedside table. Each bedroom had a buzzer in order to call for a breakfast tray if you didn't care to go to the dining room table that morning.

On the screened porch at the back door was the ice box, the only refrigeration in the house. I remember Mr. Sharp, the ice man from town, delivering huge blocks of ice to Commerce. The house also depended on a temperamental Kohler plant to generate its electricity. Inevitably, the electricity went out just as we were sitting down at the dinner table with guests.

One rainy day at the Leatherman family home, I was writing thank you notes. Being bored and having spelled grateful "greatful" on a hundred notes, I gave up the task and went downstairs to the basement playroom. Hanging on the wall were land deeds. One preceded the Treaty of Pontotoc, and another was signed by an Indian woman, She-mul-la-yo, who could own her own land under Chickasaw law. I realized I had married into the first family of Tunica County, and when I heard Richard's heavy footsteps come down the stairs, I knew I was in for a lesson about how the Leathermans acquired their title.

Richard's story was that the family farm was bought in separate tracts, like most farms, and the first land was purchased in 1828, by Richard Rout Abbay and Anthony Abbay, twin brothers from Nashville, Tennessee. These brothers married sisters, Mary and Susan Compton, Richard to Mary and Anthony to Susan.

The Abbay brothers left Nashville and went to Paducah, Kentucky, then down the Ohio River to the junction of Cape Girardeau, Missouri. They also traveled down the Mississippi River to Louisiana. They bought land in Creve Coeur, Missouri; Commerce Landing, Mississippi; and Jenrette, Louisiana. The first land bought by the Abbays in Mississippi was very close to the spot where some people believe DeSoto discovered the Father of Waters.

As the family records read, one brother, Richard Abbay, settled at Commerce Landing, where he made his lifelong home, and Anthony Abbay settled in Nashville. It was in Commerce that Richard Abbay's only daughter, Mary Susan (named after her mother and aunt) was born. Of interest today is the fact that his first land was bought from an Indian, some of which is now the location of Sam's Town Casino in Tunica.

When Richard Abbay, the twin who had chosen to live and farm at Commerce, died, his twin, Anthony, came from Nashville to settle his brother's affairs. Most of the slaves had never seen Anthony and did not know their master had an identical twin brother. When the slaves saw Anthony, the spitting image of Richard, they screamed and swooned, and word was passed among the hundreds of slaves like wildfire that "Marse" Richard had returned from the dead.

Richard Abbay's stern-faced portrait hung over the mantle in my in-laws' house. Pa, as Richard Abbay was known in the family, did not believe in the Confederacy, and when the Civil War was just starting, he sold off most of his cotton for gold instead of Confederate money and buried it in a large teapot. Not only was he able to keep the family land by doing this, he was able to acquire more after the war was over. His son, Richard Felix, who was also an excellent businessman, bought even more land.

Pa had several children. As his children married, he gave some inheritances and banished others from the family. When daughter Mary Susan ran off and married a Dr. George Washington Leatherman in Hernando, she too was banished.

As a young woman, Mary Susan did not have an easy time during the Civil War. More than once she had to flee from battles, one time to the swampy Coldwater River bottoms in eastern Tunica County, where she lived in a tent for almost a year. Another time the Yankee gunboats fired cannon balls at Commerce Landing. Mary Susan then moved to the relative safety of Port Gibson, Mississippi, to stay with cousins, and it was there that she met her future husband.

Dr. George W. Leatherman, a graduate of Tulane, served in the Civil War and afterwards became the plantation doctor for the Polk Place next to the Abbay farm. He caught pneumonia and died while making a house call in extremely bad winter weather, leaving Mary Susan with two children, a son named Samuel Richard, named after two bachelor uncles, Samuel Leatherman and Richard Felix Abbay; and a daughter who died as a teenager.

Mary Susan, widowed and disowned, had absolutely no money. It was only after her bachelor brother, Richard Felix, threatened to give up his own inheritance and leave the plantation if the father did not let his sister come home, that Pa finally relented and let Mary Susan return to Commerce Plantation with the two children.

Richard Abbay had become embittered after the death of both his wife and a granddaughter who both died in childbirth. He had given this granddaughter some land, which her husband, a Mr. Powell, had inherited at her death. But Pa hated this Mr. Powell and offered to buy the land back. When Powell named a very high price, Pa paid it, but Powell had earned his grandfather-in-law's enmity: In his will, Pa left Mr. Powell one dollar and "my undying hatred."

Years before I married a Leatherman, I had heard that Richard Abbay had a black mistress named Ellen who lived in Hernando, Mississippi. At Richard Abbay's death, he was reported to have left her a large farm near Banks, Mississippi. The men in the Leatherman family referred to this arrangement with candor, but I quickly learned as a young bride that one never spoke of the bond in front of the females. Once at a seated dinner at the Tennessee Club in Memphis, a young doctor who had married into the family brought up the fact. As usual we had climbed into the family tree, as Tennessee Williams wrote. The young man was asked by my favorite uncle to step out in the entrance hall. When they returned, we all began a second favorite topic of conversation, the cotton crop of that season.

When Pa Abbay died, he left most of his estate to his son Richard Felix, who in turn left the estate to his sister, Mary Susan Abbay Leatherman. I have enjoyed hearing my husband talk about his great-grandmother, who lived to be 96. Though she seldom ever spoke, she knew my husband's interest in history and would share stories with him.

Richard learned from his great-grandmother, Mary Susan Abbay Leatherman, that her only son, Samuel Richard Leatherman I, married Ethel Irwin, whose father, Robert Clell Irwin, was also a huge landowner in Tunica County. The two men formed a cotton brokerage company in Memphis called the Irwin-Leatherman Cotton Company, which acquired more land through additional purchases and foreclosures. When Samuel Richard Leatherman I died in 1922, Samuel Richard I's mother, Mary Susan Leatherman, and her nurse, Miss Betsy, lived for 13 years with Mary Susan's daughter-in-law (Richard's grandmother), Ethel Irwin Leatherman-Andrews. After Mary Susan's death in 1935, Ethel became the largest landowner in Tunica County.

Samuel Richard I and Ethel's son, my father-in-law, Samuel Richard Leatherman II, married Irene McNeal Morrow, and they had four children, Samuel Richard (my husband), Kate Bond Leatherman, Robertson Morrow Leatherman and Irene Morrow Leatherman. My future husband was raised on the plantation and went to a one-room school that his father built. He attended with the manager's children and some Chinese children whose father was a grocer in Robinsonville. Mr. Leatherman kindly included the Chinese children, who, like blacks, could not attend public schools at that time. In 1937, Richard went on to a fine Eastern boarding school, St. Paul's in Concord, New Hampshire, where a Latin teacher told him that he didn't know how he was going to teach "Mr. Leatherman" Latin, when he couldn't even speak English. However, Richard proved himself at St. Paul's both academically and athletically.

When I was a young bride, statesman and future presidential candidate Adlai Stevenson came to visit the plantation in late fall during hog killing time and declared its way of life a perfect example of the feudal system, whose history went back hundreds of years. In Mississippi, this system was known as sharecropping. Like England, the land was owned by the landlord and farmed by tenants.

The family farm, now known as Abbay and Leatherman, was divided into several sections, each with its own headquarters and barn. Fortunately, Richard was able to avoid family politics, because he farmed an adjoining plantation called "the Polk Place" rented by his father.

It is coincidental that both the founders of the Polk Place and my husband Richard are related to U.S. President James K. Polk. Bought by Andrew Jackson Polk following the Treaty of Pontotoc, this beautiful 1,000-acre farm in Tunica County remained in the Polk family for generations, being passed down to land agent and Polk cousin Robin Jones, until it was sold to John Flynn in 1929, whose family still owns it. Because of the fickle river's change in course, a large portion of the farm now lies in Arkansas.

Richard started farming the Polk Place for his father in 1948, and was taught to farm by an excellent black manager, Phax Long, affectionately known as "Butch." Although our home was not on the Polk Place, that is where we kept our bird dogs and horses and where we did most of our quail hunting, until quail all but disappeared, due to changes in farming practices, from the Delta. Caretaker for the dogs and horses on the place was Tom Deal, whose family had farmed on the Polk Place for three generations.

Once when we had planned to quail hunt behind the levee, my husband said we would hunt on the polo field.

"Polo field?" I asked.

"Why yes," he answered, "one of my aunts married an avid polo player who built himself a field at Commerce. Fact is, Daddy had to come home from college in Virginia to run the place, because farming seemed to get in the way of the polo player's sports."

When the polo games were finished, the aunt's husband and his friends would play World War I. They would climb in their small planes and fly over the Mississippi River to a plantation in Arkansas. There they had hired some innocent soul in a Model T to drive in circles in the fields, and they literally dropped bags of flour on him from the sky—like they were bombing the Germans. Other men of the world may have had more money than Southern men, but none could have had more imagination.

For the first five years of our marriage, all the Leathermans and their guests enjoyed extraordinary duck and goose hunting behind the levee. There was one field called "the bend" planted with 650 acres of corn to feed the hundreds of mules on the farm. The skies would look as though it had broken out in measles as the thousands of noisy waterfowl came in off the river to feed on the corn. Although you had less of a chance of getting a shot than if you were in a boat hunting with decoys, you would probably see in 20 minutes more ducks and geese than several men would see in a lifetime. To me, the geese in "V" formation were the most impressive, but sadly, I have watched one lone goose that had lost its mate circle the field as long as three days after a hunt. Only those who have experienced it can understand the awesome sight of thousands of ducks and geese against the sky with a full moon rising.

Once Richard had me hide behind a tree as he crawled around on his hands and knees, shot once to flush the ducks, and I, with my $90 Sears Roebuck automatic, had a potshot that resulted in enough ducks to feed Tunica and Desoto counties.

Although the Leathermans were aristocratic in most respects and maintained homes on the large plantations, in Memphis and in mountain resorts, you never knew which way the wind would blow with them. One minute they would argue over which calling cards you would leave – the lady's, the man's, or a Mr. and Mrs. Card — and you would not dare say "drapes"— they were "draperies".

In the next breath, having put on all these airs, they would laugh good naturedly and make fun of each other. They liked to joke that you could always tell who the richest people in the room were if a certain sister would be talking to them.

Even the daughters of Ethel Irwin Leatherman-Andrews told amusing stories about their mother. One daughter told me that after her mother had married her eldest daughter's beau, she thought she was fixed for life, but was so despondent after her second husband died of cancer at a young age that she died two years later of unknown causes.

Yet another time, Mrs. Leatherman-Andrew's other daughter said her mother told her it was a pity that the world could not see Mr. Leatherman's most outstanding characteristic – a belly button the size of a silver dollar. My husband's grandfather was indeed a very large man. Some of the men in the family were so big that they covered the whole seat of a horse-drawn buggy.

The Leathermans were also fierce competitors. I have watched a 35-year-old man send the croquet ball of a four-year-old sailing into a big cotton field and feel no shame. In the Leatherman family, they played as hard against their own children as a blood enemy in the finals of a state competition. This is how the children were taught to be competitive.

Although no pressure was put on the children to be scholars, they were expected to make good grades and did. But when the family nurse found an old report card of Richard's father filled with red "D's," we all laughed and had the report card framed and hung on the nursery wall.

In high school, Mr. Big Richard was not doing well, so his mother sent him home to live with a manager and learn to farm. This seemed to get his attention. After a few months he became more interested in his education and went on to college.

All the Leathermans were taught to enjoy life. To my husband's family money was simply a way of exchange. As long as they had enough to afford them their lifestyle, they didn't seem to care one thing about adding more. It would take up precious time that could be spent outdoors, on hunting fields, on the golf course, or reading.

The Leathermans were truthful to a point of being overly blunt. Once at a family dinner, I asked how a friend's mother died. The answer was, "She had leprosy." This blunt answer surprised me, and I said, "Really, I think you could have answered my question without saying *leprosy?*"

"Why not?" was the answer. "Why, it can be cured early now, and they have even closed the leper colony in Louisiana."

No one in the Leatherman family ever admitted to having a hangover. They would say, "I have a sore throat". There was advantage to this, because they didn't even have to pretend to sneeze or cough. Or, they might say, "I ate too much rich food last night." If a close friend drank too much, it was never suggested that they had a drinking problem – they simply had too much strife in their life. If a child did not do well in school, it was because he was really so smart he was just bored and inattentive.

My father-in-law, one of the most attractive men I've ever met, gave everyone a nickname and was adored by all the women in the family. Soon after my marriage, he asked me why I did not tell him amusing stories like I told others. Frankly, I was put off by the other women in the family vying for his attention. And besides, I was still smarting from my tenant house and no family engagement ring. They might say hell hath no fury like a scorned woman, but a scorned man doesn't like it either.

By now I was beginning to see that Richard might not have made the best choice for a career. My great friend, a historian who knows the Delta, says that more than once he has heard a 70-year-old father order his 50-year-old son to go buy him a pack of cigarettes. Not ask, but tell. The father was perfectly able to do the errand himself, but it was a matter of control. Control is the middle name of many Delta men.

Even young Delta men with good educations stood in line to play the seal-on-the-rock game, working at banks in nearby big cities before they had earned the right to farm. Eventually, with a lot of luck and depending on their siblings, they inherited the position of Big Daddy or Boss Man on the farm. It was a classic case of the old seal guarding his rock and keeping the young seal off as long as possible.

Until the quest to avoid estate taxes dictated otherwise, land was seldom passed on to an heir before death. Delta children would have no idea about the status of land and other assets until the last will and testament of the deceased was read, only to discover that the land was heavily mortgaged.

In days gone by, chattel mortgages (mortgages on personal property like mules and tractors) were handwritten in giant leather-bound books, until Tunica County began putting the records on computer. Because my brother and uncle saved many of these books, which were headed for the trash, I have read heartrending stories about how families lost farms. In French, mort means "dead," and gage means "hand." In the early days when mules were so important to farming, there was a Southern saying that you were not worth a damn until you had mortgaged your mule and burned your land (meaning clearing off the old weeds and undergrowth by burning to prepare for planting).

Don't ever ask a farmer about his crop in any given year. He will either embellish the truth or bring out his sad story about the weather, crop failures, and the cost of farming. It is like asking a hypochondriac the state of his health. On the other hand, you never ask planters how much land they farm. It would be like asking how much a person has in his portfolio.

During the Depression, there were white people in the South and there were black people in the South, but there was really only one class, *poor*. No younger person, although they may have suffered things just as hard, will understand the impact made on a person who made it through the 1929 crash. The old seals, through no fault of their own, wore Depression scars.

"When I inherited the farm, it was mortgaged. And when you inherit the farm, it will be mortgaged!" said one prestigious father to his son. These people handed down their fears and beliefs to sons and daughters.

I remember my father-in-law telling the story that my husband had broken his arm as a small child in the height of the Depression. When the Memphis doctor sent a big bill to Richard's father, Mr. Leatherman paid but added a note, "My son broke his arm, but you broke my back." The white landowner during the Depression had nothing but land, and in nine out of ten cases that land was mortgaged.

Aunt Camilla used to tell me that if a good car came as far out as our farm she would pray, holding her much-read Bible, asking God to please not let it be someone coming to foreclose on a mortgage. A lot of Delta land was not taken because banks in Memphis and the Delta did not know what to do with property – no one was buying land.

This attitude of fear and the hard truth of poverty held back the South in progress and attitudes for years after the crash. The fact is, the people as a whole almost never were healed. World War II finally helped the South economically and socially.

In hindsight, I wish Mr. Leatherman had told Richard as a young man that there is small profit for a well-educated man in farming if he does not own his own land. Not that Richard would have heeded his advice. In all fairness, Mr. Big Richard might have known that Richard was going to farm at all costs.

In 1950, cotton was the cash crop on the Abbay and Leatherman farms, and most work was still being done by mules and manual labor. But during World War II, labor left the farms and went to factories for the war effort. A few tractors began to appear to make up for the shortage of manpower. This was the beginning of the change from mule to tractor farming.

Cotton harvesting continued to be done by hand until the mid-'50s, but with labor becoming scarcer, the two largest farming manufacturers began to develop cotton pickers that were practical and efficient. While it would take ten hand pickers to harvest one bale of cotton per day, the first mechanical cotton picker could pick one row at a time and approximately ten bales a day, using just one laborer.

The mechanical cotton picker was more profitable, but not by much. I remember Richard saying that the first mechanical cotton picker that we had cost $5,000, an enormous sum in those post-war days.

Although these new machines were expensive, they offered a critical benefit: farmers were able to harvest the crop while the weather was still good. When a cotton boll opens, it has the best quality that it will ever have. The longer it stays in the field, the more that quality is reduced.

Manual labor was still needed for chopping the cotton to keep it free from weeds and grass. Then chemical companies began developing products to inhibit and sometimes completely stop the growth of weeds and grasses. The new minimum wage for farm labor was instituted in the 1950s, and a combination of the price of the labor going up and the scarcity of it made chemical weed control more affordable. Men were just not able to chop enough cotton to pay for the minimum wage. Some chopping of cotton by hand did, however, last until the 1990s.

By 1955, the mules that had been such a part of the life of the farm were all but gone. When I came to Commerce as a bride in early 1950, before the days of air-conditioning, my open bedroom windows brought the early-morning sounds of the men taking the mules out for the day, calling out "Gee" and Haw" to turn the mules right or left. And the pealing of the bells on the plantation tolled the time of day. The plantation bells rang to tell us when to get up. They rang at noon to tell the labor to stop for a rest and a bite to eat from their lunch pails, and they rang at quittin' time. A scant five years later, mules were only being used to plow water furrows through the fields for drainage. And the noisy tractors rendered the bells obsolete.

After one year of fixing up my house with the farm carpenter, I moved into what was called "Who'd-a-thunk-it." I did not think of this clever name, it went back to the days when my house site was the headquarters of Ransom Byrnes, a Scotsman who lived at Commerce in the early 1800s. When Mr. Big Richard moved the house back from the road, the cotton patch behind it became my front yard. During the landscaping, I found a cistern, confirming that this indeed had been Ransom Byrnes' headquarters.

At first there were no trees around my home. Through the years I went to the woods and dug up oaks and dogwoods to add to the many magnolia trees, true Mississippi natives I had bought off the back of a truck for $10 a piece.

Grandmother would have been pleased with the furniture in my house, because all of it had been inherited and none of it bought. Being an only daughter and only granddaughter does have its advantages.

As sharecropper houses on the farm were torn down, all of the old brick was saved. Mr. Leatherman hired two old women to clean old brick all winter long. All the Leatherman households used these bricks to enhance their homes with patios, chimneys, and porches.

Our home boasted a fireplace in every room but three. Since all the good rooms of my house faced towards the back, we built an enormous brick terrace out from my living room. This patio, though it beautified the house, could only be enjoyed from the screened porch because of the pesky Delta bugs.

In another renovation when I vaulted the ceilings in the living room and dining room, I discovered hand hewn cedar shingles hidden under the low ceilings.

Over by the garden in the side yard, we always kept chickens, the best weathermen ever. I could tell by the chickens when a rain was coming or a big wind and knew it was time to cut short my walk or my horseback ride and head home. It is no myth that old time quail hunters would check to see what the chickens were doing before deciding whether to hunt that day. If the chickens were out scratching around, the quail would be, too.

Sharecropping was so ingrained in Commerce life that as a young bride, I raised chickens on the half with my cook, Susie. Susie had first worked for my mother-in-law and had been with the family so long that she called my husband "Child." Susie selected a hundred chicks, and I paid for them and the feed. The plan was that Susie and I would divide the chickens and the eggs. Morning after morning, Susie would come in the kitchen and say, "Ole Miss, one of your biddies died last night."

Now, a biddy is a baby chicken, and our biddies seemed to me as healthy as most. After I had lost about ten biddies, it hit me that my biddies died and Susie's didn't. You can't really tell which chick belongs to whom, and when I asked Susie about this, she looked me squarely in the eyes and said, "Now, Ole Miss, you can't be serious. You know good and well I knows your biddies from my biddies."

After learning chicken economics from Susie, I marveled that the grocery stores could sell them so cheap.

Being in the cattle business, the Leatherman family rented huge frozen food lockers in the town of Tunica. On hot summer days, I would put on a winter coat and wearing gloves, go into the walk-in lockers and pick up large, well-labeled packages of meat. The beef hearts would be given to Richard's bird dogs. The heart being a muscle, the poor creatures would chew endlessly and play with them like rubber balls.

I had washing machines and dryers that ran all day, and because the sharecroppers had no indoor plumbing, the servants were welcome to do their laundry in my machines or take a shower in the servants' bathroom adjoining the kitchen. In my big square kitchen were a hotel stove and a marble-top beaten biscuit roller. Many days, we would have 17 loaves of homemade bread baking in the tremendous ovens.

When I had a backache on January 4, 1951, I simply thought it was because I had been busy most of the day having a wonderful rooster weathervane put on the roof of the house. This wasn't an easy job, since the former tenant house roof was so steep it could split a raindrop.

My baby was not due for three more weeks, but with no phone, I awakened my husband for the third time, and we both decided we should go to his aunt and uncle's house about two miles up the road and use their phone to call my doctor. The doctor, whom I had seen that day, said to drive right into Memphis. In case of trouble, Richard's aunt and uncle followed us in their car.

The doctor was busy delivering another baby, but finished just in time for me to be wheeled into the delivery room as my son was being born. I remember reaching for the gas only to have my arms strapped to the delivery table by a stern nurse. We were lucky he was born three weeks early, because the cord was wrapped around his neck and he might have choked had I carried him full term. Since Mother had lost her first two children at birth, and neither of my brothers had children, you can imagine how blessed we felt to have this perfect male child.

The birth of S.R. Leatherman IV impressed my father-in-law. He seemed to think I had *chosen* to have a quick delivery, three weeks early, and without the fuss of medication. He sent 20 potted azaleas to line the hospital hall and had a new car delivered to the parking lot as a baby gift for me. From the day I brought S.R.Leatherman IV home to his nursery and placed him in the big wooden cradle that had rocked generations of Leathermans and Abbays, I became Mr. Leatherman's pet, and the old seal could not be kind enough. Perhaps the fact that he had yet another seal to wait in line to guard the rock gave him confidence the land would stay in the family for another generation.

My mother-in-law gave me a great present of a fine baby nurse, though I couldn't stand it when the nurse locked the nursery door and took over my child. After many weeks she finally left, but without giving us any instructions.

By sheer luck, I was told about a fabulous nurse living on our plantation who had been raised by a white family in Louisiana. Esther Banks, my nursing woman, reared my three children, and they loved her. She died in the arms of my son Dick in 1970 in Tunica's small hospital, built with the help of community leaders like my father-in-law, so that the laborers did not have to travel all the way to Mound Bayou for care.

It was a treat for my father-in-law to drop by and take me, Dick, and the nurse to buy ice cream sandwiches. He continued this ritual as each successive child was added to the family. One day, while the children were in the shop with their grandfather, I read a statistical report from the local Tunica hospital that had been left on the front seat of his car. I was dismayed to see that, as late as 1959, the cause of most infant deaths in the county was malnutrition.

When Dick was christened at the Episcopal church in Tunica, I asked my brother Jack, who had been so important in my life, to be my newborn son's godfather. When Dick was still an infant in arms, Jack took my son boating on Tunica Cut-off, where he planned to teach Dick to fish just as soon as he was old enough. I can still picture Colonel holding the small baby in his arms on the back of Jack's quarter boat. Jack planned future hunts with Dick and dreamed of teaching him to shoot his Winchester Model 21 shotgun designed by Nash Buckingham.

Sadly, Jack did not live to act as surrogate father to my son. When Dick was only 13 months old, Jack died of kidney failure at age 35.

On a gray Valentine's Day, 1952, I sat in Tunica's Methodist church as the minister delivered Jack's eulogy and ended by reading Tennyson's "Crossing the Bar:"

Sunset and evening star,
And one clear call for me.
And may there be no moaning of the bar,
When I put out to sea.

My heart shrank. Raindrop-sized beads of sweat broke out in my squeezed palms and red welts surfaced on my young hands. I doubt Tennyson knew the power of his poem for one heartsick sister.

After the service, a cousin, trying to be light, said, "It always gets me when they read 'Crossing the Bar' at the funeral of a man who liked to drink."

"Funny," I replied, "That's not what I heard at all. I heard that Jack is just going on another great hunt, having crossed the Slough of Despond before entering heaven, Grandmother's OK Plantation."

God had given me great joy in my son, who though he hadn't known

Jack except through my stories, grew to be a man so like him. My breath caught in my throat each time Dick came in the back door whistling, just as Jack did at OK. Now Uncle Sterling, Mother, and Jack were all gone, and great sorrow shadowed me.

That spring, my in-laws agreed that Richard and I could take two months off in the summer. It was the dream of my husband, who had broken records in the 100-yard dash at St.Paul's, to attend the Olympic games. Coincidentally, war bonds bought for me by Uncle Sterling had come due, and the very day they matured I was at the bank cashing them in. I had the money in hand for our trip!

In early July 1952, Richard and I and another couple took off for Europe for two glorious months. Not all of our trip was lighthearted, for we saw a devastated London, where whole parts of the city were in ruins. In France, the people hated Americans, but martinis that only cost 25-cents soothed our feelings. We found that most of Italy was still so poor that a pack of cigarettes could be traded for anything, even a bus ticket. When we arrived in Helsinki for the Games, the press corps had taken our hotel rooms, and we were forced to live ten days with a family who only had hot water one day a week. I convinced my hostess to send up pans of boiling water from the stove that I would mix in with water from the tap and have my bath.

We traveled over and returned on a French boat full of happy youths. We had an unforgettable time.

After World War II, the Wild West, in the form of cattle rustling, came to the old plantation. My husband was the head of a cattle operation where the cows grazed on the levee.

Being a good bookkeeper, Richard was quick to notice that there was rustling going on, but the big surprise came when we learned that a man and woman who both worked for Abbay and Leatherman were the culprits. When confronted in court, the lady accomplice, wearing turquoise jewelry that matched her man's, pointed a red-polished fingernail at her lover and calmly said, "He did it, and I went right along with him."

Two years and nine months after Dick was born, our beautiful daughter Mary came. With a Withers face and temperament, I just say she is pure Withers.

A year and nine months later, I had Irene, who was conceived at the hunting club called Rolling Rock in Ligonier, Pennsylvania. My in-laws, who were members, asked my husband to go as their guest but did not invite me. At the last minute, Mr. Leatherman said that since I enjoyed hunting and his family hunted my land at Beaver Dam constantly, they should bring me along. Before we hunted quail, pheasant, and ducks, the guides gave us long lectures about hunting safety and ended by proudly announcing that there had never been an accident at Rolling Rock. A few weeks later, I wrote with humor to the president of the club—yes, history had been made, there had been an accident at Rolling Rock. A Texas friend, until his dying day, called Irene Miss Rolling Rock.

Once I was telling a friend about my surprise in having three children in five years, and Irene overheard me say this. She walked across the room with her little 3-year-old gait, pulled on my skirt, looked up at me and said, "Yeah, but ain't you glad I came"? That was her attitude through life – ain't you glad I came? And indeed I was. She turned out to be a real little star.

My mother-in-law in her own way made up for all her slights when she became an active member in the Memphis Junior League in order to propose me for membership. Mom, as I called Richard's mother, absolutely hated ladies' clubs and female politics and hadn't kept up with the League since she had married and moved to Mississippi. In those days, it was nearly impossible for a young woman to become a member if her mother or mother-in-law had not been one. Poor Mom not only rejoined just to propose me but even helped decorate the ballroom where the new members were inducted.

The Junior League was a real adventure for me. One of my first activities was as a volunteer puppeteer, making our puppets out of wet newspaper and then painting them. We would perform plays like *Hansel and Gretel* for public school children.

But best of all was the monthly magazine called the *Volunteer Voice*. I wrote an article every month called "Sugsie's Corner," about any topic I pleased. To this day people remember "Sugsie's Corner" and encourage me to keep writing. One admirer even went to the League house in hopes of having all my articles made into a book, but most of them have been lost.

Another project I headed was coordinating efforts with the Memphis

Symphony so the Memphis Ballet could dance to live music. The highlight was when through my affiliation with the Southeastern Regional Ballet Festival Association, I arranged for George Balanchine, one of the world's greatest choreographers, to come to Memphis and teach a ballet workshop.

On February 1, 1955, pregnant for the third time, I left Commerce for a Junior League meeting and luncheon in Memphis. I turned on the radio of my Chevy station wagon to the only classical radio station. I looked out over the bleak fields with wooden cotton houses scattered in them. These houses, small and without windows, were still used in 1955 to store hand-picked cotton until it was taken to the gin in the back of cotton wagons.

On my way home to Commerce, I switched the radio from the classical station to another that was playing my new crush, Elvis Presley. I will never forget that day. Elvis' royal voice was singing "Heart Break Hotel" in the background as I looked out over the cotton fields. Lo and behold, where there had been cotton houses that morning, now there were none. I thought I was in a dream as I passed only a few cars. The closer I drove south to Robinsonville, the small town off Highway 61, I saw and heard one, two, three ambulances and police cars coming from the south, heading towards Memphis. When I reached the railroad track that goes through Robinsonville, there stood dozens of state militia. The men flagged me down and told me I could go no further.

"There has been a deadly tornado at Commerce Landing," they told me.

"I must go through, officer," I said in shock, "I'm Mrs. Richard Leatherman, Jr., and I have a husband and two small children at Commerce, or I did this morning."

As for Richard, my first worry was that was he might not be at Commerce at all but at Como or Crenshaw quail hunting. That would mean Dick and Mary would be with Nurse and Susie.

I had to creep toward home behind ambulances, police cars, workers and machinery. Whole houses lay on the gravel road, and people huddled in groups and cried. Dead bodies were being carried out on stretchers; they were not even covered by a blanket. In the field was a car as crushed as if it had been through a trash compactor.

The commissary built in 1840 was still standing, but on either side, houses were demolished. Then I saw the most wonderful sight in the entire world. Nurse and Susie were holding my two babies in their arms, watching the chaos from my front yard. I honked and honked for an ambulance to let me pull into my drive. I parked the car, jumped out, and ran to Susie, whom I know had read the Bible till the storm was over – even as it destroyed the house next to ours.

I asked Susie and Esther if they had seen Richard. They said he was fine and had been by to see about them before leaving to help with the dead and injured. Susie said she and Nurse held the children in their arms and watched the storm out the breakfast room window. They said the storm was heading straight toward our house when it suddenly turned east and crossed the road, killing several people.

Richard and his father had been sitting in a car in front of the commissary when the tornado hit. The back of my mother-in-law's home was protected by the Indian mound; only the side screened porch was blown away. The trees told the story; you could see pieces of metal coming out of the trees in different directions. We lost the cotton gin. It was blown to Arkansas.

That night the tornado was on the local evening news and the world news. Had the farm been a city, thousands would have been killed.

Things were never the same after the 1955 tornado. For one, it cost not only precious lives but the gin, barns, machine shops, homes, and possessions. The loss cost the farm millions of dollars. The great wind swooped down and blew away a world that is long gone and remembered by only a few.

The Red Cross was great throughout the crisis. There were 55 houses destroyed, 20 people killed, and 141 injured. The schoolhouse collapsed, killing 17 children, making this the third deadliest tornado disaster in a school in U.S. history. It took months for Commerce to repair. The schoolhouse was rebuilt and named after the teacher who lost her life trying to lead the children into the ditches along the road. Mr. Leatherman gave money to replace the several black churches that were destroyed. We all helped to build a storybook chapel, designed after the one at the University of the South.

Not even a tornado, however, could stop the arrival of my baby Irene a few months later.

Chapter 11

Wink and The Children

Wink and The Children

In many Delta farming families, working for the old seal wasn't too profitable for the young ones. Our house needed renovations, and the salary Mr. Big Richard paid my husband wasn't enough to do the job. Many times I asked Mr. Leatherman to raise Richard's salary instead of doling out money to us like we were children standing on his doorstep on Halloween night.

The irony of it was that Richard was the only hands-on farmer in the family. Being land owners, the others road farmed, but Richard was out there every day like the other managers making decisions and really making a crop.

So in 1955, with our third child on the way, I decided to sell my house in Memphis in order to finance much needed living space for our growing family. My main concern was that if I sold, where would Aunt Camilla and Tennie go? They had stayed at my Memphis home, and it was there always ready for me. In hindsight, we just should have moved back to my home in Memphis and Richard could commute. After all, it would have been much easier for one man to make the daily commute than two adults and three children.

Once again, I missed my mother and her advice. As always, Aunt Camilla was lovely about moving. She lived at the Parkview Apartments in Memphis until she died in 1958. My precious Tennie went to Arkansas to live with relatives, where she died about two years later.

The day I closed the beautiful wrought-iron door on my childhood home for the last time was a milestone. Not only was I selling my past and my memories and splitting up Aunt Camilla, Tennie, and me – it was first time I took a drink alone.

Now school age, Dick went to a good kindergarten in Tunica. But when it came time to enter the first grade, we thought he would do better in Memphis, even though it would be a 100-mile roundtrip each day.

When the children started private school in Memphis, their father got up with them every morning and saw that they had their breakfast and all of their things for school. I had best not let socks get low or the right sweaters not bought, because he wanted them to have what they needed for school.

One morning, Mr. Big Richard came by for coffee, another Delta ritual.

"Daughter Jo (by now, this was my nickname)," he said, "I've found a solution for driving the children to school in Memphis. Israel Clark, who we call Wink, might be the perfect driver." Funny, I never asked Wink how he was given his nickname.

Israel "Wink" Clark was a black sharecropper on the farm who became my best friend. All the Clarks were good people, who, like so many other sharecroppers had left Alabama for the rich Mississippi Delta before the Depression. My father-in-law said Wink was better with animals than anyone he had ever known.

Wink had a special skill with mules, but he was not much good with tractors or anything else mechanical. Mr. Big Richard used to say that Wink's tractor was in the shop more than any other piece of equipment on the plantation.

Though he tried hard, Wink failed his driving test three times because he could neither read nor write. Finally, on the fourth try, Wink legally passed his written test and earned his license.

Unused to city driving, it took three weeks of me showing Wink the roads to Memphis, but then he "caught on good," as they say on the farm, and could drive us anywhere. Wink never did learn how to make a left hand turn under a red light, but because he was patient and drove slowly, he never had a wreck. To my knowledge, he never even had a traffic tick-et. Now, that might have been because Wink was so smooth that he probably could have talked the officer into a police escort instead.

I guess Wink was just born knowing how to talk to people. He was no conman smooth-talker; he spoke from a good heart and didn't have to think before he talked, because he was sincere. He was good from the top of his head to the end of his crooked old toes.

We bought a big Volkswagen bus, and Wink and the children pulled out of our drive at Commerce Landing Plantation at seven sharp every week-day morning headed for Memphis. In those slow two hours in the car each day, the children became good readers.

Wink was badly crippled by a childhood accident. As a result, his right leg was shorter than his left. I never asked Wink questions about what had happened to him. I guess I did not want to hear that a sweet young black boy had such a bad break, and no one could afford to have it set. There were lots of things that I could not bear to ask about on the old planta-tion. If I had known the truth about Wink's childhood I might have taken the one and only wealth he had–pride.

From day one, I loved Wink. He tilted like a sailboat to one side because of his bad leg. He wore his dark hair short around a broad face. His bespectacled eyes were set far apart, and he used them to their great-est advantage, looking right at you when he spoke. He was about six feet tall, and his shoulders were massive, perhaps to compensate for his leg.

Never have I met a person as pleasant as Wink, but he seldom smiled. He did have a wonderful laugh though, and you could tell the man by what made him laugh. A mean joke was not in him, for I never saw him put anyone down. This must have been hard for Wink, for he was a true judge of character. His observations were usually right on.

Once we dropped off a child in East Memphis and as we drove up their long, winding driveway he simply said, "These peoples must be rich because they have a crooked drive instead of a straight one likes usn's."

As the children grew older, my in-laws and I bought a triplex in Memphis adjacent to the Memphis Country Club, where we were mem-bers. This gave Wink a home while the children were in school, and it also gave all the Leathermans a base in the city. Only a year later, the Leathermans bought another house next to the triplex, and this gave the children even more room, for by now they were beginning to entertain their Memphis friends.

Wink drove my children and their friends to dancing class and parties before they were old enough to drive themselves. He was most appreciated at the pony club riding classes, where he would take care of the horses before the children were tall enough to put on the saddles and bridles. Animals loved Wink so much that one of the horses would eat hot dogs with mustard out of his hand, and then, if he held the bottle, even drink some cola. One day as I watched my good man Wink limp towards the Volkswagen bus as my three children piled in with books, show-and-tell objects, and even saddles for after-school pony club, tears came to my eyes. I made up my mind right then I would someday write about Wink.

We always took some fox hound puppies from the pony club for the summer and returned them in the fall. Our dogs would always be twice the size of their littermates because of Wink's good care. Wink would later go on fox hunts with the children and sleep on a cot in the stalls or I would rent a room for him at a nearby motel. In the summer when the children were older, he took them to tennis matches at towns and cities nearby. Of course I would go, too. He was most appreciated at these events, because he pulled many a city slicker's car and trailer out of a ditch.

I don't think Wink ever learned to keep score in tennis but he sure knew a lot more than I thought. Once I heard him tell my two daughters, Mary and Irene, that they could never win at doubles if they didn't go to the net.

At home on the plantation, Wink could dress all types of game and had a shed for this purpose. If I had made a clean shot at duck and geese, he could dress fowl to look like it was from a swanky butcher shop. Wink loved squirrels, but I would not go near the kitchen when he prepared these for Brunswick stew. I told Wink that a squirrel was nothing but a rat with a fur coat or better still, a rat with good P.R. The worst was when Wink would find a big turtle. I could not stand to look at that big, coiled "snake" hidden under a shell and would flee from the kitchen. New Orleans restaurants can keep their turtle soup as far as I'm concerned. And Wink pressed me too far with his foul-smelling steak and kidney pie or chitlins. I couldn't decide whether he was a gourmet or that he would simply eat anything.

My friend Wink could keep *me* in line, too. One time when I was very upset with one of the children's teachers, Wink said, "Now Ole Miss, you remember who you are. You don't be going in there starting any trouble and make it hard on those children."

I appreciated Wink's help, and furthermore, I needed his sage advice. How often I heard him say that as men aged they started acting like fools. "Ole Miss, remember: once a man, but twice a boy."

How I wish I had written down all of his wonderful sayings.

One of the most endearing things that Wink ever said to me occurred when something was missing in the house. "Well, Ole Miss, I know you know I didn't have a thing to do with that. There wouldn't be a reason in the world for me to take anything. They ain't nothing you wouldn't give me if I asked for it." How fortunate that Wink knew by instinct what some blacks had to be taught – that in the Deep South in bygone days, every black needed a white friend. I'm not making any excuses for the way things were; this was just the truth of the matter, and I'm glad we were there for each other.

Only one time did I ever see Wink get a little testy. At a national field trial for champion bird dogs, a man passed Wink on the field trial grounds and began to really "mess" with him. In the South, "messing" with someone means playing with their mind and putting in jabs. This man was telling Wink how much better his dog was than Richard's, what a fast runner it was, and that it would surely win. Wink looked at him and said, "Well, suh, if that dog can run as fast as your mouth, he will surely come in first."

Wink was the number one man on our farm for taking care of others. It was Wink who took people to the hospital, looked in on them, and tended to the funerals. He was not a big church man but I think he did more good than all of the country preachers put together. In Mississippi it was not unusual for politicians to drop in and speak at black funerals in order to gain votes. When a politician who didn't even know Nurse showed up at her funeral, Wink gently led him out and said, "There ain't goin' to be no politicking at this funeral."

Sharecroppers came back from Chicago and Detroit to bury their dead in the plantation's cemetery, and the funerals turned into celebrations. Dozens showed up, and poor Wink would serve food for two or three days. People filled all the houses. When I commented on how well the out-of-towners looked, Wink told me with complete honesty, "Ole Miss, they ain't got anything but a rented car and a new suit. They're not doing so well up there. You see where they come to bury their dead and where they send their children to be raised by their grandparents, don't you? Don't let all that talk fool you."

Above all, Wink could put me back on track when I would become upset about my husband going to field trials every weekend for several months during the winter. At the beginning of each bird dog season, Wink would say to me, and goodness knows where he had heard it, "Ole Miss, you just calm down and listen to old Wink. You can't teach a pig to sing–it does nothing but wear you out, and it irritates the pig."

God knew what he was doing when he gave the black man the speech. They can hit a nail square, flat on the head, and with it comes humor and a keen insight and even a sense of the ridiculous.

Once I asked Wink to find a new man on the place to help in the yard. I then asked if he knew the man's name. He looked at me in the most endearing way and said, "Well, Ole Miss, some days I do, and some days I don't."

One time there was a lot of talk on the plantation about two women having an affair, and I asked Wink what was going on, since one of the women was married. Wink told me. "You know how it goes, Ole Miss. There's them that likes he'n and he'n, and there's them that likes she'n and she'n, and then there's thems that stay home and likes me'n and me'n."

To understand how Wink spoke, I wish you could have heard him on a British Broadcasting Company interview about Robert Johnson, the famous blues musician and Wink's childhood friend. People come to Tunica County from all over the world to see where Johnson had been raised and to look for the legendary crossroads farther south where Johnson said he sold his soul to the devil.

Robert Johnson was reared by his stepfather, Dusty Rhodes, on the very Polk Plantation that Richard farmed. Later Johnson moved to a house on Abbay and Leatherman next to the levee. I don't even try to understand Robert Johnson's connection to Wink, but as best I can make out, Wink's aunt was married to Robert Johnson's stepfather. We just say down in the Deep South, "They were more than relations." When you get mixed up in the family tree, it's just easier to say, "We're kin to."

To hear Wink tell it, Robert Johnson was no farmer, preferring to sit on the front porch and watch his stepfather plow with Black Alice, the best mule on the plantation. But Johnson could flat play the blues, using a homemade instrument called a didley-bow, or slide guitar. These didley-bows were usually made from a piece of two-by-four board, approximately three feet long, with a nail at each end. A piece of broom wire, taken from the top of the broom that holds the straw together, was fastened from end to end, and attached to each nail. Sometimes there would be more than one wire to produce varying pitches. These country blues musicians used a snuff can as a slide or smoothed the lip of a broken-off bottle to hook over the end of their fingers to keep from being cut by the strings as they played.

Wink said Robert Johnson had a lighter complexion than he and had a "wall-eye" that wandered. He described Johnson as a "real sport." The people on the farm used a lot of words out of the Bible, and if you'll look closely, you will see that one time a Bible king said his wife was "sporting" with someone else. The Bible had an enormous influence on the black vocabulary, and many like Wink, whose name was Isreal, had Biblical names.

One year a Hollywood producer sought out Wink for his knowledge of Robert Johnson. Wink and I previewed a movie script to give our advice. To the scriptwriter's dismay, we found lots of mistakes. In the script's first scene, young men drove up to a honky-tonk with a corpse tied to the hood of a car. Wink explained that when he and Robert Johnson were teenagers in the early 1920s, not a black in Tunica County had a car except Mr. Woolf, the undertaker.

The scriptwriter was also disappointed that Wink and his friends wore bib overalls and not the type of costumes the producers had ordered from Nashville. There was even a water moccasin written into the middle of a cotton field instead of close to water. The script's straw boss was a cruel man, not at all like our gentle Phax Long.

We tried to tell them that at that time, there were no honky-tonks. The farm laborers went to each others' houses or behind the barns for their crap games. And people made their own whiskey from wheat shorts, yeast, sugar and water fermented in Mason jars. The grocer in tiny Robinsonville, Mississippi sold more sugar than a Memphis chain store! This homemade liquor was colorless, and its clear nature gave it the name "White Lightnin.'"

After we pointed out all these discrepancies in the script, we never heard from Hollywood again. I learned through the grapevine that the movie premiered later in Clarksdale – inaccuracies and all.

What Wink knew about homemade whiskey he must have learned from others on the place, because Wink himself wasn't a big drinker. I never knew him to drink on the job at all, even on very special occasions, but he did take home about a half a cup of whisky each night in a Mason jar for a well earned nightcap.

Wink was so dependable that he served at the table at breakfast and always at dinner with the children. Balancing on his good leg, he would whop his hip smack against the swinging door between the breakfast room and enter the dining room carrying a big silver tray. As Wink served, the children would always be yakking, and he joined right in the conversation. Wink would even speak with guests, not being rude; he just put in his thoughts. And do you know, I've never seen him cause any trouble with anyone.

On nights when "we were putting on the dog," as Wink said, he would wear his white coat just a little stiffer; he'd show how well he could do. He would rear back those shoulders, be very still, and you'd think he'd been watching "Upstairs, Downstairs." No maitre'd in New York could have outdone Wink, and he knew it.

Wink was a favorite of all the parents. Every fall people would call and ask if their child could be put on the list to go to the Mid-South Fair with Wink. He would take them there and let them stay as long as they had one thin dime to spend on a ride or a sweet.

While the children rode the Octopus and other rides, Wink would go find a the monkey man, who wore an outfit like a gondolier. Wink would give a coin to the monkey, who would put it in his apron pocket and then take his little leathery hand and tip his hat to Wink. That's when Wink would laugh as only my Wink could.

Every Monday night Wink went to the wrestling match in Memphis. He looked at the wrestling matches on TV every Saturday morning, too, and everyone in the family knew you did not ask Wink to do one chore on Saturday morning.

Wink called our firstborn son "the President". Once as we passed a thick, scary woods driving to Nashville, he said to me, "Ole Miss, there ain't no way I'd go in those woods." Then he cleared his throat and said, "That's wrong, Ole Miss, I would go in there if the President needed me." He called my oldest daughter "Mary Boss" because she would tell Wink what she wanted him to do. Wink called Irene "Young Miss" or "Missy".

Whenever the children were off at camp, Wink and I would drive over the levee in the afternoons to look at all the deer that had come in from the woods, running from the mosquitoes. There might be as many as a hundred deer lying in groups. It is there that we found Little Dick-Dick the deer.

I guess the mother had abandoned it, because nature has its rules, and a deer will often leave a little one if it is not perfect. Dick-Dick had one ear that was deformed, but he was perfect for Wink and me. Wink told me not to listen to any vet, to give that deer just plain milk and he would grow just fine. Once someone gave the little deer too much rich cream and he became sick. Wink and I rushed him to the vet's, and Dick-Dick, being tiny then, sat in that office just like a little pet dog up in Wink's lap.

Dick-Dick would come down the long hall and his little hooves sounded just like drumsticks hitting a toy drum. Naturally, he grew too big and he had to be, with care, put back in the woods, but often we could see Dick-Dick up around the vegetable garden. Although it was fenced in for just that reason, Dick-Dick seemed to know the trick. If he couldn't leap over the fence, he would take his deer nose and open the latch on the garden gate and head for the string beans. We saw Dick-Dick less and less, but if he didn't get shot by hunters, we knew that he could not be far. I read that deer die within eight miles of the place they are born.

In the early 1950s on the plantation, we stayed busy in the garden, canning 52 quarts of each vegetable, one for each week of the year. Afterwards, I spent long afternoons with my children at the swimming pool up on the Indian mound behind my in-laws' big house. This pool, though small, was absolutely wonderful, because it was filled with fresh water each time we used it. A huge water tank that stood on the Indian mound filled the pool with fresh, cool, artesian water each day, no need for chlorine.

A man on the farm, lovingly called "Frogman," gigged frogs and brought them in large washtubs to my back door. Frogman, with his white hair that went in all directions, was one of the most colorful characters on the plantation. Certain nights, Frogman would take Dick and his friends gigging. Although I thought these forays dangerous, my husband and parents of our guests did not. Frogman wore a coon light on his head, and so did the children. They would walk boldly in shallow water full of not only frogs but snakes, and with seemingly little effort, Frogman and the children would bring home buckets of big, greasy frogs. Often Frogman would slow down and pick up a big snake and throw him out of reach. It was no wonder that children from the city with only shopping centers for weekend entertainment stood in line to receive an invitation to visit Commerce.

My mother-in-law had given me sage advice. You have to have amusements for city folk if you invite them down to the plantation. We had hayrides, sandbar parties, catfish frys, dove shoots and skeet and sub trap shoots.

For the sub trap shoots, little round clay targets, or pigeons, would be shot out from a station in the bluff of the riverbanks, and you would go from one stand to the next and shoot at different angles. I always seemed good at this sport, because Frogman knew my voice and if I called out to him, he would slow those pigeons down as they came out of the trap.

One day out of cheerful boredom, a friend of mine and I decorated an outhouse over by the sub trap. We painted a lady seated on the "one-holer," as we used to call them. She held her arms outstretched with a dramatic ribbon holding the toilet paper. I have not had the nerve in the last few years to go back and see if my little outhouse is still there. Perhaps some casino gambler has carried it home as a souvenir.

The hunters Richard invited to our woods made a habit of stopping by to check on D. Petty, the hermit who lived behind the levee. D. was a philosopher in the guise of a commercial fisherman and though he was a man of few words, what he did say went straight to the heart of a matter. I always thought that D., an ageless man in bib overalls, had a sort of haunted look about him. Perhaps that came from his self-imposed isolation. It was rumored he had a wife in Memphis, but no one ever knew for sure.

My father-in-law always said D. and a neighboring farmer named Toby were the county's two biggest characters. D. and Toby protected the wild turkeys behind the levee, and it has been said that the two of them were responsible for bringing the wild turkey back from near extinction in the

North Delta. They literally knew the turkeys by name.

Toby, our adjoining neighbor, was the same man that the barbershop wags teased about protecting his land so vigorously from poachers with "posted" signs. Many times, he pounded at our front door and when I answered, he yelled, "Get Richard! There's somebody over there on his land!"

Willie Williams, our hostler, who had taught Richard to hunt as a child, was known as one of the best turkey hunters and callers in the world. Richard bagged his first wild turkey at age 9. After our marriage, Willie would still wake Richard up for turkey hunting by throwing rocks at the bedroom window in the pre-dawn morning. When Richard was a tow-headed youngster – long before Mr. Leatherman had built his own small levee west of the big levee to protect the land from river water – Willie and Richard would go behind the main levee, where the spring rains would have left as much six feet of water in spots. Willie always rode a great big, tall, mule, and Richard rode a short pony. When they would come upon deep water, Richard would stand on the back of his pony and follow Willie's mule. On the way back to the house after a hunt, Willie would reach down from his mule and pull up bunches of poke salad for supper.

At St. Paul's school, Richard went grouse hunting many times with a teacher, Mr. Toland, who later visited us on the plantation. Mr. Toland recounted that at a faculty meeting, he once insisted that it be written in the minutes that he had at last found a student who could really hunt, and his name was Richard Leatherman from Mississippi.

As a bride, I went turkey hunting, but with the exception of the awesome experience of seeing and hearing the woods wake up, I was perfectly miserable. Once Richard snapped at me because I stepped on a stick and made noise. I had to sit perfectly still, bathed in *Off* insect repellent behind a mosquito bar net, as I listened to millions of insects drone within an eighth of an inch of my face. I never really mastered using a turkey caller, though I even bought records trying to learn. After I almost stepped on a big snake, and since I had bagged only one gobbler in three years, I called it quits. From that time on, I never slept better than when I heard the rest of the household get up to go turkey hunting, and I could snuggle deep under my sheets and turn over and go back to sleep.

By the end of my second year at Commerce, I had seen enough game, fish and frog legs to lose interest in regional dishes, and I'm not impressed when I go to New Orleans and see rabbit or venison on the menu.

One of the things about life in the country that fascinated my three children was the rolling store, a great big truck full of goodies–things like bread and cake and a few other basics. The man who ran our particular rolling store was referred to by all the help on the plantation simply as the "Dago." Children would squeal with laughter and come running in for nickels and dimes to buy their goodies. Mr. Dago was a good old-fashioned Italian with a big mustache, funny Panama hat, high neck shirt or top collar that went around his neck with a little black tie. Mrs. Dago sat next to Mr. Dago on the truck because he was bad to drink.

Another thing that drew the children's attention was the sight of the prison chain gangs who came to work on the ditch in the front yard and on all the gravel roads in the county. In their black-and-white striped uniforms and small hats, they were watched over by guards holding long shotguns who made certain the work was done correctly. Strangely enough, the road gang worked with spirit. They seemed to have jokes that they hollered back and forth to each other, and like the people who worked in the fields, the road gang would sing.

The children were told to stay in the house on such days, but they pressed their small faces to the windowpane looking to see if they could recognize anyone from Commerce, for they actually knew some of our farmhands who were serving time. Whether I gave my children a good childhood, I cannot answer, but I certainly exposed them to reality about a certain place at a certain time in American history.

Dick, Mary, and Irene always chose our Christmas trees from the hills near Como and Crenshaw, Mississippi, where my husband did most of his quail hunting. Because of the chemicals used in farming, we had lost our good quail land along with the succulent wild berries behind the levees and the wild tomatoes that grew among the cotton rows.

I know it wasn't as beautiful as a perfect nursery tree, but the old cedar Christmas tree had meaning because my children cut it. Inevitably, the trunk of the cedar tree would be crooked, and we would have to trim it with a hatchet to make it fit in the stand. One Christmas Richard had the bright idea of putting the tree in his horse trailer instead of in the back of the pickup. This was not a good idea, because instead of Christmas greens, our house smelled like horse manure. Each time we passed the tree we squirted it with *Lysol*, which just spoiled Christmas for our cat, "Inky" who liked to lie under the tree.

We decked the tree with ornaments the children made at school, special things like little pictures of the children and plaster of Paris handprints hung on red string. Adding ornaments from my childhood and garlands of homegrown popcorn and wild berries from the field, our country tree was more beautiful to me than all the garland in New York City.

The Christmas decorations of the sharecroppers were very simple—just lights strung across their porches and a naked, brown, small tree decorated with silver tin cans from their peaches, or peas or tomatoes. No grass grew up near the house, so they swept their yards for the holidays.

Each Christmas the children and I would pick up boxes from the commissary. We put a bottle of snuff, chewing tobacco, oranges, candy, nuts, and toys into each box and delivered them to families on the farm. It was a simple Christmas.

One Christmas afternoon, we crossed the gravel road to Willie Williams' small house that sat next to the barn. When this elderly, beloved man opened the door and saw us, he said, "Lawdy be! I thought old Santie Man had just plumb forgot me."

After the excitement of Christmas, the winters are long and dismal in the Mississippi Delta. The last picking of the cotton was called "scrapping," and all too often fields never were scrapped if bad weather caught a crop. You would look out of the window at thousands of acres of dreary brown cotton stalks with four or five inches of wet cotton dangling down. There is not a more forlorn sight in the world.

To cheer us up, we kept fires going and always put magnolia leaves and nandina with red berries in a cut glass bowl on the dining room table. With these little touches, we created what we thought was a bit of style.

Another Southern tradition was to always keep a bottle of sherry in the guest room and one out on the coffee table in the living room in case someone needed a drink before the "legal" cocktail hour. During the hunting seasons we used two or three cases of whisky a month.

One way to pass time at Commerce was to do hand work. My Aunt Jeanne Leatherman tried with only a measure of success to teach me to knit. This seemed very important because we still had sheep on the old plantation as we facetiously called it. It was pure sentiment to keep them only because the flock of sheep was started by Uncle Dick Abbay. We would have the wool conditioned and knit sweaters for family members. The sheep lived in a pasture behind my vegetable garden. This was a dangerous place, but the best of the worst, because packs of wild dogs would attack the sheep no matter where they were. Many times Richard shot the wild dogs as the poor sheep just stood there while they were being bitten and destroyed.

When not entertaining, Aunt Jeanne and I would have secret adventures. Since none of our house sites were on the river, our only way to enjoy this mighty body of water was to visit the sandbars that came and went with the changing current. I spent many sandbar afternoons with Jeanne, my aunt by marriage, only nine years my senior, drinking beer, watching the sunset, and lamenting the life of the Southern woman. If it had not been for this brilliant and magnificent woman, I would have had a very lonely existence.

We talked of poor people and sad, cruel things we saw and plotted how we could join committees, help at the church and library, and get a hospital built.

I told Jeanne how just a few days before, when I was out in my garden, facing the cotton field, I watched a mother waving her hoe in the air, screaming to her two older sons to catch their younger brother, who was running as fast as his little legs could carry him through cotton stalks almost taller than himself. The two older boys grabbed the screaming child by his arms, while the mother beat the child without mercy. I held up my rose clippers and ran through the thick, inevitable privet hedge that seems to act as a wall around all Delta yards. As I ran, I hollered, "Stop that, you horrible thing or I'm going right inside to call the sheriff to arrest you!"

The oldest boy dropped his brother's arm, and looked up to me as if he had good news, "Don't you worry, Miss Sugs, soon little man will grow to be as big as mama, and then he can beat on *her*."

It was on this day that I lay face down on the black Mississippi soil, pounding my fists and pronouncing that there could be no God, at least not the caring one I saw in the Sunday school books. What was I, a young mother trying to raise three children on my husband's meager salary, to do? People in Memphis thought I lived a glamorous life because I had household help, but they didn't realize our financial world was relative.

Jeanne and I discussed how the women of the South and blacks were put in the same situation on many accounts. We had all been taught, no matter how beautiful you were or bright you were, the most important thing for a lady to be was pleasant. You could be a Steel Magnolia in the day, but by night you hung on the men's words, and you never beat them at a point, if you could avoid it. If you did, it was done so cleverly that you would have passed as a pickpocket looking like a minister.

This goes deeply into families. For example, my brother Jack married at 19, and was deeply offended when his wife wanted to get a job at the courthouse. He became irate and said he didn't want the world to think that Jack Seabrook couldn't support his wife.

Until recently, sons were given the best educations. They were sent to the fine medical schools, but if they were lucky, girls were probably sent to a two-year college with the hopes of making a good marriage. It never dawned on people in my day to let females be the doctors in the family.

As recently as 1966, in *State v. Hall*, 187 So.2d 861 (1966), the Mississippi Supreme Court wrote: "The legislature has the right to exclude women from jury duty so they may continue their service as mothers, wives, and homemakers, and also to protect them (in some areas, they are still upon a pedestal) from the filth, obscenity, and noxious atmosphere that so often pervades a courtroom during a jury trial." That says it all about women's roles on the plantation, and so Aunt Jeanne and I were hidden behind the magnolia curtain.

My engagement portrait.

Samuel Richard Leatherman III
in his youth

Our children Irene, Mary White and Samuel Richard Leatherman
IV, "Dick."

Four generations of Samuel Richard Leathermans and their spouses: (Clockwise from the top) Samuel Richard Leatherman I and Ethel Irwin Leatherman; Richard and Carroll Leatherman on their wedding day; Grace Ellzey and my son Dick (Samuel Richard Leatherman IV), on their wedding day, with Dick's daughter Carroll Leatherman II; my in-laws Irene Morrow Leatherman and Samuel Richard Leatherman, Jr., better known as Big Richard, relaxing in their Commerce home.

My sister in this life, Emma Jean Taylor, has been my helper and strength for 27 years.

Our houseman Israel "Wink" Clark, also my driver, and Henry Deal, who tended the garden. Both retired from Leatherman Farms in Mississippi and came with the family to Memphis in 1970.

Wink plucks one of the many turkeys shot at Commerce during our twenty years living in Mississippi. Wink could dress wild game to rival any New Orleans chef.

Memphis Blue Max and
Richard Leatherman

Memphis Amateur
Field Trial members,
Richard Leatherman,
President

Nash Buckingham,
second from left, is
surrounded by his
Tunica County
hunting buddies,
(from left) Jack and
Sterling, Bob
Mangum, Dick
Whittington, and
game warden Cliff
Thornton (kneeling
at right).

When the New York Times' food editor Craig Claiborne came South for a feature story in the 1960s, I served iced tea and water in the heirloom silver goblets.

Scaasi picture

Ivan Oblensky and Carroll Seabrook Leatherman at St. Regis Bar, New York apparel in Town and Country Magazine March 1962.

Symphony Ball September 14, 1963
(L to R) Helen Norfleet, Jessie Peters Norfleet, (artist Goode Davis); Carroll Seabrook Leatherman, (artist Ray Kinsler); Robert Crump, E. H. Crump, (artist E. Weber Fulop).

After our move to Memphis and the publication of my first book, The Old Man and the Dog, Memphis magazine included me in "Extraordinary People: A Photographic Tribute to Some Neat Memphians Who Are Just Plain More Interesting Than the Rest of Us," April 1985.

THE BEST BARGAINS IN TOWN ■ COMPLETE NIGHT-LIFE GUIDE
RESTAURANT KITCHENS: AN INSIDE LOOK ■ DOONESBURY

Memphis

Hidden TREASURES

A Photographic Tribute To The People And Places That Make Memphis Special.

THE·BEST·EVER·GUIDE

Richard and I flank our children and grandchildren, all together
in one place at one time: (from top) Irene and Girard Polk
Brownlow III; Grace, holding Elle, and Dick; and Mary and Oscar
Clark Carr III; and the older grandchildren, Carroll Leatherman
II, Thomas Tyne Brownlow, Oscar Clark Carr IV, Camilla Fisher
Carr, and Abbay Leatherman Brownlow.

Chapter 12

Parties

Parties

W hen Ted Turner did a documentary on lifestyles in different parts of the country, Richard and I were asked to Stovall, Mississippi, where we attended a reenactment of a Delta seated dinner party.

We drove up the Stovall's long, circular drive to the porte-cochere, where the parking attendant was holding a deck of playing cards. He took one out, tore it in two, gave Richard one half, and put the other half under the windshield wiper so the car could be easily retrieved later. This custom was a hangover from the days of illiteracy.

After a very formal wild turkey dinner, we retired to the drawing room where the reporters began to ask us questions about our lifestyle.

"Before we start," said one, stylish, professional looking writer, "I have to say, I have been in Mississippi for weeks and have visited different parts of the state. Every time the word "delta" has come up in the conversation, the person with whom I was visiting would say, *Oh, the Delta. Why, that's different from any other part of the world. It defies description, and you will have to see it for yourself.*"

Then she asked, "What makes the Delta different?"

This was a hard question to answer, and I could only reply that I felt that the Delta was making an apology to the world. For starters, with few exceptions like the Stovalls, the Leathermans and my family, as the Delta is the state's "late" child. Except for its stunning river vistas, it is as flat and plain and black as a mud flapjack. In order to make up for that, Delta people tend to over-do everything.

The women, Ole Miss co-eds included, are well dressed to the point of being overdone. The food is both plentiful and very elaborate, and in my early marriage, cocktail parties were unheard of. My mother-in-law taught me that if people were going to drive that many miles for a party, they needed something extra to do—like dove shoots, boating, hunting and dances. Delta people possess a self-awareness and poise that along with an easy air, makes them very attractive. Underneath all of this show and tell lies a very practical side, for they seem to know who they are and furthermore to like it. What I did not tell the reporter is the sad fact that the Delta she had come to see was all but gone. The good news is, that coming from frontier stock, Delta people are willing and anxious to change. Soon she would have to learn about the Mississippi she had come to see from books and movies. In truth, I think the reporter and I both will like our new South better.

As different from the Delta, as night is from day, was Como, Mississippi, that was a part of our life due to Richard's avid interest in bird dogs and hunting. It was his second home. In the 1950s the large meal of the day was still served at noon in Como. Richard was so at home there, that he could walk in unannounced to several of the large Victorian homes that faced the railroad track, sit down, and be part of the family. He loves the place so much that he says when he dies, he doesn't want to go to heaven; he wants to go to Como.

Como is a small hill country town where a few old families own most of the surrounding land. These wealthy families send their children to Eastern colleges, and when I was a young bride, there were Como women in their 80s who were Wellesley girls. Once at a Como dinner party when first married, I was the only woman there who had gone to a junior college. The five other women present were Vanderbilt graduates.

During the dove season, Como families made arrangements where there would be big dove shoots three days in a row on different farms. This would allow out-of-town visitors to have three good hunts. These hunts were followed by picnics under grape arbors the size of large rooms, and seated dinners at round tables under huge, ragged cedars, where fried chicken was followed with homemade ice cream served out of the hand-cranked freezers.

At some of these unique and varied events, you might have for entertainment choirs from the local black churches or the famous Fife and Drum Band of the late Sid Hemphill and Napoleon Strickland. It was a sound of blues notes and syncopation that grew out of a nineteenth century military tradition, but one that brought African and African-American elements to it. Who would expect a world famous small marching band in Como, Mississippi?

One of my favorite Como settings for an after-dove hunt party was the largest log house I had ever seen. This outstanding example of a log dwelling had been moved log-for-log from one farm to a new site overlooking a large lake.

Back at Commerce Landing, one of my favorite party memories was my 29th birthday, when we hosted a dove shoot, and my family presented me with a fine Winchester Model 21 shotgun with a solid gold trigger. After this shoot, we had a catfish and hushpuppies fried in large drums heated by butane burners.

As much fun as these outdoor parties were, the social event of the year was the Christmas Planter's Ball held in Clarksdale, Mississippi, shortly before Christmas day. If there was a landed gentry, you were on the dance floor with just that. Women were magnificently groomed, and some husbands even involved themselves in the choice of that evening's ball gown.

People came from all over the Delta for the party. Since it was held at Christmas time, the crops had been harvested and sold, people had some money, and spirits were high. Also, the hunting season had started, and every Delta man who owned a gun was happy. The party was often followed by a hangover brunch the next morning, where we said farewell to friends that we might not see for another year.

We loved entertaining at home. There was always humor in the kitchen preparing for parties, and the help became as excited over the party as the hostess. They enjoyed seeing people they had known for years, who would go back in the kitchen to greet them affectionately, rave over the food and most times give them a gracious tip.

There's an old Southern saying that if you dropped something it didn't fall, it just stumbled. Many a biscuit – even a Christmas turkey — has had a little touch of the floor, been dusted off, and put back on the serving platter. What is the difference? It couldn't be any dirtier than a picnic.

One time in sheer desperation with 50 guests coming on a Sunday, no grocery store open anywhere near, I discovered weevils in the flour. Knowing I needed a hundred biscuits, we cleaned it the best we could and had hot buttered weevil biscuits that the guests said melted in their mouths.

Summer parties were also spectacular. One Fourth of July Richard and I gave a large house party at Commerce Landing. With my mother-in-law in northern Michigan, we had guests sleeping at my aunt's house, our home, and my in-laws'.

Before this particular party, I had received a strange acceptance note from a devastatingly attractive gentleman. His note read, "Mr. So-N-So accepts the kind invitation he is yet to receive from Mrs. Leatherman for the Fourth of July." I figured the man had a definite reason for asking himself to a party where he had not been invited, and I would have bet my bottom dollar that it had something to do with a lady.

That weekend, everyone was learning to do "the bop", and we wore out two records of Elvis Presley's "Heartbreak Hotel."

I invited many Memphis friends down for a big hayride where we drank several cases of champagne sent by a friend. A small group of us, with our band of musicians, stayed up all night and from Miss Irene's Park on the Mississippi River, we watched the sun rise. Though I was busy, I kept watching the self-invited gentleman, but I could see nothing unusual in his behavior. My answer came on Monday when I received a call telling me that a couple I had thought were blissfully happy had parted, and the wife had left her husband for the uninvited guest.

We went to several house parties in Natchez, Mississippi, and field trials too, where my husband campaigned bird dogs. I remember how glamorous the homes were, with open windows so tall that we danced through them out onto the verandas and porches.

One particular house called The Elms was on the Natchez pilgrimage tour. This magnificent Spanish home was owned by a very good friend of mine. It had been in her family since the Spanish flag flew over Natchez. They still own it today. I stayed up all night long and had finally settled in a big tester bed for a long day's nap, when there was a rap on the door and a high-pitched voice said, "Get up, Miss. Get up, Miss, the Pilgrims are coming." I didn't realize they called the tourists pilgrims and thought I might be having the D.T.'s.

Men in the South have been shooting and dueling over women as far back as people could gossip. Probably the most publicized was called the Memphis "Jet Set Society Shooting". I cannot report first-hand what happened that Monday, because I had my gun aimed at ducks in Rose Hill, South Carolina, where a snob told me he thought I was the most attractive "inland" woman he had ever met. As for the society shooting, to quote Will Rogers. "All I know is what I read in the paper."

I can tell you that I was part of a group of young married women who were attending a music appreciation class at Rhodes College on Mondays. We ladies started a tradition of stopping by a society bachelor's house for luncheon first. Soon, various men began dropping by, knowing we ladies were there. Word spread, and the street in front of the house on Mondays looked like a mafia funeral procession, with stalkers craning their necks to see which member of the "Memphis Jet Set" (as this group came to be called) entered and left the residence. Our host thrived on such behavior, and he was delighted that he had stirred up trouble.

While I was out of town shooting ducks in Rose Hill, bigger game was being shot in Memphis. An attractive, married gentleman, quite the ladies' man, showed up for lunch, the trial reports stated. My bachelor friend, who was emotionally attached to a gorgeous widow, had had too much libation and became upset. From an upstairs window, he peppered the gentleman's backside with birdshot, according to the paper. In good spirit, they took the wounded man to a family doctor we all loved. He picked out the shot but did not report it to the authorities.

Gossip circled the town to such a point that a newspaper column called "Backdrop" mentioned it. Sunday after Sunday in Backdrop it would read, "What's Happening about the Society Shooting?" It went on and on, until finally it was investigated, and my dear friend, who meant no harm and had just been tight and thought he was pulling a prank, and the married man, just coming by to be with the gang, were made victims of a terrible trial.

I never went near the trial, but one poor friend had to hide on her farm in a neighboring state the entire winter, hoping to avoid a subpoena. The society bachelor served time at the penal farm. His friends brought him scrumptious meals from the finest restaurants in Memphis, like Justine's. He used to laugh and say, "I went from Yale to jail."

After a short time, Tennessee Governor Buford Ellington pardoned him. The governor was a very savvy politician. The day he pardoned the bachelor he told the gentleman responsible for getting him sprung, "Today I'm going to pardon your friend. You must go alone and pick him up in your car, because every son-of-a-bitch in Tennessee is going to take credit for obtaining this pardon, and this is a personal favor to you."

Two weeks later, I was at a seated dinner when a very prominent and arrogant man made the statement that he was responsible for the pardon. I used my husband's favorite expression.

"Wrong!" I said, "I was waiting at his front door when a certain influential gentleman brought the bachelor home."

I had known before the society shooting ever took place that a young, 29-year-old mother of three did not need a Monday morning hangover drink. The Monday morning drink wasn't the only thing that needed to stop. I needed to stop being tagged as belonging to the "Jet Set" of Memphis.

One night with my husband gone, I said that I was going over to join my friends—the ones who were in the ruckus and the society shooting. My precious son looked at me and said, "Momma, don't go over there." Those were the only words he said. I knew this child had heard. I knew he had feared for his mother.

The whole affair made my friend and me closer and although it was a sad and needless mess, it prompted me to find help, stop drinking and lead a very different life. Some good comes from all happenings.

A trip with friends to Cumberland Island, Georgia finally convinced me to seek the help I needed. During the nights with no air-conditioner, I would get up by myself and go down through the huge house and into the private indoor swimming pool about four in the morning, when it would be so still that even the frogs seemed to quiet down for a few minutes. Dashing over rocks and stones and hoping not to step on long, great rattlesnakes. The indoor pool smelled of sulphur and I would plunge in. Then I would go back, crawl in my bed without even drying, and I could be comfortable and sleep until the morning, when I knew at any hour we wanted, we would start off with an enormous breakfast. Later drinks were served at noon on the beach before a late lunch and while other sensible guests fished or took hikes, I partied on and on and on.

The most memorable night of the visit, my host and I decided that we would join some commercial fishermen as they threw their nets. We were the last up that night, and nothing would do but that we fish with these people. It was fun, pulling in those nets, and in a democratic mood, we had found our new best friends. While we were one of these good, earthy, island fishermen poaching out there on the beach with the full moon, we were all God's children, and we had formed a fraternity. Naturally, nothing would do but that we had our new friends, if they chose to be our guests, return with us to the Carnegie mansion where we were staying. Having had a good deal of our champagne, they seemed to think, "Well, why not? Would it hurt to go up and see how the Carnegies lived?" So off we went.

We were in a Model-T Ford owned by my hostess' father and kept on the island, and they were in rundown vehicles that were wired-together, and rusted from the ocean's salt. The doors of the house were left open, since there was a house full of people, and we had no trouble coming right in the huge entrance hall. Before we knew it, we were all dancing. But that wasn't good enough.

My host and I decided it would only be fitting for us to do our routine, a dance to "Colonel Bogie's English March," to which we sang *Rat's Ass, that's all the band could play. Rat's Ass, we do it night and day.*

What could be a better idea than to climb up on the Carnegie's enormous dining table. We could push aside Papa Carnegie's chair, which was off-limits, a throne, and no one was allowed to sit in it. But as I recall, before it was pushed out of the way, I had stepped on it and was atop the table with a beach towel and my host. We did our routine. What laughter, what screams, what a way to forget that I had lost Mother, Jack and Aunt Camilla.

Unfortunately the party and I both were wearing down. The last night I was there, I had gone into a large downstairs bathroom to find a very long snake wrapped around the toilet. By then, I had what I would call a very bad hangover from having been on the island way too many days, and so I flew home.

The crops at home looked more beautiful to me than the Atlantic

Ocean. It was near dark but not too late for Richard to drive me over behind the levee. It looked like a scene from *National Geographic*. I caught a glimpse of the river as we drove on through deeper woods to the sandbar, where I stepped out and looked at the Mississippi. We crossed back over what I call the "Bend," the place now filled with casinos. The cotton was in full bloom and almost ready for harvest. I was *home*. Maybe the East coast snob was right: attractive or not, one thing was certain–I was an inland woman.

As beautiful as home was, it was not the answer to my real problem. Deep down I knew the parts were not fitting in the puzzle of my life.

Chapter 13

Last Chapter

Last Chapter

For my birthday in September of 1959, I was given a big dove shoot and it turned out to be not a happy time for I did not stay awake to bid my guests good by.

Throughout the fall I clung to my sanity as though I were dangling off the edge of a cliff. That Christmas was not a happy one either, and I was riddled with guilt about my three small children. Even our Como cedar tree looked a bit neglected. On Christmas morning I even forgot where I had hidden some of the children's toys, and Nurse had to help me find them. Richard wanted to give me a 10th anniversary party on December 29, but I told him I wasn't up to it.

New Year's Eve meant nothing, but I do remember one nosey friend asked me why I drank so much. Her question haunted me.

It was a rainy Monday morning, January 17, 1960, and the Delta sky was almost as dark as the soaked brown dirt that was now a mud puddle several thousands acres wide. The sky and earth were so much alike that there seemed to be no space in between. I prayed for the strength to make my first step toward a new life. Sitting in my living room, I cried over the pictures of Mother, Jack, and Aunt Camilla, while listening to a Puccini opera. I realized that I must be very sick to be crying over the dead with a gin bottle in my hand, when I had three healthy children to think of.

I had crawled into a pit. Stumbling to the phone, I called the farm office and asked the bookkeeper to find Richard on his car radio, because I needed him at home at once.

When Richard opened the front door, I cried out, "Help me, Richard. Here I am, Monday morning in this shape, for God's sake, help me."

Richard and the children's nurse steadied me so I could dress, but I could manage only a nightgown and an old black raincoat. With me slumped over in the backseat, begging the nurse to take care of my children, Richard drove to a family doctor in Memphis. My head dizzy with the fake courage of warm gin, I felt I could lick this problem as Richard carried me through the back door of the doctor's small clinic. The doctor told me that he remembered seeing me at the train station, heading to New York with the school set and that I was both the prettiest and happiest young woman there. And now I stood before him, pitiful and messy. I used harsh language and did not even try to hide my fear and anger.

The doctor said of course he would help me but it was too bad that I had come now, for only a week before he had sent a friend of mine to a good, attractive hospital. Since it would never do for both of us to be in the same place, he would send me to a world-renowned, but stricter, hospital up East.

"Doctors send their families to this place, and this is where they go themselves," he said.

My stomach swirled with the nauseating combination of shame, fright, and relief as we crossed the state line back into Mississippi. After all the years of playing make-believe and pretending bravery and complete control, I had melted. I had lost myself trying to impress people I did not like and please people I did not trust. Somewhere back in my childhood were Miss Lee and Tennie and OK Plantation, and the hospital was the only way back to my people and my kind of world.

I ordered a gin and tonic on the plane to the hospital, and my poor husband asked desperately, "When are you going to stop drinking?"

"In about two hours, when I sign into that hospital, you idiot!" I answered.

With the help of a little gin, I committed myself for what I thought was 30 days at the Institute of Living in Hartford, Connecticut. I kissed Richard good-bye, and my attendant led me to a strange house with bars on the windows, called Williams Cottage. As I walked into the den, two patients stopped watching television to gaze at me like a new cow at auction.

Another attendant led me upstairs to a sunny corner room with a small porch, which served no purpose during the frigid January except to give me a place to cry where no one could hear me.

I was fortunate that I did not arrive drunk and have to go the detox side of the hospital, where one eats only with a spoon, and a toilet is in the middle of the room.

I had not been in the cottage overnight before I learned that the earliest anyone ever left this place was six months for drinking, eight months for drugs, or two years for a complete psychological analysis.

Sitting alone in my room after the attendant left me, I watched the snowfall like flour through a sifter. Thoughts of making snow cream with Mother and Willie, our Memphis housekeeper, came slipping into my mind. Snow was a big event in Memphis, Tennessee, when I was a child. Bringing large tin pots full of cold snow inside and adding custard to it before it melted was a treat. Where had my childhood disappeared?

A rap on the door preceded the entrance of a tall, rather thin dark-haired man with perfectly clear skin and color in his cheeks that a schoolgirl would kill for. With little formality and no hint of friendliness, he pulled up a chair, sat down, and pulled out a gold cigarette case. He opened it towards me before he lit his smoke, but with no charm left after just trying to keep from bawling, I told him I did not smoke.

"If I did smoke," I told him, "I would already have been smoking before you arrived."

Then the man crossed his legs. This was his habit before he began therapy. I would notice this repeatedly over my time at the hospital.

His first words to me, in a voice completely devoid of emotion, were, "Tell me, Mrs. Leatherman, who are you here to spite?"

Although I was surprised, I answered him very quickly and with candor, "Some dead and some alive."

At this point, I nicknamed him Dr. Malateste, which means "bad head" in Italian. From that day to the last day five months later, Dr. Malateste never once stopped being the doctor. Young and anxious, I tried to alter our relationship at the beginning, but he was never to be my friend or confidante.

During the first two weeks at the Institute, I was on "constant," which meant I could never be without an attendant when out of my room. I saw my doctor only three times a week for 45 minutes each time. In between these very short appointments, I went to class or took long walks. They were not strict about going to class, but it was very much encouraged. Since I was dying of homesickness and utterly distraught, I would drag myself to class rather than just walk and weep. I could not fathom that because I had lost control of my drinking, I had been forced to leave behind my three magnificent children, my husband, and a fun country home.

I did not eat for the first three weeks because I could barely swallow. I lived on a little bread and milk. After a time, I did begin to eat, and I even slept a little better. The fact is, in a matter of days, the thick walls looked almost good to me. I was protected from myself. There was no way I could continue to do harm to either myself or my family.

One day I entered the doctor's office looking and acting cheerful. Really I was dying on the inside, feeling like two big hands were squeezing the blood out of my heart like a housewife would squeeze water from a kitchen sponge. I told him that the people from Memphis and home in Mississippi had sent me bunches of flowers and support letters and even gifts. To this, the man glared back with piercing blue eyes and said, "So the little queen of the plantation is reigning in the insane asylum." I literally could not believe the brutality of the remarks the man made.

We blundered through meeting after meeting. After about two months, the doctor asked what I thought of him. "How could I like anyone as cruel as you?" I replied.

"You may think I am cruel, but I have good news for you. This weekend you may have a visitor," the doctor told me. I was stunned.

He said, "Aren't you interested in who it is?"

I replied, "I would assume it is my husband."

"Do you want to see him?"

"Of course I do."

"Would you like to spend the night out with him?"

I said I would and he agreed. Then I stood speechless after his final crude taunt. "Are you the master in the sex act?"

"That I cannot answer," I told him, "but if I wait to start an argument at bedtime and I am undressed, the arguments do not last as long."

One of my first psychological tests was to draw a man and a woman. Naturally, I drew them as stick people–nothing but little straight stick bodies with two legs, two arms, and a little round head. Walking the campus one day with a brilliant doctor who was also a patient, he asked about my test. I told him how I had drawn my little stick figures. To that, the doctor replied, "Lady, do you realize you're in one of the most Freudian hospitals in the world? If you did not give your stick people anything like bosoms, you're going to be in here for the rest of your life."

Needless to say, after three months, when I was given that test again, my figures were more lifelike. This time my stick woman had bosoms, and my stick man had a pecker that was as long as a fire hose. Maybe that is why I was released from the place a month early.

I talked to Dr. Malateste about my mother's illness and death. I had never faced it and avoided facing it by keeping my life at a distractingly hectic pace. I drank first to forget my mother being sick, but then lost control. After my mother died, I lost my precious brother Jack to alcoholism.

I told my doctor about when my brother, a handsome and fine man, had been a patient at Dr. Wright's clinic in Byhalia, Mississippi. Dr. Wright was pre-Alcoholics Anonymous, and he believed in the old withdrawal method. The first time I went to the clinic as a young, innocent woman to see my brother, I was confused to see patients in dressing gowns with their tired, sad eyes glued to a clock that hung on the wall. I later learned they all watched the clock because at a certain time, they would be given a drink.

A famous Mississippi writer had also been a patient there. Each time before this man came, he would have two young black boys tie whiskey bottles in the branches of trees. The writer then did not have to wait like the other patients, but he could take a walk, pull down a branch and have a drink.

With Dr. Malateste, I gradually began to discuss a part of my life I had shared with no one. It was the fact that I had missed having a sister. Mother's first two children had been female and had died. If I'd had a sister, we could have shared Mother's ill health. Older brothers were not the same as two sisters drinking colas and talking about the rest of the family. A sister would know everything, and I would not have to play pretend with her. An older sister would be kind, pretty and popular and would break the ice for me in a snob Southern world.

When I finally did find someone to be as close to me as a sister, she is not at all what I fantasized to my doctor about. Instead, she is a very intelligent black housekeeper who came into my life 27 years ago.

In between talks with Dr. Malateste, I encountered the other staff and my fellow patients. I became very attached to the lady with whom I ate three meals a day at our table for two. She was a wonderful English woman named Lady Mann, who owned an enormous estate on Long Island. She never told me why she was there–never. But I knew she wasn't an alcoholic. Alcoholics, when relieved of their drug, laughed and walked and seemed normal. The desperately mentally ill patients acted and looked miserable.

Eventually the doctors said that Lady Mann could go home, and a huge black car came to retrieve her. The chauffeur put a mink throw over Lady Mann, and I told her good-bye with many tears. She had made this place bearable.

The next morning, there was my Lady Mann sitting at the table with me. I never said a word to her about what happened, and she never mentioned it. I later heard it whispered that poor Lady Mann had traveled some distance from the hospital before she asked the chauffeur to turn around and take her back.

The nurse in charge of my cottage seemed to take an immediate dislike to me. She was a huge black sergeant of a woman that I gave one of my nicknames. "Bully" abused me unmercifully in front of the other patients and would make rude remarks about my clothing and my Southern accent. One morning when Bully was gone and had left her door unlocked, I went into her office. You see, this cruel woman very often kept my mail for two or three days before she handed it to me. When I entered the office, I saw my chart lying on her desk, and I could not wait to read it. It started like this, "Mrs. S. Richard Leatherman, 31, white, upper middle class, plantation type. She is a born leader, but she can be a follower, too. She has other patients waiting on her hand and foot and even rearranging furniture in her room." Then came the good news. "Mrs. Leatherman has a fair to very good chance of recovery." It was worth the other part to read that.

When I went into group therapy, there was a Doctor Webb there. He asked if anyone in the group had a problem with drinking. I said I did. The others looked horror-stricken that I would admit such a thing. We sat in a circle, and I sat next to Dr. Webb.

"Why do you sit next to me?" he asked.

I answered, "Because I want to get well and leave here."

One night I left a boring movie at the Institute with permission, of course, and walked to my cottage. I looked up into the sky. It was crystal clear and blue. Snow was falling. I simply said, "God, I do not know who You are or where You are, but if You will take this monkey off my back, I promise I will never forget the favor, and I will repay You in any way I can." It was years later that I learned this is the first step in Alcoholics Anonymous.

Next to my all-female cottage was an all-male cottage housing what must have been very sick men. In the five months I stayed at the Institute, I never saw one of them. One ice cold winter night, the shriek of fire trucks awakened me, and I could see from the window that the men's cottage was going up in flames. Bully started waking the female patients and herding us downstairs, but she kept fumbling at the locked door, trying one key after another. My moment had arrived. I snatched the keys and with my right arm held out straight, pushed Bully as hard as I could against the wall. Then I opened the door and led the group out like the pied piper.

After I had been at the hospital five months, the doctor asked me if I really wanted to return to my life on the old plantation.

"It is obvious," he said, "that it must not agree with you, or you would not be here."

It did not take me five seconds to answer that I wanted to return to the plantation, to my husband who had written me every day for five months, and to my three children.

I loved my children so much that I could not speak of them or mention their names for the first two months I was there. When the doctor brought this to my attention, tears swelled in my eyes and I said, "Doctor, I would think you would know you can tell more about someone by what they don't say than by what they do." Later, when I was better, I never stopped talking about them. I let everyone in the cottage see their pictures.

When I received a letter from my 9-year-old son on his birthday, I dissolved.

"If you come home," Dick wrote, "I will fix you your coffee and bring it to your bed." If I ever made it out of that place, I promised with the help of God, I would never fall into this trap again.

After five months, the doctor told me he was going on vacation. Rather than start over with a new doctor, I asked if I could just go home. He said he would bring it up before the board of 40 psychiatrists, and the next time I saw him, he said that I could go home. I asked him on my last visit if he thought I would ever drink again, and this clever, strange, man simply said, "Mrs. Leatherman, you will never drink again unless you decide to."

It is strange that I can remember verbatim what was said to me at that hospital. I can close my eyes and see the rooms. I can smell the snow, the galoshes; I can hear the radiators pump. I can see the anguish on the patient's faces, the hope in some and the hopelessness in others.

I am surprised that the doctor did not warn me about the adjustments I would have to make at home. He did not tell me to see another doctor in Memphis, nor did he tell me to go to AA, since they did not have it in the 1960s at the Institute of Living.

I did return to my husband and my three children, but things were vastly different. Life would take on a different meaning, and I would see things in a very different light.

My precious maiden aunt Camilla had given my first cousin, my two brothers and me land when I was only 15. On the other hand, my husband, the heir apparent with his siblings, was not given an acre until his father died at age 72.

After the owners of the Polk Place leased to another planter, Richard was made manager of the Bayliss Place, which was part of the family partnership. I had been renting the land Aunt Camilla had given me at Lake Cormorant to a Withers first cousin. He agreed to sell Richard and me an adjoining parcel given to him by Aunt Camilla, and also a gin we called "Old Cranky". Richard and I were now partners in a farming operation.

When I returned to the old plantation in June 1960, my re-entry into life was not as smooth as I had hoped. That first summer I let my children go to Charlevoix, Michigan, to spend a month with their grandmother as they always had. I was later sorry that I had let them go, but the up side was that Richard and I could have some concentrated time together.

Charlevoix was a lovely resort, but I had come to realize that my family should be together, even if it was a long, hot summer. From that time on, I either rented a cottage in Michigan where I could be with the children, or they went to camps.

It took courage to refuse invitations to family dinners at both Leatherman households on the farm. Once sober, conversation at the long cocktail hours lost its charm, and I needed to be home with my children.

I told my mother-in-law how I felt — that it embarrassed me when she would say in front of the help, "Have dinner early. Mrs. Leatherman, Jr. doesn't drink." But I noticed that the cocktail hour dragged on, and dinner was never served early.

Mrs. Leatherman had a hard time accepting that if I did come to dinner (which was seldom) I would prefer to come only with her son, who cared nothing about a drink, and like me, wanted dinner served earlier so we could be home before the children went to bed. My good friend, Aunt Jeanne, missed having a drinking friend, and in all honesty, I missed our times together, too. As the months passed we all learned that you can lunch and do other happy things with someone without drinking.

Early in our marriage, I rode in the field trials with Richard. But then my life became more and more involved with the children's activities, and he became more involved with campaigning dogs. It became increasingly hard for me to go with him to weekend field trials. Even if I didn't have the children's interest as my priority, now that I didn't drink, I did not enjoy the company of that hard-drinking crowd.

Thank goodness field trial season only lasts December through March. The rest of the time Richard would be there with me on weekends. We saved every Friday night for the children. This was the time we encouraged them to bring home their friends from the Memphis schools and do all the fun things on the plantation.

I learned funny things that are a vital part of life. I learned that once my children traded a pair of my stockings to Nurse in exchange for three of Wink's cigarettes. I deliberately played along, since all children are going to try a cigarette some time. We just hope they don't stay with it.

Time spent with the children in the car was my favorite. On one trip to Memphis from the farm, I wondered why everyone was looking at my car. I looked into the rearview mirror to see who could be following and why they were so intrigued with my car. What I saw in the mirror was one of my children's houseguests with a girdle on top of her head, made to look like rabbit ears. There was one laugh after another. And I soon found the best company in the world was my children and their friends.

In the station wagon, I could eavesdrop and hear what the children were really doing and thinking. The more time I could spend with my children and their friends, the happier I was.

There was one drawback to these country weekends: mothers in Memphis. The fact was that our country house is over an hour from some Memphis homes, yet I would receive calls on Saturday morning that little Lulu had a dentist's appointment, and would I mind bringing little Lulu in right away? In the 20 years I lived at Commerce, not one person in Memphis brought a child down to Mississippi. No parent seemed to know that the highway went both ways.

Never have I had hunters, visitors, or children that they did not leave something in the country. At seven one night I received a call from a woman who the previous weekend had left a dress at my house that she wanted to wear to an important engagement that evening. She thought nothing of asking me to bring it to Memphis.

I practically lived in Memphis in the daytime; my children went to school there, and after I came back from Hartford, my social life was centered in Memphis. My appreciation of our apartment increased as the children grew older and wanted to take part in many Memphis activities. When they started dating, it became a lifesaver.

Soon after, I started modeling in Memphis. Several of my friends did this. And though it was not taken as seriously as today, we could buy designer clothes at a discount and have fun seeing our pictures in the paper all the time. By now I was very interested in writing not only for the Junior League, but for a magazine called the *Delta Review*. I was a contributing editor to the *Review*, the literary magazine that was published in Mississippi by a Frenchman. It was off to a great success, trying very hard to be like the *Paris Review*, for about two years. But alas, the publishing business is very iffy financially, and the gentleman backing us finally had to stop the magazine.

In the very early 1960s, *Town and Country* came to Memphis, and they were gracious enough to include me in articles on Memphis, though I lived in the Delta. I had pictures taken in front of the Memphis Art Academy, and Justine's, the famous restaurant, and the ancestral home where I'd had my debut in 1947 on New Year's afternoon. They also were gracious enough the next year to ask me to fly to New York, where they did a picture of me at the St. Regis bar. This picture was lifted from the magazine, made into a flyer and put into every bedroom of the St. Regis for two or three years. I wish I had a dime for everybody who thought they were being clever when they told me they had been in the bedroom with me at the St. Regis.

The *New York Times* food editor, Craig Claiborne, ventured to the South to write a book on Southern cooking. When my turn came to play hostess, instead of preparing an elaborate meal, I simply invited Mr. Claiborne into my kitchen to cook with our then cook, Bessie.

I was worried about impressing this New Yorker until I found out that Craig Claiborne was the double first cousin of my brother Jack's wife, Alyce Claiborne Seabrook, and that he had gone to Mississippi State.

We served not a drop of wine, only iced tea and water in our heirloom silver goblets. A large picture appeared in the food section of me serving water in the silver goblets. Later these goblets were displayed in a drinking vessel exhibit on Fifth Avenue sponsored by Hallmark. More than the goblets, though, Mr. Claiborne was impressed by my Grandmother Seabrook's marble-top beaten biscuit roller.

Other, unexpected enjoyments came my way. At a fashion show in the early 1960s, I wore one of the first pantsuits shown. When I came to the end of the runway, I kicked up my leg to show that this voluminous piece of fabric that looked like a skirt was really a pair of pants. A photographer snapped the shot, and it was in the middle of the newspaper's front page that afternoon.

In 1963, a cousin and I were co-chairmen of the Memphis Symphony Ball. We had no money to spend, but I insisted on having Peter Duchin, because he was the rage at the White House and a great favorite of Jackie Kennedy. I thought he would bring in the tickets, and bring in the tickets he did. The theme of the ball was "The Portrait Ball" and it was held at the Memphis Hunt & Polo Club. I don't suppose there has ever been – before or since – as much bad art under one roof in the South. At the inception of the ball I told all to send their portraits to hang on the wall if attending. Many came without a portrait, but several portraits that were painted for the special occasion were still wet when hung that day.

In 1964, I was very surprised to be named one of the ten best-dressed ladies of the Mid-South. I was particularly pleased, because I was the youngest woman ever chosen and after three years on the list, made the Mid-South Hall of Fame of the ten best-dressed. My mother-in-law asked her husband how Sugsie could afford to dress so beautifully. He told me, "I replied, she has her own income."

On July 31, 1966, I was featured on the front page of the Sunday supplement of *The Commercial Appeal* as one of the "Women Men Would Remember."

I had been a member of the Memphis Garden Club since 1956. You might say I was born into the Memphis Garden Club; it was founded in 1921 by my father's first cousin, Elise Vance Norfleet.

In 1966, when I was recording secretary, our local club hosted the Garden Club of America's national meeting in the spring. Not a stone was left unturned. I asked the Secretary of Interior to come, and he accepted. It was a thrill to meet him with the mayor of Memphis at the airport.

One night during the annual meeting, we had dinners in members' houses. Never have you seen such table settings. There was one snag. We had the bright idea to have an attractive male for each visitor. Many old friendships among members were shaken because of the hostesses fighting over men.

After my return from the Institute in 1960, I had prayed for oneness with God. Although I was happy, I had never had a true conversion, even though I received the help I needed that night at the Institute when I left the movie early. A few years later, my prayers were answered: I became deeply involved with halfway houses for the rehabilitation of women. There is no way of describing the pleasure that I received from being some small help to these women who would otherwise have been out on the street.

In the late 1960s, there was no place for a female to go to rehab without an insurance policy or private money. It was, in fact, hard to even enter a hospital unless you said it was "nerves." You could not use the word "alcohol."

Our goal was to have a nice house with a very simple program, simple food, furniture that was donated and to have a place where women of all races could be rehabilitated, all for $17.50 a day. This did not come easy; there was very little money available.

I was on the board with a group of nice, good, solid, sober men, but I was the only one who had gone to any college, in my case, two years of junior college. I soon learned that if you want to do anything, you must have help from the state and federal government. In order to have this help, you must feed paper to the bureaucracy. Many hours I would sit in a waiting room watching as the civil service workers put on false fingernails and painted them over and over. When finally ushered into a frightfully large room and confronted by high officials, I would be turned down for funding again and again.

Once I went to the Memphis mayor's office for help, since we had been classmates at Miss Lee's. He said quite frankly that his job as mayor was to keep the fire and police departments going and not to take care of drunks. To this I replied, "It costs the city $125 a day to keep someone in jail and only $17.50 to help them be sober."

The day the City funding was passed out, I received a call from the mayor, saying our program had not been funded.

"Thank you," I replied, "but I don't understand. Another prominent politician just called to tell me we *have* received our funding."

After my cool reception from the mayor, I had asked another man for help. He visited the halfway houses and was impressed with our work. It was then that I learned that before funding is distributed, the politicians go in a backroom and exchange favors. Luckily this man had been our champion.

We did not know how to run the house according to rules of the Human Services Division of the City of Memphis. We were brought up before the feds, the state, and the city for 101 faults. One day I picked our director up at the halfway house to go before the review board, he stepped in the car wearing a what looked like a $300 leather coat and a diamond ring. I told him that I thought he could have dressed down a little, since they thought we were absconding with the money anyway.

As punishment for our infractions we had to close the rehabilitation facilities for both men and women for a few months. The flashy-dressing director was relieved of his position and absurdly sentenced to community service, the exact thing he had been doing, because we wee found guilty of breaking some federal, state, and city codes for half-way houses.

I laugh when I remember thinking we were going to teach these poor, shaking, quaking, despondent women how to dress and how to find a job in 28 days. I asked one of them what was the thing she thought about most, and very honestly she looked at me and said, "Where I'm going to get my next cigarette." I soon learned to stay away from trying to make them into supersonic receptionists in a month and just tried to help them go one day at a time without a drink by going to AA meetings.

My happiest moments were when I would take a bit of Christmas over there–just a little shampoo and a few simple toiletries, magazines, coffee, and cake. I suppose I liked myself better at that moment than at any other time.

For a while I served on the both the city and county Drug and Abuse boards. It did not take me long to realize I was in over my head on those boards, and I could do more good at the Serenity halfway houses that I had helped to found. At that time our recovery rate was as high as Betty Ford's and other expensive places.

Next I enrolled at Memphis State University. When I was in my forties and wanting to write, I knew that I needed to go to school and learn the rules, even if I wanted to break them. I was fortunate to attend classes under a very fine creative writing teacher. He taught me a great deal about writing, and he taught me so much about life. After almost two years, my favorite teacher told me to stop coming to college and go home and write a book. "Do not become confused about dangling participles and correcting things. I have taught here for many years, and you have talent. You are a storyteller. Go home. Take out some white butcher paper, and tell your story."

The Christmas of 1969 I gave a large open house for all the managers, gin operators and bookkeepers and their families on Abbay and Leatherman Plantation. As I prepared for this, the last party I would ever give at Commerce, I thought of all the times I had entertained, and remembered the three excellent cooks we had over our 20 years there. After Susie, Richard found a lovely field hand who, though she had never cooked in any kitchen but her own, learned to follow recipes from the fanciest cookbooks, because she could read and write. It should have come as no surprise to me that when I walked in to the kitchen one morning, Lilly May was not there. Only the week before she had returned some furniture I had loaned her, explaining that her husband, who was a terrible drinker, might damage it. The winter before, her husband's best drinking buddy, was found frozen just a few feet from his front door, where he had passed out. Frankly, I was surprised that something had not happened to Lilly May's husband. When it finally registered that my friend and her children had left in the night – probably headed for Detroit or Chicago — I lay my head on the kitchen table and cried. I had become about as good at crying as my Aunt Camilla.

Then a strange thought came to me; maybe Lilly May was fortunate that in her station of life she *could* just plain disappear. For I, like most women who are truthful, had myself sometimes thought of leaving, but the complications would have been overwhelming. When I would have these thoughts of abandoning this way of life, I had only to make a long list of men I knew, and not a one of them could match Richard. The truth of the matter is, married life is not easy.

As a young bride, I had once given a tea for the managers' wives, and had been told it was a bad idea to fraternize with the managers and their families. This was not for a snobbish reason. It was explained to me that this could have caused great jealousy among the employees in the family operation. But now I could entertain them because we were leaving.

That fall, Richard saw an opportunity to work for his mother's side of the family in furniture manufacturing. Due to his older uncle's health, Richard was offered a good position. As much as he loved farming, Richard could not ignore what the new position could mean to the children and their educations – and we would still farm our land at Lake Cormorant.

When he told the family his intentions, Aunt Jeanne said it seemed that her youngest son was the only Leatherman left who wanted to farm. My mother-in-law said, "Wrong. I've had two sons who wanted to farm, and your husband has had two nephews who were told there was no place for them. The truth of the matter is that timing is of the utmost. Family farming is like playing musical chairs. One must wait to grab a chair, and age and circumstances rule. Your son is the youngest son of a youngest son, and there will be a place for him."

There could have been no way to convince me as a young bride that my husband of 20 years would not die a Mississippi planter. Nor would Richard have believed it if a fortuneteller or one of God's own angels had told us that our first born son, a sixth-generation Tunica Countian, would choose furniture manufacturing over farming. Dick had loaded boxcars at the Memphis Furniture Factory in the summer since he was 14. Since there were no Withers' heirs, there would have been land for Dick. Was at long last our muddy blood, that flowed through generations of pioneers and men of the soil, being purified?

Giving the party before leaving Commerce was easy compared to packing our things. My eyes fell on the large Tiffany bowl filled with silver dollars, called "bow dollars" by Southerners. At Halloween, whoever came to our door for trick or treat, it was a silver dollar they received instead of candy. I packed slowly, savoring my memories of Delta customs. How could I put away records when all I wanted to was stop and play them? The birth bracelets worn by my three newborns sent me back to an earlier, happier time.

As I packed books that filled shelves in every room, I noticed stickers that said the books belonged to Sugsie Leatherman. At this very time and place I made a big decision: when I started my new life in Memphis, I wanted to be called Carroll. Slowly I strolled down the long hall with paper and pen in hand, sat at the dining room table and wrote a letter that was as solemn as a will. It took four minutes to write the note but years of thought, and it told the world that I had not been comfortable with whom my family and the world had chosen me to be.

In it, I defined the end to a name that had caused me trouble in explaining it, yet it had stood me apart from others in a way that was almost legendary. I must admit the young men in the East adored the name. But when I visited or traveled, my nickname was a burden and far too many times, I had to explain how you spelled it, how you said it, and the history of it.

For many years I had wanted to be called by my given name and after my return from Hartford, I had made many changes in my life and why not my name? Why not leave nicknames like Sugar Child and Baby Doll behind with all the other past mores of the Delta? I closed the door on a time and place, and it was my written good-bye to that life.

I quickly found that it took more courage to stand up for my name change than stopping smoking or drinking. There were three articles written in local newspapers about my name change — which might have flattered some people but embarrassed me to the point of calling the editors. Some people responded with notes of support and some with notes of insult. Others wrote they were not going to call me by my given name–end of discussion.

I had great support from my husband, and I soon learned who my real friends were. I do take it as a compliment that many people did not want to lose a fun-loving, amusing and interesting young Southern girl. They would miss her, and to tell the truth I would miss her, too. My whole life had changed and I felt Miss Lee and Grandmother, who always called me Mary Carroll, would approve. The hurried note was ready to be copied and mailed at a much later date. It was short, but strong:

> *March 19, 1971*
> *Dear Friends:*
> *Let it be known that Mary Carroll Seabrook Leatherman, often called "Sugsie," after much thought, has decided to use her given name "Carroll" for the rest of her life.*
> *There are several good reasons for this. The first one is the fact that I am named Carroll and the second one is that I want very badly to be called Carroll.*
> *The name Sugsie is hard to say and frankly, is not even spelled like it is pronounced. It was a nickname and no one even knows where it came from. So, please don't ask. I would make a safe guess that it was given me because I loved sweets when I was a child or maybe if we stretch our imagination a little, it had to do with my nature.*
> *I am 42 and have a son in college. Really, don't you think it is time that I am called by my given name? My husband is in a new business, and we meet new people all the time. Frankly, my old nickname was a burden to both of us.*
> *May I reiterate that I am very serious about being called Carroll? If at first you forget or make a slip, I will understand. But, after a proper length of time, if I feel you are not trying,*

I will help you out with a few hints; such as, when the phone rings, and you ask for me by my nickname, I will say there is no such person and hang up. If addressed by my old nickname in person, I will correct you and say, "Carroll, please," or maybe look blank and not even answer.

This is very important to me. Remember, calling me Carroll will be a free gift. There are not many of those around these days. I know you will do it.

Sincerely,

Carroll Leatherman

P.S. Please pass the word. "Carroll" that is, to your family and friends.

On moving day, Richard came to me and said he was going up to his mother's to look at the ballgame on TV and to come fetch him when we were ready to leave. It was late. If we were to go to Memphis and unpack, we had to keep moving. I drove up to the big house and found Richard in the basement looking at old books and deeds. I could see where he had moved the first deed written in 1828, for it was crooked on the wall. "Time to go," I said, avoiding his eyes. "Yep, sure is," he said, and we walked out of Commerce never to return except as guests.

The trucks from the furniture factory were at last loaded with generations of furniture, family art, and memorabilia. If those trucks had stopped at the weigh station on Highway 61, they would not be nearly as heavy as my heart. Richard led the trucks, and Wink and I were last in the caravan.

As we turned onto Old Commerce Road, the farm bell across from the house tolled as a salute to Richard, a kind of going-away gesture, but to me it seemed more like a death knell. As we passed, I did not look at the commissary that my great-grandfather John Paxton Carruthers had helped build in 1836. I was riding on the very road where he and his colleagues had intended a railroad from Commerce to Hernando. As the car turned north on Highway 61, I did not dare look in the rear view mirror or turn to look back. Instead I slumped down in the car seat and closed my eyes.

Sometimes it is God's mercy that keeps us from seeing into the future. No one, least of all our little band of gypsies heading north in 1970, could have imagined that Commerce, a river town that fell into the Father of Waters in the 1860s, would become, in the 1990's, the third largest gaming center in the world.

Mississippi has had gambling, legal and illegal, for a long time. There were Mississippi River boats carrying passengers–and gamblers–up and down the Mississippi River through much of the nineteenth century. In the twentieth century, the Gulf Coast of Mississippi had ships that docked on the coast, yet carried gamblers out past the 12-mile international limit where state law did not prevail. For many years the Mississippi Gulf Coast counties had tried to convince the Mississippi legislature to pass casino gambling laws.

Mississippi, however, would not pass the laws or legalize gambling. Tunica's House member Clayton Henderson suggested to his fellow representatives from the Gulf Coast counties to include all the counties bordering on the Mississippi River, and give each county the option to vote in or to reject gambling. To everyone's surprise, both chambers of the Legislature passed the bill, and the governor of Mississippi signed the bill to legalize gambling in 1990. The Tunica County Board of Supervisors promptly accepted gambling, and no one asked for a referendum.

However, DeSoto County, Mississippi, also accepted gambling, but the citizens of DeSoto County did ask for a referendum. The resulting vote in DeSoto was 66 percent con, 34 percent pro. A second vote was held two years later with almost the exact same vote tally. That second vote finally decided that DeSoto County, which lies between Tunica and Memphis, would not have gambling, giving investors confidence that Tunica County would have a virtual monopoly in Mid-America, at least for a time. Several other Mississippi River counties approved gambling, but none has had the success of Tunica County.

"Splash Casino was the first to open its doors at Mhoon Landing in October of 1992, later joined by the Lady Luck Casino only eleven months later."[3] Investors arrived in the community and quickly acquired rights to all available casino sites, from Mhoon Landing north to the Tunica County line. Farm values skyrocketed as national gaming companies acquired prime locations and planned world-class casinos, entertainment complexes, hotels, golf courses, restaurants, and even a sporting clay facility. In fact, since the inception of gaming, total capital investment of the casino industry has exceeded $3 billion.

Our family received several offers. As *The Tunica Times* reported in a 2002 retrospective on gaming, "Mr. Richard Leatherman was in his office meeting with the representatives for Jack Binion. That day they were determined to make Mr. Leatherman an offer. Just minutes after Leatherman accepted Binion's offer, he received a call from another casino developer offering him much more per acre. Mr. Leatherman told him he was sorry. "If you had called me twenty minutes ago, I would have talked to you, he told them."[4] Binion's representatives were astounded that people in the South would keep a verbal agreement. They said everywhere else in the world if you didn't have a signature on a piece of paper, the deal would have been off."[5]

Other Tunica Countians had similar experiences. A *Times* reporter interviewed Paul Battle, Jr., then president of the county board, along with his son, who is currently a supervisor: "People would come out to the house to talk to Daddy about building a casino," Little Paul Battle began. "Donald Trump came down. That was when his Taj Mahal was about to fall through, and he met with Dutch Parker at the John Deere place. Can you visualize Donald Trump ever sitting in a John Deere office? The people who had land along the levee were all uptight and thought their property was going to be selected for a site."[6]

Nine casinos currently operate in Tunica County, employing over 16,000 people. The county's unemployment rate has dropped drastically and has remained in the low single digits since 1993. There has been a steady increase in child support collections and a decrease in the number of residents receiving welfare benefits as well as a decrease in the number of residents receiving food stamps. Amazingly enough, today more jobs exist in the Tunica casinos than there are residents in the county.

I wish now that Wink had seen all that has happened in and around Old Commerce and could just once go in one of the casinos, play the slot machines, and be served a drink on a silver tray by a cute cocktail waitress wearing a short tuxedo pants and mesh stockings.

A lot of water in the history of casinos has gone under the bridge. There are casinos that made good, and some which did not survive. Tomorrow, who knows? Tunica County bet on gambling and is still taking bets that are sure to pay off in ways no one has dreamed.

As Wink and I neared Lake Cormorant, I thought of Uncle Tom and Lulu, whose mother had killed her father so long ago. To the west lay the little town where the Cannonball would drop off Handy and the Memphis crowd for Mother's parties.

In the cotton fields were a few mechanical cotton pickers, forlornly trying to harvest the last of the crop. To me, these ungainly green monsters looked like alien creatures from outer space. My mind traveled back to OK and the laborers who picked cotton by hand when I was a child.

I touched Wink's glove, which covered his gnarled hand just like the white gloves that would cover them as he lay in a coffin in Mississippi years later, and said softly, "Wink, do you remember that Sunday afternoon when you drove me to Starkville, Mississippi? I was frightened for you to be seen sitting in the front seat wearing your cap and me sitting in the back."

"Why was that, Ole Miss?" Wink asked.

"Because there were people who would resent that–you driving a white woman and wearing a chauffeur's cap," I told him.

Wink turned to me and said softly, "Ole Miss, what you and I do ain't none of their bus'ness."

I guess no one could understand the relationship Wink and I had after all our years at Commerce. We had gone through a lot together. Though he was born in Alabama and I in Tennessee, we were both children of the Delta, our holy ground, with mud squeezing between our toes. We knew how we felt in our hearts.

As we turned into the drive at our new home in Memphis and parked, Wink came round to open the door for me, as he had done hundreds of times before. His final good-bye wasn't sentimental, for that wasn't Wink's way. He simply offered me his hand. Then Wink turned to his Ole Miss and said, "Only God knows what's in the future, and he ain't going to tell."

I keep a picture of Ole Winkie man wearing a cap and a blue jump suit that he wore over his gray chauffeur's pants and jacket. Beside this picture sits a small china pig to remind me that I "can't teach a pig to sing". When I leave this place, I sure wish my Wink could come down from the heavens above and drive me in that golden chariot to the hereafter. Wink and I have a lot of catching up to do.

[1] Minutes of the Board of Supervisors, I,60; see entry 2, Inventory of the County Archives, No. 72, Tunica County, Mississippi Historical Records Survey, June 1942

[2] *The Tunica Times*, October 17, 2002, by Catherine Cupples

[3] *The Tunica Times*, October 17, 2002

finish this quote:by whom

[4] *Tunica Times*, "The Second Wave," October 17, 2002, Sue Watson

[5] *Tunica Times*, October 17, 2002,Recollections by Sue Watson

[6] *Tunica Times*, October 17, 2002, Recollections by Sue Watson

Wink's funeral, Commerce Landing graveyard behind
Commerce Baptist Church.

Award

Courage Under Fire

*Andrew Coffey, speechwriter for General Creighton W. Abrams, U.S. Army, for
meritorious achievement in ground operations against hostile forces in the
Republic of Viet Nam, was awarded the Bronze Star for heroic action.*

Carroll Seabrook Leatherman, a short story writer, composes and resides in Memphis, Tennessee, and Mississippi.

Carroll Seabrook Leatherman was born and raised in Memphis, Tennessee, where she attended private schools and later graduated from a girl's school in Florida. She graduated from Finch College in New York City.

As a child she spent her weekends and summers at OK Landing, the family plantation located on the Mississippi River and the Beaver Dam Lake. It was here that she gained a love for wildlife and the outdoors. It was also here that she recalls a collection from her fondest memories.

Another of Carroll Seabrook Leatherman's Books

THE OLD MAN
AND THE DOG

The most touching dog story since "Old Yeller."

The Old Man. . .And The Dog is a poignant, heartfelt tale, based on the true story of "Miss One Dot," 1979 Grand National Bird Dog Champion, and her relationship with her handler, "Mr. John Gardner."

… like Old Yeller's, Miss One Dot's story was written to be enjoyed by all of us.

Suzanne Biffle
The Dallas Morning News